DIPLOMAT IN EXILE

FRANCIS PULSZKY'S POLITICAL ACTIVITIES IN ENGLAND, 1849-1860

by
THOMAS KABDEBO

EAST EUROPEAN QUARTERLY, BOULDER
DISTRIBUTED BY COLUMBIA UNIVERSITY PRESS
NEW YORK

1979

EAST EUROPEAN MONOGRAPHS, NO. LVI

Thomas Kabdebo is Social Sciences Librarian
of the John Rylands University Library of Manchester

Publishing this volume was partially subsidized by the Brothers Szathmáry, Lajos and Géza, who live in Chicago, USA, in memory of their Great-Grandfather Captain Szathmáry István, who fought under Kossuth's flag in Bem's Army and became blind from the heavy wound he suffered.

The writing of this volume would not have been possible without the untiring enthusiastic help of Mrs. D. Forgács who lives in Budapest, Hungary.

ACKNOWLEDGEMENTS

My sincere thanks are due to Miss Pauline Adams, Archivist of the Harrowby Archives, to Mr. Ian Angus, for the use of the Xerox machine, to Mr. Bentley-Bridgewater, Secretary of the British Museum, to Professor J.H. Burns for time and attention and advice, to the Central Research Fund of the University of London for a travel grant, to Professor S.B. Chrimes for urging me to do a thesis, to Mrs. C.S. Csapodi of the Széchényi Library, to Dr. F.G. Cushing, to Dr. T. Dénes, to Mrs. D. Forgács, to Dr. I. Gál, to Mrs. M. Haines, to Dr. Éva H. Haraszti, to Mr. E.E. Hitchock of the Central Photographic Unit, to the 6th Earl of Harrowby, to Miss Vera Hollander, to Mr. Z. Jagodzinski, to Mrs. T. Kabdebo, to Mr. Neville Masterman, to Mrs. Romola Nijinsky de Pulszky, to Professor L. Országh, to Dr. L. Péter for free consultation, to Mr. J.W. Scott, Librarian, and to the Library Committee of University College, London, for a leave of absence during the summer vacation, to Miss Margaret Skerl, to Mr. A. Tattersall, Secretary of University College, London, to Mr. J. Weissmann and to Miss Judith White.

FOREWARD

The activities of those Hungarians who, after their nation's fight for freedom had been crushed in August, 1849, by the Austrian and Russian armies, sought refuge abroad to carry on the struggle as exiles, make a story which is not merely romantic, but also one which historians of the following years cannot afford to neglect; for few as they were—the important figures among them a mere handful—they constituted for nearly two decades a factor big enough to find a place in the calculations, not only of Austria, but of every major European power. It is true that they never finally pursuaded any Power to commit itself irrevocably to effective championship of their ideal of an independent Hungary; true also that in Hungary itself the elements favouring an honourable settlement with Vienna ended in command of the field. But they had played a genuinely important part in the manoeuverings which preceded these final results, which they also certainly influenced; Francis Joseph would assuredly not have accepted either Napoleon III's overtures after Solferino, nor those of Ferencz Deák a few years later, but for the threat to his rear that the Hungarian emigres had kept active.

The story has not often been told, except in episodes, by Western historians, and the non-specialist reader will be grateful to Mr. Kabdebo for what a purist would have to condemn as a blemish in his work: that he frequently departs from his nominal theme to describe events in which his titular protagonist, Ferencz Pulszky, had little hand, or none at all. But the specialist will further find in Mr. Kabdebo's monograph a valuable corrective to the picture presented by many of his predecessors, who have tended to train their spotlights on the single figure of Lajos Kossuth. To do this is to yield to a natural temptation, for Kossuth was not only the leading figure among the emigres, but also by far the most pictureque one; but it leads to a measure of historical distortion, and certainly to injustice towards some of those helpers without whose devotion Kossuth could never have acquired the nimbus that he wore with such a grace. Among those helpers, Pulszky, the subject of this monograph, certainly earned the special attention which Mr. Kabdebo has devoted to him. Few of Kossuth's companions showed him a loyalty so patient, or so enduring, and few did so much to help him. Especially in the key years from 1849-1851, when Kossuth was languishing in internment in Anatolia, the task of representing the ideals for which the emigration stood, fell inevitably on other shoulders. So far as Britain was concerned, it was on Pulszky that this crucial duty— all-important in those crucial years—devolved, and he carried it out in a way which altogether belies the common picture of him as a born second in command. He perhaps did not gladly seek the initiative, but when, as in 1849, the situation forced it on him, he accepted it, and hampered as he was by every kind of difficulty, he yet succeeded in truly remarkable fashion in awakening that sympathy for Hungary, and understanding of her case, which then found expression in the triumphal reception accorded to Kossuth. This is a story which is even less well-known than some of the emigration's later activities. Mr. Kabdebo's account of it will be new to most readers, and they will find it not only historically valuable, but replete with human interest.

C.A.Macartney

LIST OF ABBREVIATIONS*

Bp. = Budapest

B.P.L. = Birmingham Public Library

Correspondence, 1847-49. = Correspondence relative to the Affairs of Hungary, 1847-1849.

Correspondence respecting refugees. = Correspondence respecting Refugees from Hungary within the Turkish Dominions.

D.A.B. = Dictionary of American Biography.

Diary = Memoirs of a Hungarian lady by T. and F. Pulszky.

D.N.B. = Dictionary of National Biography.

Directory = Hungarian National Directory (i.e. Magyar Nemzeti Igazgatóság.)

É-K. = Életem és Korom (3rd. ed.) by F. Pulszky.

F.SZ. = A forradalom és Szabadságharc levelestára, compiled by E. Waldapfel.

HANSARD = HANSARD'S PARLIAMENTARY DEBATES.

K-e.A. = A Kossuth-emigráció Angliában és Amerikaban, by D. Jánossy.

K-e.O. = A Kossuth-emigráció Olaszországban, by J. Koltay-Kastner.

K-e.T. = A Kossuth-emigráció Törökországban, by I. Hajnal.

K.H. = *See*: O.L.K.H.

KOSSUTH, L. Irataim. = Kossuth, L. Irataim az emigráczióból; (ed. by I. Helfy and F. Kossuth.)

M.I.L. = Magyar Irodalmi Lexicon.

M.T.A. = Magyar Tudományos Akadémia.

Notebook = Pulszky's MSS. *Notebook*, 24 April 1859-29 July 1859.

N.R.A. P.P. = National Register of Archives. Palmerston papers.

O.L. K.H. = Országos Levéltár. Kossuth Hagyaték. (i.e. Kossuth Collection. Hungarian National Archives.)

O.SZ.K. Pulszky Coll. = Országos Széchényi Könyvtár. Pulszky Collection. (i.e. "Pulszky analecta" os "Pulszky levelezes" in the Hungarian National Library.)

O.SZ.K.-U.C.L. = Orszagos Szechenyi Konyvtar – University College London. Photocopies of correspondence between Pulszky and F.W. Newman, 1849-1890.

P.R.O. = Public Record Office.

SZINNYEI = SZINNYEI, J. Magyar irók élete és munkái.

TANÁRKY = Tanárky Gyula naplója.

U.C.L. = University College London.

White, red, black = White, red, black: sketches of society in the United States by F. and T. Pulszky.

* All items are listed in full in the Bibliography.

Variant spellings in documents quoted* and names used in translated forms.

Bălcesco = Bălcescu
Czartoriozky = Czartoryski
Dénes = Dionys = Dennis
Eperies = Eperjes
Esterhazy = Eszterházy
Ferencz = Ferenc = Francis
Fülöp = Philip
Galac = Galatz
Haas = Hás
Hapsburg = Habsburg
Ignác = Ignatius
István = Stephen
János = Jánosh = John
Jellasich = Jellashich = Jellachich
Kásszony = Kaszonyi
Kiutahia = Kutayya = Kiutayah = Kiutahya
Komárom = Komorn
Lajos = Louis = Luis
László = Ladislas = Leslie
Martinovits = Martinovics
Mednyánsky = Mednyánszky
Miklós = Nicholas
Montecuccoli = Montecucculi
Pozsony = Pressburg = Bratislava
Sándor = Alexander
Sebő = Sabbas
Sulzefszky = Sulczewsky = Szulczewski
Sumla = Shumla
Theresa = Therese = Teréz
Tür = Türr
Walewsky = Walewski
Widdin = Vidden

*The grammer, style and orthography of sources is left uncorrected in direct quotations.

CONTENTS

INTRODUCTION

Historical and diplomatic contacts

The first traceable Anglo-Hungarian contacts date back to pre-Norman times. Edmund Ironside's two sons were brought to the Court of St. Stephen where the older son, Edward is supposed to have married Agatha, the King's daughter.

As geographically speaking, Hungary lay 'en route' towards the Holy Land, it is not surprising, that a Hungarian king, Ladislas I—later canonised by the Pope and now generally known as St. Ladislas- was asked in 1095 by English, French and Spanish envoys to lead a crusade. Later, Henry II of England established contacts with Béla III of Hungary who took for his second wife Margaret, widow of Henry, the son of Henry II. Richard I of England had Hungarian knights fighting at his side and Endre III, the last issue from the House of Árpád, sent an envoy to Edward I on the matter of a common expedition to the Holy Land.

Learning, religion and war prompted, and remained the focal point of these early connections.

Hungarian students studied at Oxford from the thirteenth century onwards, and Hungarian church dignitaries exchanged visits with English ones several times during the Middle Ages. In the XIV century, Louis I of Hungary kept Edward III of England informed of his campaigns, while in the XV century, Emperor Sigismund, King of Hungary acted as intermediary between Henry V of England and the king of France, and so he spent four months in England.

When, a century later, the Turkish menace became imminent, Louis II of Hungary asked for armed assistance from Henry VIII and from Cardinal Wolsey, a troop of bowmen came and fell at Mohács; more effective English help came at the re-taking of Buda some 150 years later, in 1686. In the intervening period, which saw the division of Hungary and the expansion of England, a Hungarian Protestant, John Tolnai Dali came to England with his companions and remained here for years, returning only to propagate Puritan ideals, while the tidings of Thomas Cranmer's martyrdom travelled abroad to be included in a long poem by the Magyar religious poet Sztárai (1583). Theologians from Debrecen, and from various parts of Transylvania often visited England—a fact worthy of a mention in Milton's *Aeropagitica*. These visits from Erdély* were quite frequent until Maria Theresa took measures to prevent them, not entirely successfully since they continued right through the XVIII century. Count Francis Széchényi, who subsequently founded the Hungarian National Library, had visited England in 1787.[1] A herald of what was to become a new era, he met the famous Adam Smith and recommended the election of Jeremy Bentham to the then newly founded precursor of the Hungarian Academy of Science, in that year.[2] Actually, Bentham's first Hungarian acquaintance was the antiquarian baron, Joseph Podmaniczky, whom he met in 1779.[3] The compliment paid to Bentham by Széchenyi, was returned to his son: Count Stephen Széchenyi, as a letter in the Brougham collection of University College testifies, was elected a member of the Society for the Diffusion of Useful Knowledge.[4] With him a new phenomenon appears on the horizon of British-Hungarian liaisons: he was the first Magyar statesman conscious of translating his experience in England to the economic advancement of his homeland; but before considering his policies, we should briefly survey the careers of some of those statesmen of Hungarian birth who were employed by the Austrian diplomatic service in Britain.

Whereas during the Middle Ages and until the Turkish conquest Hungary was a free and independent Kingdom, from the introduction of the first Habsburg ruler in 1526 to the Congress of Vienna in 1815 a period of prolonged constitutional conflict set in; on the one hand the Austrian rulers were trying to subjugate the country to a semi-colonial status within their empire, while on the other hand, the Hungarian nation, insisting on ancient and inviolable privileges, upholding local institutions and maintaining local government was claiming the share of a partner endeavouring to achieve equality. By 1815 the Habsburg Monarchy had abandoned Alsace-Lorraine and Belgium, had withdrawn to mainly German territories, but did not and could not shape itself to form anything resembling a national state.[5] And since according to the treaties of 1815 Austria had received neither a Constitution, nor had statutes been established to that effect, Hungary was not really threatened with

---

*Erdély = Transylvania = Partium

becoming against her own laws and constitutional development an integral part of an Austrian Empire. By the summoning of the Hungarian Diet in 1825, an ever-widening gap was opened between the Austrian territories governed by a paternal system and the emerging Hungarian State in possession of a free constitution. As far as external questions were concerned, the state of things allowed only a united platform; foreign affairs were part of the Emperor's personal prerogatives. Hungary as a separate state could have neither independent foreign relations nor any diplomats representing her as a separate entity.

The first of the notable Hungarian diplomats in the service of the empire was Count Antal Apponyi, whose initial appointment took him to the Court of Ferdinand III Prince of Tuscany in 1815; from there he proceeded to Rome ten years later, and finally to Paris, where he stayed, as ambassador, until the revolution in February 1848. His son Rudolf Apponyi, was appointed ambassador in Lisbon in 1846. The Eszterhazy family might be counted as a rival in diplomatic successes: Prince Paul, who as a young man had taken part in the conference of Chatillon, became Ambassador in England after Waterloo thus satisfying the expressed wish of the Prince of Wales. The Prince warmly assisted a commercial co-operation between Britain and his homeland and urged the establishment of an English Consulate in Budapest. He promoted István Széchenyi's English connections. Of the other Eszterhazy diplomats representing the Empire in Europe, Prince Nicholas deputised for the Austrian monarch at the coronation of George IV in 1821. But it was Széchenyi who, from a Hungarian point of view, made the real breakthrough. Some writers attribute the beginning of the so-called Magyar 'reform era' to Széchenyi's visit to England in 1815. The Count recognised that if Hungary was to play any role in European politics, she had to be content with the existing framework of diplomatic relations- for the time being. His motto was well known: he wanted his own nation to achieve cultural equality with Western Europe.[6]

Széchenyi pursued a policy in cultivating the acquaintance and friendship of English statesmen. He was on good terms with Lords Castlereagh, Canning, Palmerston, and Aberdeen, and was a friend to a succession of English Ambassadors in Vienna: to Lord Steward (1814-1822), to Sir Henry Wellesley (1823-1831), to Frederick James Lamb (1831-1841) and to Sir Robert Gordon (1841-1846). The Count, though a radical reformer himself, belonged to the Hungarian conservative party, yet felt particularly at home in liberal Holland House. In his opinion, the economic co-operation of England, Austria and Hungary was a vital necessity from Hungary's point of view. The Englishmen who visited Hungary after 1815 shared his view in so far as they agreed that the Monarchy had an important role in keeping Russia at bay with the active help of England. John Paget the scholarly English doctor who had first travelled around and then settled in Hungary was very much in favour of close commercial ties.[7] In his book on Hungary, he called the attention of the English public to the welcome amongst Hungarians of the Anglo-Austrian commercial treaty, engineered by MacGregor as a counteraction to the German Zollverein. Another traveller, David Urquhart, "author of the revelations of Russia" as he usually styled himself, came to the same conclusions. An English merchant and diplomatic agent, A.J. Blackwell, went as far as 'prescribing' the strengthening of Anglo-Hungarian ties as a basic course British foreign policy should take in Eastern Central Europe. This thesis of Blackwell's had drawn the attention of Sir Robert Gordon to him and made the British Ambassador to Vienna decide to get Blackwell to establish an Anglo-Hungarian Commercial Agency in London. Only the court-diplomacy of baron Kübeck and Metternich, who were anxious lest the Hungarian opposition should find a possible ally in the English, stopped the founding of a British Consulate in Budapest in the 1840's.

The mode of Kossuth's orientation was basically different. He had sought the transformation of the status-quo - and as a first step towards this aim, he directed his whole parliamentarian propaganda, trying to secure the constitutional independence of the country.

His plans for Hungary's foreign relations included the wooing of German nationalist circles in order to find a balance against the influence of the Austrian Government, with a view to achieve national independence. On the other hand, he was also aware of the necessity of an English political alliance against the Panslav-Russian danger. Lastly, he collaborated with the Polish revolutionaries, which might have seemed a hazardous course to take even then.

The Hungarian political fermentation was followed with interest by Sir Robert Gordon. Soon after the opening of the 1843 Parliament we find first Sir Robert then his agent Blackwell in Pozsony. The

Opposition is very much aware of the English approach (perhaps attaching too much importance to it), and Blackwell not only makes the acquaintance of Klauzál, Batthyány and Kossuth, but is introduced even to Archduke Joseph, the Palatine, and later, in 1847, to his successor in deputising the King, Archduke Stephen.[8] Yet, Blackwell's political fortune had suffered a setback with the change of Government in England. In 1846 Aberdeen was replaced by Palmerston and Sir Robert Gordon by Lord Ponsonby. One of Blackwell's memoranda, submitted to the new English Ambassador in Vienna, tackles the question of nationalities within the Habsburg Empire. Blackwell forecasts the dissolution of the Monarchy and the emergence of Hungarian power. In other words, he thinks with the mind of the Hungarian liberal opposition.

In 1848 the Habsburg Empire was in fact showing signs of disintegration. But this process was countered by the Austrian imperial machinery which though less able to fall back on a homogenous national force could still muster an army welded together by discipline. Confronted with constitutionally independent Hungary- strengthened with the laws enacted on 11 April- and having granted a constitution to its own Austrian nationals on 15 April, the Empire had to find a legal way of allocating the functions of the government. Given two separate governments, certain functions remained united and inseparable. This was the framework into which the first Hungarian foreign ministry, owing its existence to the April laws, had fitted. Headed by Prince Eszterházy and furnished with an Under-Secretary of State, Francis Pulszky, this ministry, according to Blackwell, was "by the person of the King",[9] destined to influence the communal affairs of the Empire, and, as a consequence, treat with foreign states as well. Although not invested with a separate power it still acted as and was recognised as a foreign ministry. As Daniel Irányi put it: "Francis Pulszky, Under-Secretary of State for Foreign Affairs, was Under-Secretary of State for the relations between Austria and Hungary, whose minister was Prince Eszterházy."[10]

Considering the facts that on one hand, Austria had continued to maintain her ambassadorial offices for the whole of the Empire, and on the other hand both Kossuth, the Magyar Chancellor of the Exchequer, and Szemere, the Magyar Home Secretary, entrusted separate Hungarian envoys to represent the country abroad, the confusion was steadily mounting. The Hungarian motive was at first simply to counteract the

Panslav movement within the Monarchy. Ladislas Szalay and Dionys Pázmándy were entrusted on 14 May 1848 to represent the Magyar Diet on the Frankfurt Conference in search of German assistance. Their mission was countersigned- through Eszterházy- by Pillersdorf, the Austrian Prime Minister, though we should note that while the Hungarians speak of their two "ambassadors" the Austrian documents refer to the "envoys of the Diet". But at the same time, Szalay received a separate authorisation from Szemere to present his credentials in England.[11] Meanwhile the Austrian General Radetzky had been victorious over the troops of Carlo Alberto; the Viennese Camarilla had successfully incited both Serbs and the Croats on the southern frontiers of Hungary, the Hungarian Prime Minister Batthyány, and the 'foreign' minister Eszterházy resigned, Pulszky was dismissed but stayed on in Vienna on the expressed wish of Kossuth, to represent the Committee of Defense. On the instigation of Bach, Szalay's mission was cancelled by the King on 7 September 1848.

The Hungarian reaction, as acted out by the Diet's representations abroad, was (mainly, but not only, through the predominance of Kossuth's influence) to regard themselves as independent Hungarian diplomats adopting an increasingly anti-Austrian attitude. In August Kossuth had secretly sent a diplomatic agent, Theodore August Wimmer to England with the task of buying arms for Hungary and finding a way to negotiate with Lord Palmerston. Kossuth had hoped to obtain a loan from England. The first object was set on foot, the second was doomed to failure.

We have to discern one important point when considering the "secret", "semi-official" and "official" instructions of diplomats representing Hungary between May and September 1849. While the Eszterházy 'foreign ministry' was still in existence the representation abroad had an undoubtedly legal character, in the eyes of both governments, though the representatives themselves may have carried secret instructions, as was the case with Szalay and Pázmándy. Furthermore, we know that these independent ambassadorial representations, in Paris for instance, were contemplated by Pulszky, in his capacity as Under-Secretary of State, who would have liked either Ödön Beöthy or Szalay to undertake the responsibility for it. Instead, the Prime Minister, Count Louis Batthyány nominated his friend Count László Teleki for the ambassadorial post in Paris.[12] When Teleki leaves Pest for Paris on 31 August he stops in Vienna for four days, where Louis Batthyány and Francis Deák on behalf of the Hungarian Diet, made a last attempt at reconciliation with the Austrians, by entreating that the Croatian army of Jellashich should be stopped by the king. Batthyány himself could have had neither any illusions of his attempt to negotiate with the Court nor any doubts about the rectitude of his actions to ask for the help of France against Vienna. So, when the final break comes, Batthyány resigns, and Szalay's mission is cancelled on 7 September, the Hungarians are not entirely unprepared: Teleki arrives in Paris on the 8th and tries to present his credentials. Although he failed to get official recognition even as a Hungarian Ambassador, his successful contacts ranged from the French Left, to the exiled Polish Aristocrats and the English liberals; at home he came to be regarded for a while by Kossuth and the Committee of Defense, as the country's virtual foreign minister.

After the first mission of Szalay's, which never materialized, and the secret commission of Wimmer, which came to nothing, Szalay was personally instructed by Kossuth, to represent independent Hungary in England and present his credentials to the English Foreign Secretary. Szalay, on his way to England called on Teleki in Paris, and the two diplomats, came to London in December in the hope of a personal interview with Palmerston.[13]

. . . "The establishment of commercial relations between the two countries might be of great importance to Great Britain herself",[14] starts Kossuth in his letter of introduction. Enumerating the economic advantages, he sums up by saying that Szalay is "authorised to open preliminary negotiations with the British Government".

The reply from the Foreign Office is dated 13 December and signed by Lord Eddisbury, the Under-Secretary for Foreign Affairs:

> Sir,
> I am directed by Viscount Palmerston to acknowledge the receipt of your letter of the 11th instant, and in reply I am to say that Viscount Palmerston is sorry he cannot receive you. The British Government has no knowledge of Hungary except as one of the component parts of the Austrian Empire; and any communication which you have to make to Her Majesty's Government in regard to the commercial intercourse between Great Britain and Hungary should therefore be made through Baron Koller, the representative of the Emperor of Austria at this Court.[15]

Szalay did not give up at the first rebuff. His second letter to Palmerston is dated 15 December. In it he refers to the conception that Hungary never formed a part of the Austrian Empire. He quotes article 10 of the Diet of 1790-91 which is instituted "De independentia Regni Hungariae" and expresses a further hope that England will draw the inference that Hungary is "capable of forming a sufficiently great and extended political organisation."[16] He entertains the hope that the question of his official reception might be adjourned until he is able to furnish the British Government with more information on the actual state of Hungary.

Lord Eddisbury's[17] second letter, in Palmerston's name, reiterates the essence of the first one: "H.M. Government can take no cognizance of these internal questions between Hungary and the Austrian dominions".[18]

CHAPTER ONE

AN EMISSARY IN LONDON

1. The Origin of Pulszky's Mission

The examination of the exact details of Francis Pulszky's mission to England presents one of the truly complicated problems of Hungarian history in the period 1848-49. In order to set it in proper perspective we have to examine the question in Pulszky's own writings, in biographical accounts, and in the light of historical sources offering conjectural evidence.

Preliminary points.

On 28 February 1849 Francis Pulszky landed at Ramsgate, having travelled under the assumed name of Lipót Kánitz,[1] Galician Jewish merchant. Among European countries, England was unique in so far as neither her laws referring to aliens nor the Home Office regulations of the period had required more than a declaration from the ship's captain, of the names of passengers holding no British passports. In practice even this was often omitted. Kánitz- alias Pulszky- was duly granted a landing certificate, which is still preserved, together with his passport, in the Hungarian National Library.

In earlier accounts, Pulszky's mission- the reasons for his coming to this country and his activities here- were set against the failure of the preceding enterprises of the Independent Hungarian Government in connection with Britain. As we have seen, László Szalay's rejection by the Foreign Office was in fact a statement along the official lines of Lord Palmerston's foreign policy that seemed unconditionally to protect the interest of Austria in December 1848. But the rejection came to be interpreted, subsequently, as a snub to the Kossuth administration.

On this last issue, we should take into account that both before the April laws, in the forties, and almost immediately after the establishment of the Independent Hungarian Government, the question of setting up an English consulate in Pest had been brought up and dropped. The first attempt was thwarted by Metternich's diplomacy, the second, in May 1848, when the Prime Minister, Louis Batthyány brought it up in the form of a concrete proposal to Blackwell, was foiled by Lord Ponsonby.[2] On the first occasion the proposal would have fitted into the old framework of Anglo-Austrian diplomacy and in the second case it could have run along the modified channels of a triangle of Austrian-Hungarian-British relations. But after Hungary was declared to be in a state of rebellion it was most unlikely that where Paul Eszterházy and Louis Batthyány had failed, Louis Kossuth and Ladislas Szalay would succeed.

Furthermore, it did not help Anglo-Hungarian relations in 1848 either, that the Austrian Ambassador in London had successfully appealed to the British authorities to stop Kossuth storing arms and ammunitions in England. Kossuth had actually bought the *Implacabile*, a disused British vessel in the Mediterranean and had it brought to Britain where it was promptly sequestered by the Austrians.[3]

Pulszky's own accounts of his mission contain certain hints that he was sent to rectify matters between England and Hungary. The longer of these reports is given in the last three chapters of the second part of his memoirs, *My life and times*,[4] written thirty years after the events, but still of great historical value if used critically. The shorter one, written in 1860 for the biographical dictionary *Rank and Talent*[5] and subsequently published with some alterations, deserves to be quoted in this context in its original form, as preserved in the MSS. Collection in the British Museum,[6] for it sums up the background as well as the motives of Pulszky's mission to England:

PULSZKY, Ferencz Aurel de Lubócz and Czelfalva. . .[7] was born on 17 September 1814, at Eperies, in the County of Sáros and educated at the Protestant College of his native town of which his family had continued to be a munificent supporter. He studied Law, as customary in Hungary with all those who prepare themselves for a parliamentary career, and took high honors in passing his examinations as an advocate in 1835. Having been one of the founders of the first debating society in Hungary, which was prosecuted in 1836 by the Government, he escaped arrest only by leaving the country on a tour through Continental Europe and the United Kingdom. After his return he published his observations on England in German[8] and on Germany in Hungarian.[9] In 1839 he was elected to the Hungarian Diet,[10] just when his essays *On the history of Hungary, On currency* and *On the regulation of the Danube* had attracted the attention of the public. Though he made but one single speech on the Diet he became a most useful member in Committee, and in conjunction with Francis Deák and Maurice Szentkirályi[11] he drew up the code of Commercial Law and Bankruptcy, which received the Royal sanction in 1840. He was upon this elected member of the parliamentary Committee for the codification of Criminal Law, and Fellow of the Hungarian Academy. Engaged for three years upon the Criminal Code,[12] Pulszky did not try to get a re-election in 1843, but re-visited about that time Italy and Germany, married in 1845 and retired to his splendid country seat, devoting his time to country politics, political essays in Kossuth's paper and the management of his extensive estates.

In 1848, at the first intelligence of the revolution at Vienna, he hastened to Pest and for the time when the old baron (sic) of the Government had abdicated and the New Ministry was not yet confirmed, he was appointed by the Palatine, Archduke Stephen,[13] one' of the three commissioners for the maintenance of public order all over Hungary. At the final formation of the Batthyány[14] Cabinet he became Under-Secretary of State for Foreign Affairs under Prince Eszterházy,[15] who having lent his name to the national movement and unwilling to incur any serious visit, left the management of the relations between the Hungarian Cabinet and the Austrian Ministers in Pulszky's hands.[16] At the approach of Jellashich,[17] when Count Batthyány had resigned, and the Palatine fled and Hungary was, according (sic) to the plan of the Court party, to be driven into Anarchy, he was dismissed by the Emperor from his office on the eve of the second Vienna revolution (6 October). The Hungarian Diet sent Pulszky back to his post at Vienna, which was about to undergo a siege. He remained there, until he saw that the imbecility of the leading politicians tamed the energy of the besieged population and the talents of General Bem,[18] who commanded the defense. He succeeded to evade the vigilence of the besiegers, went to the Hungarian army, where he met his friend Kossuth, and together with his chief took part in the battle of Schwechat and the retreat of the army to Hungary. His extradition was insisted upon by Prince Windischgraetz in the capitulation of Vienna, and not being found in the captured town, a sentence of death was recorded against him.[19] At the end of the year he was sent to England, in order to prevent the intervention of the Russians, who had already garrisoned the frontier towns of Transylvania. After many hairbreadth escapes he managed to cross the Austrian dominions . . .

In his *Memoirs* Pulszky refers to two members of the Hungarian parliament, István Bezerédy[20] and Ödön Beöthy[21] who at the end of December urged Kossuth to send him abroad, "All the more he should do that" (the author echoes their argument), "since if the Austrians won, no-one is as much implicated, beside Kossuth, than I, who am regarded as the inciter of the 6 October Vienna revolt.". . .[22] "Kossuth then wrote a brief authorisation to Palmerston and another to Madocsány, Lord Lieutenant of the County of Árva." ". . . He made out a passport for me . . ." ". . . My plan was that as soon as the approach of the enemy forces the Government to leave Pest, I would get out through Galicia and Prussia. I counted mainly on the sympathy of England believing that as soon as I will be in London, I will be able to arouse English sympathy for Hungary and perhaps to find ways whereby to get arms smuggled into Hungary, because our greatest trouble was the lack of weapons . . ."[23] ". . . Gyula Tanárky, our faithful land-steward, accompanied me to the Hungarian border, an Austrian passport was in my pocket, bearing the name of Kánitz, which I had bought from a traveller . . ."

In the next chapter, Pulszky relates his stay in Paris from mid-January to the beginning of March 1849, his encounters there with Lamartine, George Sumner, William Sandford and F.W. Browne, with various Polish, Roumanian and Russian emigrants, and with the Hungarians Kmetty, Kiss, Irinyi and Szarvady, all of whom called on Teleki, the Magyar envoy at the French capital. Teleki, says Pulszky, "thought it necessary that I should go to England."[24]

The first group of historians gave credit to Pulszky's statements about Kossuth's authorisation despite the fact that documentary evidence was lacking. Still writing in Pulszky's lifetime, József Ferenczy, the author of the first short (and still the only) biography of Pulszky, re-echoes his hero's arguments of the subject.[25] The bibliographer

József Szinnyei,[26] Pulszky's personal friend, rephrases the same arguments, English versions do. the same. Pulszky's escape- as related by himself- comes down to us from Miss Susan Horner,[27] and in summarised forms, from Thomas Watts[28] and from the writer of an article in 1858 in the Illustrated London News.[29] None of these present new data.

Pulszky's mission came under close scrutiny in a short history of Hungarian diplomacy by Jenő Horváth,[30] and a still more detailed analysis of its causes and reasons were given by the same author in a treatise on the political relationship between Kossuth and Palmerston. Horváth argues that Kossuth, having sent Szalay to Palmerston but receiving no news from him "instructed Pulszky to follow him across the Channel". Furthermore, he conjectures that Pulszky probably suggested to Kossuth that his approach to Palmerston might be successful since his wife's family and that of Lord Lansdowne's (who was then a cabinet minister) were on friendly terms with one another, while to Count Teleki he ad- duced the need for repairing Szalay's failure in December. Horváth thinks that Pulszky's immediate "pretext" for proceeding to London towards the end of February was that a near relative of Lord Eddisbury, Captain Frederick William Browne, offered his services to the Hungarian Government and was appointed Major of the General Staff by Count Teleki on 26 February 1849.[31]

This last argument about the "pretext" we can quickly eliminate: Pulszky himself relates in his *Memoirs*[32] that F.W. Browne had called him previous to his departure from Paris and volunteered to take letters from Teleki, Szarvady and Pulszky, copied with microscopic hand- writing on very fine paper and sewn into his coat-buttons, through the Austrian camp to Kossuth. It is more likely, therefore, that Browne set out for Hungary from Paris, on 27 February, the day after his secret nomination as major of staff, when Pulszky left the French Capital for London.

The two major monographs and source publications on the sub- sequent period; István Hajnal's *Kossuth emigration in Turkey*[33] and Dénes Jánossy's *Kossuth emigration in England and America*[34] discuss the merits of Pulszky's mission without taking sides as to how it originated. Éva Haraszti, author of the work *English Foreign Policy against the Hungarian war of Independence*[35] again quotes the *Memoirs* as her only source. On the re-publication of the *Memoirs* in 1958, the literary historian, Ambrus Oltványi, faced the problem once more, in the following terms: "In the last months of 1848 (Pulszky) works at Kossuth's side directing the affairs of the revolution for a while, then Kossuth entrusts him again with a diplomatic mission: he is nominated as English envoy of the Hungarian government. The details of his new mission are not quite clear. Twenty years later, after his return from emigration, a political adversary of his, Lajos Csernátony accuses him, that fearing the consequences of an Austrian victory, he had left the country on his own choice. Kossuth confronted with this *fait accompli*, entrusted the diplomatic mission to him since by that time he was already staying abroad. This statement is not corroborated by convincing evidence and Pulszky himself most vigorously protested against it, yet it still cannot be completely disclaimed. The stoic heroism of a courageous contempt for death does not really characterise Pulszky, who was well aware that his role in Vienna alone would make him one of the first targets of the Court's revenge."[36]

The view that Pulszky left the country without an authorisation and without the knowledge of the Hungarian government was taken up both by Zoltán Horváth, in his work on *László Teleki*[37] and Eszter Waldapfel in her dissertation *The Independent Hungarian foreign policy 1848-1849*.[38] Horváth's main evidence against Pulszky's authorisation is an exchange of letters between Kossuth and Pulszky in 1861 following a quarrel over the right policy of the Hungarian emigration for the liberation of the country. Kossuth writing from London on 12 January 1861 to Pulszky in Turin, acknowledges that their policies part company and adds: "I never remined you of December 1848". Pulszky, in his reply from Turin, dated 17 January, protests against such threats, but without specifying what they consisted of.

It appears that the above correspondence was an 'edited' version by Kossuth and his original letter (not known or not referred to by Horváth and Waldapfel) had been more clearly phrased. Gyula Tanárky, who had followed Pulszky into exile and there became the tutor of his children as well as his secretary entered the following lines in his diary for 3 February 1861, as a direct quotation from the same Kossuth letter: "At the end of 1848 you left me- I have never remined you of that. But time may come that I will".[39]

Further indirect evidence is offered by Waldapfel. When Csernátony accused Pulszky in 1868[40] of having left Kossuth in 1848, Kossuth did

did not defend him, neither did Madocsány, Lord Lieutenant of the County of Árva (referred to in the *Memoirs* as having seen the authorisation), came forward to his assistance. Bertalan Szemere, the Home Secretary of the 1849 government, -later, in the emigration, a political opponent of Kossuth and Pulszky- calls Pulszky a "cowardly runaway" in an open indictment delivered against the 'Kossuthites' in 1853.[41] Lastly, we should consider, that the 28 February session of the Debrecen Diet listed the names of those officials who were sent abroad on foreign missions by the government. Pulszky's name was not on that list.

As a conclusion about the origin of Pulszky's mission we share Waldapfel's view that Pulszky had escaped from Hungary and stayed in Paris and London 'illegally', that is to say without an authorisation from either Kossuth or any other member of the government at home. He secured letters of recommendation from the Hungarian plenipotentiary, Count Teleki, whom he himself had persuaded that he would be able to find a direct link to Palmerston. Acting on his own initiative he crossed the Channel, started to mobilize the press and secured interviews with the English Foreign Secretary. His official authorisation as Hungarian envoy to England sent on 15 May 1849 and signed by the Foreign Minister came as a late recognition of service.[42]

2. Contact with Palmerston.

Departing from Paris, Pulszky wrote a letter to Kossuth on 26 February,[43] informing him of his intentions to see Palmerston and to win the sympathy of England for the Hungarian cause. Self-appointed to carry out this double task he proceeded with great care and circumspection. He took up residence in a boarding house in Golden Square, London, in order to improve his spoken English at dinner-table conversations during communal meals, and set out at once, using his letters of recommendations, to make social contacts.[44] Through his old friend, D.J. Vipan, the traveller and archaeologist, who had a few years back visited the Pulszkys in Hungary, he got an invitation to Lady Lovelace, Byron's daughter, next day, and in her salon he was introduced to personalities ranging from members of the Society for the Diffusion of Useful Knowledge to members of both Houses of Parliament. Pulszky the scholar attracted the interest of two geologists, Leonard Horner and Sir Charles Lyall; Pulszky the writer was welcomed by Professor

Francis Newman, by John Forster,[45] the editor of the *Examiner*, by
Eyre Evans Crows, the editor of the *Spectator*, and the Morning
Advertiser, respectively; Pulszky the advocat shared common grounds
of interest with W.L. Birkbeck and Joshua Toulmin Smith, constitut-
ional lawyers; Pulszky the politician was kindly received by both the
Marquis of Lansdowne,[46] Lord President of the Council, and Lord
Dudley Coutts Stuart, M.P. for Marylebone.

But as the many-sided Hungarian was to carry out a diplomatic mission, the link with Lord Dudley Stuart, achieved through the joint
recommendations of Teleki, Prince Czartoryski and Thomas Banfield,
appeared to be the most important in the first period after his arrival
in England. Stuart was instrumental to his first reception by Lord
Palmerston in Downing Street on 14 March. Lord Dudley had carefully prepared Pulszky for this reception: as direct official diplomatic
relationship between Hungary and England was out of the question,
he was warned that he could only be received as a private individual.
Not to raise his expectations, that Britain's policy might take an anti-
Austrian turn, Dudley Stuart quoted him a fashionable phrase by the
well-known Czech historian, Palacky: "if the Habsburg Empire had not
existed it would have to be invented".[47] We know, that Pulszky at the
time, was convinced that the concept was outmoded, but still wonder
whether he was a slow as subsequent historians to point out that Palacky
had in fact stolen and re-employed his motto from a witticism of Voltaire
about God. The good advice to Pulszky, was followed by a letter of
introduction from Stuart, dated 9 March, and a note on the tenth - via
Banfield,[48] informing Pulszky that Palmerston was ready to receive him.

The encounter between the English Foreign Secretary and the
Hungarian politician was due not only to the latter's diplomatic skill
and his good connections but to the slightly more favourable political
climate following the first Russian attack on Hungary and the Hungarian
victories over the Austrians which made this attack necessary. Not that
Palmerston himself "had protested" against the first Russian intervention,
as Pulszky was to interpret his favourable reception to the Hungarian
Government.

When the English Foreign Minister had learned about the Russian
attack, first, from Sir Stratford Canning, the English Ambassador in
Constantinople, and later on 9 February, from Nesselrode, the Russian

Foreign Secretary, his reaction was far from protestation. But the liberal press was soon bringing reports fo the Hungarian victories of Kápolna, Branyiszkó, Tokaj, and previously russophile politicians, like Richard Cobden, became converted to the Hungarian cause. Kossuth's letter of 24 February, showing the strength of the Hungarian resistance had been conveyed by Pulszky to Palmerston.[49] This letter- which was originally sent to Teleki in Paris, then copied by his Secretary, Szarvady, and sent by him to Pulszky who translated it into English- sums up the Hungarian military operations. It also expresses the wish of the Hungarian Governor that Teleki should represent Hungary at a Congress summoned at Brussels to regulate the affairs of Italy. When Teleki decides to go to Brussels he wants to recall Pulszky from London, to stand in his place in charge of the Hungarian Office in Paris. But Pulszky, whose presence has been announced by the press[50] and who hopes for a further interview with Palmerston, stays in London.

The second interview took place on 1 May,[51] when, despite the quick victory recently gained by Radetzky over the Italians at Novara, Windischgrätz suffered defeat after defeat in Hungary, and with a great part of the country re-conquered by Görgei, the situation looked hopeful for the Magyars.

Moreover, after the interview, on 8 May, Palmerston warned both the Austrian government through Baron Koller, and the Russian government through Buchanan[52] of the undesirable consequences of a new and major Russian attack on Hungary, of which Pulszky forewarned him.

Yet despite the suspicious signs, Pulszky must have been convinced that some extra and inner pressure was needed to activate the English Minister on behalf of Hungary- hence his supporting the idea of gaining further interviews, for the time being, and concentrating on mobilizing the English press and public opinion. Reinforced by the successes on this front- Colloredo, the Austrian chargé d'affaires in London bitterly complained to Schwarzenberg in June that Pulszky had gained the sympathy of the whole English press, with the exception of the *Times*- Pulszky visited Palmerston twice at the end of July, first in the company of a special envoy of Kossuth's, Colonel Bikessy, and later together with Teleki. The immediate purpose of the first July visit was to interpret the dethronement of the House of Habsburg by the Hungarian

Diet to Palmerston; while on the second occasion, the Magyar diplomats made a last attempt to secure British diplomatic intervention, against the military combination of Austria and Russia in Hungary.

Meanwhile Pulszky's efforts had been recognised by the Hungarian Government, and as much active assistance was provided as circumstances and difficulties in communication permitted. The messengers came either via Galicia, Germany and France, or through Constantinople, with considerable delay either way. Teleki supplied Pulszky with funds from Paris, with the knowledge of the Hungarian Foreign Minister in Debrecen. A diplomatic messenger, Fejér- his real name was Csernátony- arrived in London with instruction from Kossuth at the end of May.

Pulszky's official credentials sent in May, arrived in June; his nomination to be Ambassador, and the letter addressing him as such, was dated 14 July,[53] but he received them only after the armistice. In June he was instructed by K. Batthyány to offer, officially, new and more favourable trade agreements between Hungary and England than had existed between Austrian and England. His good sense and Dudley Stuart's warning prevented his attempting to present his credentials to Palmerston.

Knowing how isolated the Hungarian Government was, he would execute instructions from home using his own discretion. This fairly independent attitude was displayed when he delayed sending Kossuth's Declaration of Independence to Palmerston until 19 July,[54] three months after its issue, and with his own modifications in the text. He moderated Kossuth's tone in the course of translating the document into English.[55] From the reactions of his friends Pulszky judged well that the dethroning would be an unpopular measure in English official circles, though it has since been proved that it neither provoked the second Russian attack, which was a foregone conclusion by that time, nor had it changed the disposition of England towards Hungary.[56]

Pulszky's efforts at representation in London were concerted with those of László Teleki in Paris, who tried to achieve the recognition of Hungary through private contacts with Ledru Rollin (while he was still a political force), Droyn de l'Huys, and Tocqueville.[57] As they would not receive him officially his contacts with the Polish emigrants, particularly Prince Czartoryski and the various exile circles of Prussians, of Roumanians, grew more frequent and he called Pulszky twice to Paris to participate. Pulszky took part in a meeting of exiled politicians on 19 May, and he went ot Paris in July again, for a day, presumably to sound Tocqueville as to whether France would join in a protest against a Russian intervention with England, provided England would also be disposed to do so. Both Pulszky and Teleki were somewhat more optimistic on this issue, then the situation warranted. Pulszky, writing to Kossuth on 27 July is the more realistic of the two, when he informs the Governor that "Lord Palmerston and Lansdowne are kind to us but they are apprehensive of wars. Against us they do nothing, for us they might offer mediation, at the most. If we can survive until the winter public opinion will force the Government to act, as it hates the Russians, but wishes to see a strong Austria. . ."[58] In Teleki's opinion: "Palmerston is a good friend of ours and despises the Austrian Government . . . He welcomes the active manifestations of the public opinion since he wishes to act in our favour which will be easier for him if he knows the support of the public is behind him."[59]

How far was the optimism of these Hungarian politicians justified as regards the attitude of Palmerston?

Although the basic assumption, that Lord Palmerston thought a strong Austria necessary for the balance of Europe, remains unchallenged, it would be untrue to say that his policies regarding the Hungarian question were static. We may in fact discern at least three phases in Palmerston's policies towards Hungary, between November 1848 and August 1849. At the end of 1848 while the Hungarian struggle could still be viewed 'as an internal affair of the Austrian Empire', Lord Palmerston held aloof. His 'partiality' towards Italy, which was deemed particularly dangerous in the eyes of English Court circles, was in fact part and parcel of his grand political conception. In Sproxton's terms, he regarded Italy not as the shield of Ajax but the heel of Achilles of the Austrian Empire, and exactly the reverse applied to Hungary. Consequently he waited for the peaceful termination of the Austro-Hungarian struggle and made the first move only when the introduction of a third power, Russia, transformed the domestic question into a European one. Six days after his first interview with Pulszky he instructed his Ambassador in Vienna, Lord Ponsonby, to draw the attention of the Austrian Government to the recent entrance of Russian troops from Wallachia into Transylvania.[60] His main argument was that Austria should look further into the future and see that if a strong power like Russia was to be in possession of the Principalities, instead of their being held by a weak power like Turkey, the security of the Austrian Empire from attack on its eastern frontier would be very essentially diminished. Naturally, the English apprehension of a growing Russian influence in Eastern Europe which would threaten the balance of trade as well as the balance of Europe had to be translated into different terms.

At the same time Palmerston, who- despite his pragmatism- had often been guided by ideas and believed in liberal principles, does not seem to be entirely unconcerned about the fate of Hungary. In January he still entertains hope that the revolt of the Magyars "may turn out to be a fortunate thing",[61] not only affording a opportunity but actually imposing the necessity of entirely reconstructing the organisation of Hungary- a re-construction founded on the principle of equal rights and equal duties. In this manner, "Austria would revive from her ashes and become a far more really powerful state than she has ever been under the narrow-minded and coercive system by which she has for the last half century been governed." Obviously, the possibility of such a desired transformation becomes very distant if Austria regains her hold over Hungary by Russian assistance. Such a contingency would "have a bad effect present and to come".[62]

Lord Ponsonby, the recipient of Lord Palmerston's despatches in Vienna, proved quite unable to understand the subtlety of his superior's arguments. In his unimaginative execution of his ambassadorial duties he only echoed the voice of the Austrian Cabinet ministers, making the wrong pronouncements, wrong conclusions, wrong forecasts. Commenting on the Vienna disturbances in the summer of 1848 he pronounced that "nobody likes national liberty", At the preparation of the Croatian attack he forecast that the Croatians would subdue Hungary.[63] On the eve of the hostilities, in October 1848, he thought that the Hungarian army was a "humbug".[64]

It may well be the measure of Palmerston's displeasure and influence of intelligence gained from Hungarian sources, that Ponsonby was given a leave of absence from 21 April to 31 July 1849. On the other hand, this may still be an entire coincidence, as Palmerston was to use Ponsonby in the beginning of August, as we shall see, entrusting him with the most important task in the Hungarian affair up to that date.

In Ponsonby's absence, it was the chargé d'affaires in Vienna, Magenis, who was briefed by Palmerston to re-employ A.J. Blackwell in order to transmit to H.M. Government "more correct and detailed inform- ation as to the important events which are now passing in Hungary." He should take up residence in Styria, as his presence in Hungary "would be liable to misconstruction by both parties engaged in the war".[65] The great caution and inscrutability displayed in smallest details, is much more characteristic of Palmerston's policy in this phase, than the extremes of cynicism or anger over the Russian intervention. According to Buol, the Austrian Ambassador in St. Petersburg, Palmerston remarked to Brunnow, the Russian Ambassador in London: "Finish it quickly", when he had heard of the Russian intervention.[66] On the other hand Pulszky's archaeologist friend Vipan speaks of Palmerston's outburst of anger upon the same issue.[67]

Whatever sentiments Palmerston may have betrayed in private con- versations (if he really did so), he was certainly non-committal in public. When on 11 May R. Bernall Osborne, M.P. for Middlessex, confronted him with the questions whether there existed a treaty which would have bound England to prevent Russian intervention, and whether England should mediate between Austria and Hungary, Palmerston replied that there was no such treaty and that England would only mediate if Austria wished her to do so.[68] The problem came up again twice in the House of Lords, on 15 May and 6 June, where Lord Lansdowne and Lord Russell took the task of reassuring the members on a point which they feared most; the Czar had no intention to *conquer*. But, as if not quite convinced by his own arguments, Lord Lansdowne invited Pulszky to his house on 22 June. Pulszky determined to oppose Russian inter- vention by demanding the recognition of Kossuth's government.

Late as it came, the change in Palmerston's attitude seems to have been brought about by three internal factors. First, a full debate in the Parliament on 21 July,[69] when Osborne, Monckton Milnes, Roebuck, Thomson, MacGregor and Dudley Stuart pressed him with questions and demands on the Russian intervention. Secondly, the manifestations of sympathy at public meetings: on 23 July,[70] with Dudley Stuart, Osborne and Cobden taking part; on 25 July, with Pulszky and Teleki invited by the Lord Mayor;[71] and on 30 July in Marylebone with Dudley Stuart in the chair, and thirdly, his interviews with Pulszky, Bikessy and Teleki.

It is noteworthy that Palmerston stated in his summary of the debate of 21 July that it was his expressed wish to see peace between the contending parties of Austria and Hungary, and he was ready to mediate. As if bound by this promise, the Foreign Secretary sent an official dispatch[72] and a private letter to Lord Ponsonby, just back from his leave, on 1 August. He requested the Ambassador to read out the text of the dispatch to Prince Schwarzenberg, which contained the following points: 1) The war which started off as a minor conflict has become a major European transaction. 2) The Hungarian population of both Hungary and Transylvania are involved and their army of about 150,000 men. The Russian and Austrian army together has about 300,000 men. 3) It is very important to note, "no material changes should without urgent necessity take place in the distribution of territorial possession established on the Continent of Europe by the stipulation of existing Treaties". 4) Although it is likely that ultimately the numerical superiority of the Austrian forces will prevail 5) it is not impossible that the Hungarians, by dogged resistance, will make a truce with them on their terms. 6) The latter might lead to a dismemberment of the Austrian Empire which would be regarded by H.M. Government "as a great public calamity". 7) Britain would rejoice if this conflict might be brought to an early termination by an arrangement which on the one hand would satisfy the national feelings of the Hungarians and on the other hand should maintain unimpaired the bond of union which has so long connected Hungary with the Austrian Crown.

Whereas point 7 of the official instructions contain only a hint, Palmerston's private letter to Ponsonby, on the same day, states his wishes explicitly, "if you should have reason to think that the friendly intervention of a Third Party might in any respect be acceptable to the Austrian Government as removing difficulties of any kind, Your Excellency is authorised to give the Austrian Government to understand that H.M.'s Government would feel great pleasure in attending without the least delay to any intimation which they might receive of the wishes of the Austrian Government to that effect".[73]

But as if still not convinced that Ponsonby knew the real arguments in favour of negotiations, another private letter was sent by the Foreign Secretary next day.[74] In it, Palmerston prepares Ponsonby for the adverse

reaction of the Austrian Court circles to the English proposal of mediation, and urges him to persevere. Referring to his conversations with
Hungarians in London- he does not name them- Palmerston thinks, that
if the Magyars were assured of the maintenance of their separate nationality and constitution they would submit to the Emperor as King of
Hungary. He argues that Austria would ultimately regret the submission
of the Magyars by aid of a Russian army since it would sow a crop of
future insurrections in the land. Such a victory would be followed by
vengeance, and reducing Hungary to impotence would mean for Austria
to paralyse her own right hand and eventually to surrender her position
as a first rate power. The Foreign Secretary considers, relying on the
advice of the Hungarians in London, that Kossuth would be willing to
come to terms with the Austrians, and that Blackwell, who knows
Kossuth personally, would be the best person to be employed to sound
him. As for the Austrians, Ponsonby should not allow them to put him
off "with stale pretences about non influence, and you must say, moreover, that the feeling in England is becoming so strong and general upon
this matter that it is impossible for the British Government to avoid
making every endeavour in its power to persuade the contending parties
to come to an amicable arrangement".

As far as the Hungarians were concerned Palmerston was right, they
had on several occasions shown willingness to negotiate. The Foreign
Secretary himself may well have remembered that Blackwell had
contacted him, through Ponsonby, about the Hungarian Government's
wish for English mediation. More recently,[75] Kázmár Batthyány had
contacted all Hungarian diplomatic agents, Pulszky amongst them, about
peace proposals and Kossuth himself had asked Stiles, the American
chargé d'affaires in Vienna, to sound the Austrian Cabinet.

But all efforts of peace proposals or mediation were futile with the
Imperial Government.[76] Schwarzenberg refused to read Palmerston's
despatches: the Austrians demanded unconditional surrender.

3. The Hungarian Propaganda Committee.

When Pulszky came to London in March 1849 everything that was
happening in Hungary was transmitted through either the Viennese press
or, at best, through German newspapers, mostly biased against the
Magyars. The outcome of it all was that the British press was talking

about the Hungarian affairs in 'Viennese terminology': the Magyars were rebels, they were continuously defeated by the Imperial troops who came to Hungary to re-establish law and order. Such was the language of General Welden's circulars, Prince Windischgrätz's proclamations, and the articles of the Official Viennese Gazette. Even one of the most liberal British newspapers of the late forties, the Daily News, lacked direct reports from Hungarian sources, kept a correspondent only in Vienna,[77] and, at best, quoted the Breslau Gazette for fragmentary reports on Hungarian victories, at Gyöngyös, Szolnok, and Czegléd.[78] From March onwards, when the name of Pulszky was announced to the readers of the Daily News, this situation started to change.[79] "The struggle which continues on the banks of the Danube and the Theiss every day attracts more attention to the position and affairs of Hungary, but public opinion as to the character of this struggle is formed from imperfect information, and from impressions which induce false conclusions," said Pulszky in his first article in the British press. Pulszky who was no novice in newspaper reporting- he had his training in the Allgemeiner Zeitung- and was an expert on constitutional law, immediately sprang to action and set forth the basic tenets of the Hungarian struggle. The changes that took place in Hungary on 11 April 1848 guaranteed the constitutional liberty of the Hungarian nation and were sanctioned by the Emperor. After the battle of Custozza, against Carlo Alberto, the Viennese Court declared the April laws null and void, and soon forced war on Hungary through Jellashich. As for the character of the Hungarian movement, it is lawful and parliamentary rather than revolutionary, even though one third of the country is occupied by imperial troops. Pulszky sums up his article by observing (a) that the Hungarian question is closely connected with the great Eastern question (b) that the question is political and should not be decided by the sword; rather, Austria's objective should be federation. He signed his first article- signatures were uncommon in the Daily News except in the letter-column, where his was printed- as Francis Pulszky, late Secretary of State for Foreign Affairs. Well disposed as the newspaper had been towards Hungary, it was now put in direct contact with Hungarian printed sources by Pulszky, such as the *Közlöny*,[80] the organ of the Hungarian Government and the *Honvéd*, the army newspaper, and from mid-March onwards, the Daily News became the warmest supporter of the Hungarian cause right through the struggle of the Magyars for independence.

Pulszky's old friend Vipan was also a contributor to the Daily News, and it was through him that the ex-minister had soon gathered a circle of devoted English friends, that came to be known in June as the Hungarian Propaganda Committee. A letter from John Mitchell Kemble to Pulszky, dated 29 March, shows the first signs of the thought of a press campaign by these friends of Hungary. Kemble, who was already a well known historian, and was working, at that time, on his Saxons in England, published later in that year, invited Pulszky, L.W. Birkbeck and Vipan to dinner. These four people became the nucleus of the Committee.

At the beginning of May, after the second interview between Pulszky and Palmerston, we see the dominant questions formulating in Vipan's mind, which set the direction of the pro-Hungarian propaganda "Can Hungary resist 180,000 men",[81] of the Czar? And the practical question, what can we do to help Hungary? Vipan advises that the friends should distribute the tasks, Birkbeck should talk to the editors of the newspapers, he has little time to write articles, Kemble should write some of them and Pulszky needs a messenger and translators. Three days later[82] he urges Pulszky to write or dictate new articles now, when- in his opinion- Lord Palmerston needs the pressure of public opinion to force him into action against the Russians. Birkbeck devises a programme consisting of five points to tune up public opinion in favour of Hungary:[83] 1. The demands of the Magyars are moderate and just. 2. The demands of the Croatians and Slovenians should be dealt with in peaceful negotiations. 3. The Hungarians do not even want indemnification for their losses caused by the war. 4. It should be proved to the public that Russian intervention in Hungary is against the principles of international law. 5. The tolerance of the Hungarian middle-class should be set against the intolerance of the Croatians. Articles on these lines should be written for the Globe and for the Standard of Freedom.

The problem by the middle of May was how to explain the dethronement to the public, or rather, how to explain that this extreme measure of the Hungarian Government was justified. The organs, according to Vipan, should be the Edinburgh Review, the Observer, the Spectator and the Globe. The news of the Hungarian Declaration of Independence appeared in the Daily News[84] with the enthusiastic comment "The

14 April 1849 is an eternal era in the history of Hungary."[85] More reasoning is needed for the weeklies and the periodicals, such as the *Edinburgh Review* and the *Examiner*, argues Vipan in his letter of 14 May;[86] the writers (Pulszky for the former, Birkbeck for the latter), should stress that a united Hungary with 14 million people should be stronger than a disunited Austria with 31 million.

In the same letter Vipan praises the translators, Stolzmann and Bachman, and complains that Pulszky is never found at home. We can deduce from these letters that Pulszky wrote his articles in German, and employed two translators who put these into English, and from these 'roughs' Kemble produced the final products. So within the little circle, Pulszky provided the information, Vipan the ideas, Kemble the style, and Birkbeck the distribution. By the end of the month, the little group had supplied half a dozen newspapers and periodicals with articles, but the problems were mounting and the members were not content with the results.

The lack of books written in English about current affairs in Hungary made three works, which were recently published in France, very popular. Soon everyone in the group owned a copy of Boldényi's[87] and De Gérando's[88] books and Count Teleki's pamphlet *Question Austro-Hongroise et l'intervention Russe.*[89] These works mention a point that Vipan got hold of, a point that will be emphasised in Parliament, by the defenders of the Hungarian case, that will be propagated widely in the press, and will be echoed in nearly all meetings called together for the Magyars: Hungary was the only country which had an ancient constitution comparable to that of England.

In the beginning of June the group decided to form a Committee which could deal even more effectively with the dissemination of information. The Hungarian Propaganda Committee had elected Birkbeck chairman, Kemble secretary and assembled eight times between 4 June and 16 July. The meetings were held in Pulszky's new lodgings, at 122 Jermyn Street. From the Minutes of the Proceedings, preserved in the Hungarian National Library, we can follow the work of the Committee.[90] At the first meeting of 4 June, Nicholas Kiss, Hungarian Colonel, was also present as well as Pulszky, Birkbeck and Kemble. Vipan had complained of ill health lately, and moved to the country keeping contact through letters with the other members. The meeting decided to stress the point that the Hungarian movement was neither republican, nor Polish-orientated, but had a 'national' character. The *Examiner*, the *Standard of Freedom*, the *Spectator* and the *Observer* should be notified accordingly. The falsifications of the anti-Hungarian press (i.e. mainly the *Times*) should be corrected in an article by Pulszky, to appear every Saturday in the Daily News. Duly, Pulszky's article appeared, under the cover-name 'Hungarus' on 4 June: "Sir, the credit which your impartial paper justly enjoys, has excited in me the wish to rectify every week the intentional and unintentional errors, with respects to events in Hungary, that find their way into the English newspapers. . .". The first bunch of these errors concerns the allegations that the Poles are dominating the Hungarian movement, and the value of the Hungarian paper-money.[91] A week later[92] Pulszky, now using the signature 'Hungary' corrects information about the Russian advance, which is slower than reported to be, and about the respective behaviour of Austrian and Hungarian forces towards the population. On 22 June, in an unsigned article, Pulszky published a list of the chief officers of the Hungarian army, showing their respective country of origin. On 26 June, signing himself as "Hungary", he gave an account of recent military operations, and exactly a month later, signing himself as 'Hungarus'[93] he refuted the charge made by the *Morning Chronicle* that some Hungarians sympathised with Russia.

At the second meeting of the Committee, held at Jermyn Street on 7 June, two new members were present: Charles Pridham and Thomas Banfield. Next day[94] Vipan, who had missed the meeting, wrote to Pulszky that the British Government had received intelligence regarding Kossuth's intentions to create a federative state with the Principalities under Turkish suzerainty. In Vipan's opinion, Palmerston had nothing against such a confederation, provided it was strong enough to withstand the might of Russia. Three days later,[95] Pulszky replied to Vipan. He thought that if Eastern Europe was reorganised in such a way that Hungary would benefit by it, it would bring peace to Europe. Despotism reigned in Austria whereas the freedom of the press was secure in Hungary. Austria operated with strict customs law and with other trade restrictions, while Hungary pursued a policy of free trade. In Galicia, the Russians took over police duties and postal administration, because the Austrians had proved unable to make law and order. Only the peoples themselves, acting by their own free will, could secure lasting peace. Pulszky offering these thoughts, wrote to Vipan, to utilise them for the Hungarian cause.

At the third meeting, held at the same place on 11 June, the newcomers were Colonel Bikessy, Mr. Fejér[96] and Mr. Somerer. Regarding the press, they sent material since the last meetting to the *Examiner*, the *Morning Herald*, the *Globe* and the *Daily News*. At the meeting they decided to ask for a list of the most important newspapers in the country, from Taylor.[97] Two letters were read, one from Vipan, and one from Dawson. The later was written by a gentleman from Birmingham, who had collected money for the Hungarian cause and was now asking the Committee what he should do with the collected sum. The Committee entrusted Colonel Bikessy and W. Banfield to meet the gentleman from Birmingham next day.

The fourth meeting took place on 14 June, in the presence of J.E. Taylor[98] but in the presence of Pulszky who had gone to Paris.[99] Banfield gave an account of their meeting with Mr. Dawson, the gentleman from Birmingham. The outcome was that Mr. Dawson had decided to go to Hungary in order to be able to report personally to firms in Birmingham about the state of things there. Banfield agreed to write to the *Mining Journal* on the question of trading with Hungary.

On 18 June, the date of the next meeting, Pulszky was present again, and was entrusted to write an account of the war, interspersed with anecdotes for the *Observer*. Vipan was to write on the Russian intrigues for the *Examiner*, and J. Crosse on autonomy in Hungary, for the *Spectator*.

The sixth meeting, held on Monday, 25 June, drew up, as usual, the press programme of the week, which included contacting two more publications hitherto not supplied with articles. It was decided that Pulszky should write anecdotes for *Bell's Life* and Kemble should contribute an article for the *Nonconformist* on religious toleration in Hungary.

The Committee suggested that Pulszky should write to Lord Palmerston on behalf of Colonel Bikessy, seeking an interview with the British Foreign Minister. A letter from Prince Czartoryski to Dudley Stuart was read out and a discussion followed on the possibilities of public meetings to be held in the West End.

Pulszky and Vipan exchanged letters in the days following the Committee meeting. Enumerating his arguments for the next contribution to the *Examiner*, Vipan wants to forewarn readers that if Hungary is defeated it will be due entirely to the Russian intervention, so unpopular in England.[100] If the Russians win it will be the end of free trade and of civilisation in Eastern Europe.

Two guests, arriving from Paris, William Sandford and Count László Teleki, were present at the next meeting at 122 Jermyn Street, held on 9 July.[101] When Teleki had met Droyn de l'Huys in May, in private, he told the French Foreign Secretary that if the great powers failed to protest against Russian intervention, the Hungarians would try all propaganda methods abroad to save their country.[102] The discussion in the Committee revolved around the propaganda methods to be transmitted through the press to bring pressure to bear upon the British Government to recognise Kossuth's Administration.

The Austrian Government was aware of Pulszky's influence in the British press, and Colloredo, the Ambassador in London, decided to act. On 10 July, an article appeared in the *Times*, signed by "a Hungarian", which purported to represent conservative Hungarian views, condoning Austrian policy in Hungary and condemning Kossuth and his extremists. Calling attention to this article, Vipan wrote to Pulszky next day[103] urging him to reply to this article in the *Times* since it might have the effect of dividing the British public. Although Pulszky took up the challenge[104] and wrote a letter to the *Times* on the following day, Vipan's next letter shows[105] that it did not repair the damage, as the English attach particular importance to the principle of *audiatur et altera pars*. The *Spectator*, for instance, ceased to publish pro-Hungarian articles. Neither the British public nor Pulszky[106] and his circle knew at the time, that "a Hungarian" was a Magyar Count, Antal Széchen, employed by Schwarzenberg and Colloredo. His subsequent reports[107] to Prince Schwarzenberg, which are preserved in the State Archives in Vienna, show that Széchen wrote four pro-Habsburg essays on the constitutional questions of Hungary. Széchen's main thesis, as expressed in these essays, was that Chapter 10/1791[108] secured the rights of the Hungarians to self-government only and not to constitutional independence, as claimed by Kossuth, whose victory- the new laws of April 1848- was achieved by extortion.

The eighth meeting of the Hungarian Propaganda Committee, the last for which Minutes have survived, was held on 16 July. Birkbeck, Teleki, Pulszky, Fejér, Sandford, Kemble and Wimmer[109] were in attendance. After the review of the material to be sent to the usual run of journals, Sandford called attention to the *Illustrated London News* and undertook the task of writing an article for it. The Committee prepared a number of suggestions which shall be put forward as resolutions by the orators of the public meeting to be held on 23 July. The Committee adjourned until Friday, 20 July.

We have no evidence proving that the Committee met again although some of the members remained active in the next phase, when public meetings for the Hungarian cause were in the centre of their interest.

The continuity of Anglo-Hungarian relations, which had existed up to the Treaties of Vienna, was preserved by Hungarian aristocrats serving in the Austrian diplomatic service in England. When in 1848, Hungary acquired a new status within the Austrian Monarchy, her politicians sought to establish direct political links with Britain. After repeated failures, Francis Pulszky, formerly Hungarian Under-Secretary of State in Vienna, self-appointed Emissary to England, succeeded in meeting the British Foreign Secretary in private, but could not achieve recognition for the independent Hungarian Government. His good social contacts enabled him to establish a Propaganda Committee in London. This mobilised the English press to support the Hungarians, when the Habsburgs, bent on the depriving Hungary of her independence, called in the Russian army. Although Pulszky could not persuade Palmerston to protest against the invasion, his representation and the press propaganda he engineered made Palmerston decide to mediate between Hungary and her enemies. As the Austrians demanded unconditional surrender, the war continued.

The first Hungarian Minister in London put up as resilient a fight on the fields of diplomacy and 'back-door diplomacy' as the nation had done on the real battlefields.

CHAPTER TWO

THE EMIGRANT

1. Relief for the Exiles.
> *Sympathy without relief, is like to mustard*
> *without beef.*

(*Daily News.* 17 August 1849)

In the beginning of August it was evident that Hungary would not be able to hold out for long. Palmerston's official despatches and private instructions sent to Ponsonby in Vienna, on preliminary steps leading to peace proposals, attempted to obtain the diplomatic co-operation of Prussia through Lord Westmorland, the English Ambassador in Berlin. But the Prussian Foreign Minister, Schleinitz, was just as slow, and even reluctant, as the French Foreign Secretary, Tocqueville, to join in with mediatory proposals[1] as if waiting for the inevitable end.

Meanwhile Kossuth and the Hungarian Government took desperate measures in trying to get official recognition and political acceptance by England. Kázmér Batthyány in his letter to Pulszky of 14 July 1849,[2] proposes a federative alliance of the Danubian States, headed by Turkey, which could replace Austria in the European balance policy. Kossuth, who had already considered the idea of a federation, with Hungary as its centre, had also instructed his finance minister, Francis Duschek, to devise a new scheme of Anglo-Hungarian treaties, was now ready to offer even the Hungarian crown to a member of the Koburg family. As no positive response was forthcoming he intimated to Bem that at the last resort the Hungarian throne could be offered to a member of the de-throned Habsburg family, other than Francis Joseph.[3]

When Kossuth wrote to Bem on 14 August, he was already fleeing the country, having resigned the leadership to General Görgei. When Pulszky, on 16 August, communicated the latest despatches of the Hungarian Government to Palmerston,[4] he was still unaware of the surrender of arms by Görgei on 13 August. The news took a long time to travel and even longer to register. In 13 August issue of the *Daily*

News[5] a report from the Vienna correspondent of the paper still hails the recent victories of Görgei and those of Bem. Reports of the pro-Hungarian meetings show that on 14 August a great assembly in Birmingham, presided by Samuel Thornton, still demanded the *independence of Hungary*[6] and the Manchester meeting of the next day[7] echoed the *Free Trade with Hungary* petition. On 16 August a meeting in Westminister, with Charles Lushington in the chair, Lord Nugent and Dudley Stuart present, welcomed "Madam Pulszky[8] who had personally defied the bayonets of the Czar," meaning she had recently escaped from Hungary to join her husband in London. And when, finally, the news of the surrender reached London on 21 August, and the Daily News informed its readers on 23rd, the public, as Sproxton says, "worked itself into a perfect frenzy for the Hungarians". The meetings continued throughout August, September and October.[9] The "demands" were substituted by resolutions and petitions sent to the English Government expressing anxiety for the vanquished. At the end of August sixteen members of the Parliament, headed by Lord Fitzwilliam, handed in a memorandum to Lord Russel and Palmerston, requesting the British Government to thwart the wholesale destruction of Hungary by Austrian vengeance.

When the Austrians gained control of the whole of Hungary- by the end of September, Pétervárad and Komárom, the last two fortresses held by Hungarians had also capitulated- they instituted an unprecedented reign of terror over the country. Thirteen of the leading generals[10] and the former Prime Minister, Count Louis Batthyány, were executed, civil and military officials were imprisoned, women who were implicated in the freedom-fight were flogged and tortured. Upset by the news, Teleki writes to Pulszky on 13 September and again three days later:[11] "The news from Hungary are depressing. If only you could do something for those who are detained..." But Pulszky's own uncle, old Gábor Fejérváry, the collector of antiquaries who had never meddled in politics, was detained too, and was only set free on the condition that he would stop all contacts with his nephew in London.[12] Pulszky's three children were safe in Vienna with their grandparents the Wagners, but were refused passports to come and join their parents in England. Kossuth's wife went into hiding inside the country, but his children were captured and detained. The ex-Governor himself was granted asylum in Turkey together with some of his ministers, and about 5,000 troops.

But the first Hungarian refugees did not come from Hungary and had reached Toulon before the contest ended. They were a squad of Hungarian Hussars who had originally served in the Imperial Army stationed in Italy but when the war broke out between Austria and Piedmont they went over to the Italian side. After the armistice they were sent over by Italians to the French who wanted to enlist them for the Foreign Legion. Only a minority complied, while the majority, 110 soldiers, were assisted by Teleki[13] while his money lasted. In July they were shipped over to Folkestone.[14]

The second group of Hungarian soldiers to come out to the West were the defenders of Komorn.[15] With their commander, George Klapka, they were granted a free pass by the besieging general, Prince Windischgrätz. These soldiers went to Hamburg first, in October, then came over to Britain in November with the intention of finding employment or emigrating to America from here.

The third set of emigrants was an admixture of diplomats, agents on political or commercial missions, aristocrats with independent means who took part in the freedom fight but could escape in time, highranking officials who had managed to escape either direct from Hungary, or from Kossuth's entourage detained in Turkey and finally, employees of the Paris and London agencies of Teleki and Pulszky.

At the time of Klapka's arrival Pulszky and Wimmer were working on a memorandum requesting the release of Kossuth's children. "Pulszky lived in a good distance from the middle of the town, in a very neat little house in Peterborough Square,"[16] writes General Klapka in his *Recollections*. "He instantly made us acquainted with the political situation in England and revealed to us everything for our benefit as well as for our nation's advantage. As a first thing he tried to dissuade some of my companions to hope for financial assistance from the people who were interested in our case. . . . Everybody should try to make his own living," (said Pulszky). "His words had the effect of a cold shower and produced the good result that the majority of the soldiers from Komorn decided to continue their journey to America, as soon as it was possible. Újházy (a colonel in the army) was leading them and their plan was to establish a Hungarian colony overseas."

Those who wished to remain in England, as Lieutenant Colonel Mednyánszky and Colonel Szabó, and indeed Klapka himself, were introduced by Pulszky to his friends, notably to Lord Dudley Stuart,

Cobden and Cockburn, among the English politicians, and to Mazzini, Ledru Rollin and Louis Blanc, among the distinguished foreigners.

The Folkstone group of Hungarian refugees was catered for by a committee which announced its fromation on 21 July in the Daily News:[17]"We, the undersigned, having formed ourselves into a provisional committee to afford relief and support to the distressed Hungarian soldiers and to collect subscriptions...earnestly invite the contributions and co-operations of all parties, who either from sympathy with the Hungarian cause or on the broad grounds of humanity and benevolence, may be disposed to concur in the object of the committee." (Signed) "Lord Nugent, M.P., Chairman; Lord Dudley Coutts Stuart, M.P., C. Lushington, M.P." etc. . . .

Altogether twenty-six members from the two Houses of Parliaments signed the article in the Daily News. This English Committee, which was formed to help the first group of Magyar soldiers, came to provide the basic financial and social assistance to all the three Hungarian refugee groups assembled in Britain by the end of the war. The Committee resolved to provide financial assistance to all Hungarians for three months while they could get acquainted with the circumstances in Britain, could learn the language and could find employment. Those who were incapable to take advantage of this help could get their travelling-fares to go to America and some pocket-money to last a month.[18]

Some of the Hungarians, indeed, found employment and made a living from themselves in Britain. Their former army commanders-Klapka and Szabó in particular- were in favour of their staying together or as closely connected with one another as was possible, in the hope that if a new insurrection were to start in Hungary they should be ready to join in. Others could not get used to the idea that emigrants were expected to work, and so waited either for a pension similar to what the Poles had received in the thirties or had blamed Pulszky, who had the best connections, for not having found work for them. To resolve the mounting difficulties an Association of the Hungarian Political Exiles was formed in London under the chairmanship of Klapka and with Pulszky as vice-chairman. This Association functioned in co-operation with the English Relief Committee for the Hungarians, until the arrival of Kossuth in England in October 1851, when it was re-organised on new lines.

The Association was formed in the beginning of January 1850, and according to Tanárky's short entries in his diary,[19] it discussed political questions in the *first period*: should the Hungarians give up their 'national supremacy' and form a federative alliance with the neighbouring small nations.

An unpublished document, the *Minutes* of five general and twelve committee meetings of the Association, preserved in the Department of MSS. of the Hungarian National Library[20] provides us with data regarding the *second phase* in the operation of the Association from 19 February 1850 to 30 April 1850.

The reason for calling together a General Meeting on *19 February* was that Klapka had decided to leave England and asked the General Meeting to elect a new committee with a new chairman. The eighteen members present first elected István Gorove, former Minister of State, as chairman, but as he refused office, Pulszky was elected chairman by a second secret ballot. Mayer, a furrier who had found employment in London, was elected treasurer, Dióssy, a tradesman, became secretary, Gorove, Mednyánszky and Szabó, members of the executive committee.

A similar association had already been functioning in Hamburg, in Sumla (Turkey), with the detained Kossuth as chairman, and in Paris, where Gorove, when he took up residence there, became president.[21]

It it perhaps sadly typical of political emigrations, and the Hungarians of 1849 were no exceptions, that as a first measure a "Court of Honour" had to be created to settle dissensions among the exiles.[22] Pulszky relates in his *Memoirs*[23] how a troublesome Captain Géza Miháloczy, recipient of Pulszky's overcoat, repeatedly slandered him, accused him of partiality in distributing relief and finally challenged him to a duel. Pulszky remarked that he was "not going to perforate his own overcoat with a bullet" but as the captain kept on pestering him, he decided on a duel with swords.

The *General Meeting of 24 February*, confirmed the constitution of the previous meeting in the presence of nineteen members, and decided to deal with the petitions for relief on the next committee meeting. Some of the members were lucky or enterprising enough to help themselves. Gyula Tanárky, Pulszky's one-time manager of his estates, who had succeeded in smuggling out his employer's children at the close of 1849, became the tutor of the children in London, and Pulszky's personal secretary. Manovil, who was a Hungarian Jew, received regular help from a succession of Anglican priests who were trying to convert him to the Christian religion.[24] B. Mauksch, former editor of a revolutionary journal in Arad, became a stock-broker, Mednyánszky was employed by a Greek merchant. Usually those with knowledge of languages succeeded sooner or later.

Material and moral assistance was forthcoming from at least two emigrant sources. The printing press requested formerly by Guggenheim, who had been a printer in Hungary, was bought for him by Herr Bamberger, editor of the Londoner Deutscher Zeitung.[25] A former lieutenant in the Polish Army, Charles Szulczewski, who became one of Prince Czartoryski's secretaries, co-operated with Lord Nugent and Lord Dudley Stuart to provide for the first Hungarian refugees, the soldiers from Italy.[26]

Pulszky as chairman coveyed his special thanks to all the helpers. His attention extended from the small details of sending the addresses of cheaper lodgings to exiles, and entertaining requests from the exiles in Paris, to refute falsifications on the Vienna papers as quoted by the English London Press.

The Association repeatedly warned its members against various unmerited claims for assistance, and against impostors collecting aid under false pretences. The *General Meeting of 30 March* refused a request for aid from Imre Rosenthal, a Hungarian scholar who was not an exile. The *Committee, meeting on 15 April*, regretfully turned down a financial plea from Polish exiles in London for the "Committee could scarcely cater for its own nationals". Discussion took place on the *Committee meetings of 8 and 15 April*, about dealing with "unknown persons who misused the Hungarian name and the sympathy towards the Hungarians".[27] One of the "grandest" of such imposters was Ephrem Leo Jacob Koricosz,[28] 'prince of Armenia', who claimed to have descended from Mary of Hungary, daughter of Louis I of Anjou and from Jacob VI Prince of Armenia. Koricosz turned up in London in the autumn of 1849 when the sympathy for the Hungarians was at its height and claimed that he was an implacable enemy of the Czar, who had disinherited him as Armenian ruler and oppressed his 'brothers' the Hungarians. He gained the confidence of Lady Jersey, Lord Dudley Stuart, László Teleki, and even the astute Pulszky himself. Pulszky introduced him to

Charles II of Braunschweig, and it was only several years later that Koricosz was unmasked as the son of a Dutch merchant called Joannis. Another of the would-be impostors, "Comte Jean Sobolewski" who had solicited the favours of the Prince of Braunschweig, was disclaimed by Pulszky.[29]

On the *Committee meeting of 25 February* the Chairman gave an account of the distribution of £335 as financial relief to thirty-nine exiles of whom nine were provided with travel fares and sent to America. Applications of small sums of money for starting up a business, or buying joiners' implements, or a lithographic press, were listed and added to further travel-fare requests and petitions for a monthly aid or repayment of debts. The total sum requested -£176- was communicated to the English Committee. It appears that the English Committee considered these requests monthly, though they were not always able to give the whole sum requested by the Hungarian Association. On *1 March Committee meeting* a letter from the English Committee, signed by Mr. Willich[30] (sic) was read out, informing the Association that they could have only £150 out of £176 that had been requested.

We learn the details of further requests for financial assistance from the Minutes of *4, 11, 15 and 25 March Committee Meetings.* Among the persons first applying for assistance was Ödön Beöthy, a former Hungarian envoy to Bucarest, Captain Gyula Számwald, aide-de-Camp of the British officer Richard Guyon, who became general in the Hungarian army, and Baroness von Beck "who had accomplished several missions in the service of the Hungarian Government".[31]

The Committee of the Association expressed its gratitude on several occasions to those members of the British public who were prominent in displaying their sympathy for the Hungarians. The name of Lord Dudley Stuart is mentioned at practically all the meetings, Birkbeck, former chairman of the Hungarian Propaganda Committee in 1849, was twice sent letters of thanks for his continuous interest and activity, in March and April 1850. Special sentiments of appreciation were conveyed to Judge Johnes in Wales, by the Committee, meeting on 8, 15, 22 April.

The Welsh had been particularly enthusiastic for the Hungarian cause. Their non-conformist ministers interpreted the Hungarians as Protestant Magyars struggling against Roman Catholic Austrians. Furthermore, their attitude towards England was that of the *ruled* towards the *ruler*, so they easily identified themselves with the Magyars fighting for their independence.[32] Public opinion in the Welsh language was moulded by the weekly newspaper *Yr Amsereau*, whihc had been published in Liverpool since 1843 under the editorship of an Independent minister in that city, Rev. William Rees, better known as Gwilym Hiraethog. In the English language, it was the *Carnarvon and Denbigh Herald*, a liberal newspaper circulating in North Wales which gave its most vocal support to the Hungarians. The prime mover behind the Welsh sympathy was Arthur James Johnes who appeared in the columns of the Herald as "Cambrensis". He was a judge in the County Court of North West Wales, a radical, a disciple of Bentham, a great believer in education and the freedom of the press. It was he who organised the first meeting of sympathy at Liverpool in mid-November 1849 which was followed by other meetings in rapid succession, at Bala, Aberystwyth and Bangor. Judge Johnes regarded the meetings not merely as beneficial to the unfortunate Hungarians, with whom he most sincerely sympathised, but also as offering proof to the English that the Welsh were alive to the cruelties of the Autocrats, quick to feel in the name of humanity and Christianity for the Hungarians, and progressive enough to make full use of press and platform to register their opinion on the matter.[33]

On 15 April Szabó and Mednyánszky from the Committee members, and Lieutenant Colonel Kékessy and Dr. Glück from the ordinary members of the Association, decided to travel down to Wales and hand over a letter of thanks to Judge Johnes personally. They met the Judge at Cerrig-y-Drudion. A week later they were back in London to inform the Committee Meeting of 22 April, that Mr. Johnes was ready to find employment for those members of the emigration who could speak English. Although the Hungarians had not asked the Judge for financial aid, Johnes now drew up an Address to his fellow countrymen asking for their subscriptions on behalf of the refugees, starting off the list himself with a donation of £20.

The last *General Meeting* of the Association, whose Minutes are preserved, was held on 3 May in the presence of thirty-two members. On this meeting it was decided that there will be a change in the constitution of the Association and to avoid dissensions the English Committee will be asked to distribute financial assistance directly to those in need. The members of the executive Committee having resigned, the General

Meeting elected a new Committee as follows: Chairman: Pulszky; Treasurer and Secretary as before; ordinary members: Ödön Beöthy, Andorfy and Captain Ágoston Grisza.

In the two years from the summer of 1849 to the autumn of 1851 when Kossuth came to London there were 313 exiles[34] of the Hungarian War of Independence who came to, or passed through, London. Some of these were only guests from Paris; others -158 of them- sailed to America. Twenty-six of the emigrants were Poles who had fought in the Polish legion in Hungary. Eighty or so was the total number of Hungarian exiles who decided to stay in England. Many of these continued to shower requests on Pulszky[35] long after he ceased to be the chairman of their Association.

2. Literary activities.

> "O Magyar, to thy country act
> A firm and faithful part!
> She gives thee strength; and if thou fall;
> She hides thee in her heart."[36]

General Klapka relates in his *Recollections*[37] how he turned to Pulszky for advice in his financial difficulties at the close of 1849 in London. "When I described my position to Pulszky he said that in the circumstances I have no other way out than to write a book within the shortest possible time. For my *Memoirs* could get especially good royalties for me. Then he dropped the word at *Chapman and Hall*, publishers, and promised to let me know the details soon.

"Nothing could have embarrassed me more than the offer. Straightaway I said to Pulszky that I would find it impossible to write a serious work in the short time I had in my disposal.

" 'But you have to do it,' he answered, 'if you don't want to starve' . . . The contract was signed within a few days. I had £100 in advance and was to have another £100 as soon as I will have finished the manuscript . . . The English translator, Mr. Wenkstern,[38] a correspondent of the *Times*, accomplished his work efficiently and so, completely exhausted, I finished my work in six weeks . . . The Library of the British

Museum contained . . . historical documents relating to our country
and from these what was necessary for us. So my first 'Memoirs' were
born.[39]

As financial difficulties made Klapka write, the same reasons applied
to Pulszky himself. He had a choice though. Lord Lansdowne who had
been kindly disposed to the Pulszky family asked him what he was going
to live on in England. Pulszky answered[40] that he was to live by his pen.
Lord Lansdowne then offered to open a credit account for him at a
bank. Pulszky declined saying that he would not make debts he might
never be able to pay back.

But Pulszky had another strong motive also urging him to write.[41]
Even though the military struggle had ended the fight had to be continued for the cause of Hungary. The Austrian embassy[42] in London
brought out a half-official "Esquise de la guerre in Hongrie" (London,
1849), which accused the Hungarians with cruelties and transgressions
of the law during the war. A book by Lewitschnigg[43] brought out in
Hungary, abused "Kossuth und seine Bannerschaft" for lawlessness.
Such attacks should not remain unanswered, particularly at the time
when the Magyar constitutional rights were so openly ignored by the
Austrians re-establishing themselves in Hungary.

The works that had so far appeared on Hungary, and were known
at least by a section of the public were, with a few exceptions, travelogues,
written by Englishmen. Robert Townson's *Travels in Hungary* was more
than fifty, and Richard Bright's travelogue was more than thirty, years
out of date.[44] Of the accounts and descriptions of Beattie, Miss Pardoe,
and John Paget,[45] the last was the most trustworthy but even this lacked
political actuality. A taste of Hungarian poetry (not quite authentic)
could be gained from John Bowring's little anthology[46] and Hungarian
folklore was introduced by Mrs. Gore. The only eye-witness account
of some of the events connected with the war was a thin book comprising
three lectures by T.G. Clark, a Scotsman, who had resided in Hungary
for eighteen months, between 1847-49.[47] Sympathetic as he is towards
the troubles of his former hosts, Clark feels non-qualified to pass judgement on the issues at stake, leaving this for more competent observers.

Pulszky, as former Under-Secretary of State for Foreign Affairs and
envoy extraordinary to England was certainly better qualified than most
to write a book on Hungary, but even he looked upon the last dramatic

phase of the struggle from outside, as it were, since he had left the country
in January 1849. His wife, on the other hand, joined her husband in
July 1849, having lived through the vicissitudes of the War in Hungary.
So in a way, the combined experiences of husband and wife were needed
to produce a work which could satisfy most requirements: a historical
background from the Hungarian point of view, facts regarding the constitutional issues and an eye-witness account of the events of the War.
Such a book was the "Memoirs of a Hungarian Lady" (henceforth referred to as the *Diary*), written by Mrs. Pulszky[48] with the cooperation
of her husband.

This literary partnership[49] which blossomed out in London in the
fifties, producing two further works: *Tales and traditions of Hungary*,
and *White, red, black* in 1851 and 1853 respectively, had the background
of an exceptionally happy marriage. Theresa Pulszky -nee Walter- born in
Berlin in 1819, was the only daughter of a wealthy German banker. Even
the circumstances of her acquaintance with Francis and his proposal
of marriage to her had a literary setting. Theresa's interest in Francis
was awakened by his article in the *Frankfurter Allgemeiner Zeitung*,
which she had read. Francis proposed to her during the preparation of
a Salon-performance of *A Midsummer Night's Dream*. He describes the
occasion vividly in his *Memoris*: . . . "I took her hands and said: 'I love
you. Will you be mine?' She was startled, her cheeks turned red, withdrew
her hands from mine, and said as she ran away into the library: 'Speak
to my mother tomorrow' . . .[50]

Theresa had kept a diary. There are nineteen volumes of this unpublished work in the Széchányi Library. Her entry for that day in 1844
reads: "Apr.25. Morg.6. Freitag. Lieben Gott ich danke Dir! Verdienen
kan ich mir Seligkeit die mich erfüllt . . .[51]

In October 1849 we find Theresa busy[52] writing her second book
in English. The first was a translation of Lermontov's *Hero of our days*[53]
into English, in 1847 when the Pulszky couple was still in their country
estate in Szécsény, Hungary. We learn from the family secretary, Tanárky,
that the *Diary* was being copied up by him for the publisher at the end
of November, 1849.[54] It was published in the beginning of 1850 and was
an instant success. According to the *Edinburgh Review* it cannot fail
to interest all classes of readers, those who open a book only for amuse-
ments and those who look for something more enduring. The *Globe*

compared Mrs. Pulszky to Madame de Staël. The reviewer of the *Morning Post* praised the joint effort of the Pulszkys for the interest of history, the charms of romance, the richness in social illustration and topographical description that are contained in the volume. Apparently the reviewers either missed or were too polite to point out the subtle Hungarian propaganda that permeates the work.

Even in her dedicatory remarks to *The Marchioness of Lansdowne* Mrs. Pulszky expresses her wish that her "unadorned narrative may help to rectify some erroneous notions spread abroad respecting Hungary".[55] This rectification starts with Francis Pulszky's long introductory essay on the history of Hungary. The factual outline of this essay goes back to a work Pulszky published in his youth: *Ideas to the philosophy of the History of Hungary*.[56] which remained, however, unfinished. "The reason was that because of censorship, I could not even hope to express my views regarding the rule of the House of Habsburg," said Pulszky later.[57] His views were certainly condemning. In the *historical introduction*, the third period of Hungarian history: "under the Kings of the Houses of Habsburg and Lorraine," is contrasted with the first two periods, "under the House of Árpád" and "under Kings from different Houses" with the main conclusion that the Habsburg rulers were repeatedly trying to curtail the ancient constitutional freedom of the Hungarians. From the earliest Habsburg rulers, such as Ferdinand's successor, Rudolph, the King's policy was "Faciam Hungariam prius mendicam, dein germanam, postea catholicam".[58] The constant violation of the Constitution, such as religious intolerance, increase in taxation, governing without a Palatine[59] or failing to convoke the Diet produced insurgence, revolution, civil war, one after another. In 1606 Stephen Bocskay was at the head of the Malcontents, the terror measures of Leopold I provoked the Zrinyi -Frangepán conspiracy; in 1703-1712 it was Rákóczy's turn to fight for the liberties of Hungary and finally, in 1848, as if to fall in the well established pattern, Kossuth did the same. Never distorting the facts but emphasising mainly the painful lessons to be learned from three centuries of Habsburg rule in Hungary, Pulszky produced a masterpiece of propaganda writing.

The main body of the book, Theresa's *Diary* is an exceptionally well-written narrative of her life in Hungary, from her very first impressions, which were those of an intelligent foreigner to the description of their life in the country where she took her place as a wife of a progressive Magyar landowner. Throughout the first volume Theresa employs a simple and successful stylistical device of conjuring up historical tales at every topographical description so that the cultural information provided, would impregnate the mind of the reader. And furthermore, these traditions usually relate to those figures of the Hungarian past, who are depicted as constitutional heroes in the historical introduction, such as Mathias Corvinus, Bocskay and Kossuth. In the prodigious notes which accompany they text explaining the government (Vol.I. P.50-51), the nobility (Vol.I. P.52), or the Palatine (Vol.I. P.111), we can detect her husband's hand.

The events of the war from the invasion of Jellashich in September 1848 to the epoch of Hungarian victories in the spring and eary summer of 1849 are depicted in the last three chapters of the first, and the first eight chapters of the second volume.

The chronology of events, which includes the description of the Vienna insurrection of October 1849 and Francis Pulszky's share in it, is interrupted by a long appraisal of the patriotic and constitutional character of Count Louis Batthyány.[60] This chapter is a word by word reprint of an article in the Daily News, 16 November 1849, which Pulszky wrote to refute the Austrian charges of treason against Batthyány and his alleged complicity in the murder of Count Latour. To justify the execution of Count Batthyány, the Austrian writers in the Cabinet and in the press alleged that the Vienna revolution and the assassination of Count Latour were provoked by Hungarian advice and bribes.[61] Louis Batthyány in particular, has been charged with having, by means of Francis Pulszky, corrupted the Austrian press, parliament and soldiery.[62] These charges which had originally appeared in the Wiener Zeitung were given credit in the *Quarterly Review*[63] and were believed in by the Viennese Ambassador, Lord Ponsonby. Pulszky did not stop with the defense of Batthyány and himself at the printed word, but took out a writ against the Editor of the *Quarterly Review* and won the lawsuit.

The Viennese action and accusations and his Ambassador's credulity evoked the indignation of Lord Palmerston too. In a letter from the Foreign Office, dated 19 October 1849, he wrote to Lord Ponsonby:[64] "I am sorry that in your Despatch about the execution of Batthyány you put in, the wicked and base excuse . . . for the murder of that unfortunate Hungarian . . . that he had anything to do with Latour's murder which if I remember right was the result of a popular tumult . . ."

The last chapter of Mrs. Pulszky's work deals with the *catastrophe* from the surrender of arms by Görgei to the unlawful execution of the Hungarian generals in Arad. This act of vengeance was not only proved to have been unlawful murder by statutory quotations in the Pulszkys' book, (Vol.II. P.278), but were condemned by Palmerston himself.[65] "I say murder, because it was such; for if ever there was a rightful resistance to unlawful exercise of arbitrary power it was that of the Hungarians against the illegal and unconstitutional abrogation of their ancient Constitution by the Viennese Government." Palmerston's tone is indeed more passionate than those of the ten appendices of documentary evidence proving the same points at the end of the first joint work of Theresa and Francis Pulszky.

The literary partnership of husband and wife bore its second fruit a year after the publication of the first one. The *Tales and Traditions of Hungary*[66] appeared in three volumes in London, 1851. The first volume contains diverse literary material, entitled *Popular tales and traditions of Hungary* while the second and third volumes contain a novel by Francis Pulszky called *The Jacobins in Hungary.*

"The poetical genius of a people is expressed in its traditions"[67] state the authors in their introduction to the collection of popular tales from diverse parts of Hungary. Ever since the Grimm brothers directed public attention to the fact, that many popular tales and proverbs are fragments of ancient mythology, the habit of collecting these tales became widespread. Pulszky published three small pieces of Northern Hungarian tales of his own collecting as early as 1840.[68] In the collection of twenty tales published by the Pulszky couple, they attempted to gather Hungarian traditions of manifold kinds whihc belong to the different nationalities who inhabit the country. The Slovak tradition is represented by "Yanoshik the robber", "Pan Twardowski" shows Polish origins, "Ashmodai" come down from the Talmud, the "Nun of Rauschenberg" is a tale that survived among the German inhabitants of the Carpathian valleys, "the hair of the orphan girl" a Hungarian Cinderella, and "The Maidens' Castle" belong to the Magyar lore. Whatever their original form may have been, these tales and legends are presented in a straightforward lucid English prose, which suggests that they are not so much translations from Hungarian texts but re-creations. Their rich vocabulary and the felicitous turns of phrase show Theresa's hand, though the very final touches, the stylistical corrections were done by Professor Francis Newman.[69]

Already in the *Diary* the Pulszkys translated a Hungarian poem into English verse: Mihály Vörösmarty's 'Appeal'[70] as an illustration of the Hungarian patriotic genius. In the *Popular tales and traditions* the authors wanted to illustrate the life of the Hungarian peasant and the turn of his imagination as portrayed by a leading Hungarian poet. Their choice fell on Sándor Petöfi's long narrative poem: 'Jánosh the hero.'[71] Their selection could have been due to two factors. Firstly, Francis Pulszky had been a serious and appreciative critic of Petöfi,[72] and secondly, the fate of the poet was inextricably bound up with the Hungarian War in which he died. Theresa Pulszky's translation of *Jánosh the hero* is preceded by a long introduction, and a short lyrical poem of Petöfi's translated by Francis Pulszky.[73] While Pulszky's rendering of "My Death" imitates the style of the Odes of Walter Savage Landor, and is just about adequate, Mrs. Pulszky transformed the original Hungarian Alexandrines into English blank verse and produced a fairly successful version.[74]

The Jacobins in Hungary, in the latter part of *The Tales and Traditions* was written by Francis Pulszky alone.[75] In his youth, the story of the Hungarian Jacobins was a living part of recent historical tradition among the liberal nobles at his home town, Eperjes. The fate in 1795 of Ignác Martinovics, the Abbot of Sasvár, and his six companions Hajnóczi, Laczkovich, Szentmarjay, Shigray, Solartsek and Öz was execution for conspiring against Royalty. They had formed two secret societies,[76] whose members, many Hungarian writers, lawyers and other intellectuals, were imprisoned on charges of distributing a 'revolutionary catechism'[77] translated from the French. The conspirators, some of them former officials in the relatively progressive state-machinery of Joseph II, seem to have been motivated partly by frustration, for being dismissed by Joseph's successor and partly by commendable idealistic fervour, that feudal laws and the existing framework of monarchical despotism should be changed. Although all the participants were Hungarian, it is a credit to Pulszky's use of his sources, that he avoided making the protagonists 'nationalists' to suit the purpose he wanted to serve with his historical novel. Based on Fraknói's[78] researches, De Gérando's "De l'Esprit public en Hongrie"[79] and on I.A. Fessler's "Die Geschichte der Ungarn[80] he spun a fairly straightforward story employing the technique of putting the sub-plot woven around a minor historical character in the focus. The portrayal of the fortunes of a young lawyer, Solartsek, who gets involved in the conspiracy by accident, as it were, and his sorrowful end, gave ample opportunities to Pulszky to display his expert knowledge of Hungarian Criminal Law[81] and expose the wanton action of the Austrian Chancellor who, unconstitutionally, had the prisoners committed for trial before the Royal Board. The analogy between the unlawful trials by the Austrians, before exceptional courts, of the Hungarian Jacobins in 1795 and the Hungarian Generals in 1849, is driven home by the author[82] and so the novel scores as another superb propaganda achievement even though it cannot qualify as a good novel.[83]

One of the minor figures in the Martinovics conspiracy who was convicted for, and served seven years in prison, József Pruzsinszky, became after his release, the family tutor of baron József Eötvös. Pulszky claims, that Pruzsinszky implanted many of the anti-feudal and liberal ideas into the mind of young Eötvös who in 1848 became minister of Public Instruction in the Batthyány government.[84] Pulszky had been a lifelong friend of Eötvös, who dedicated one of his novels: *The village notary*- an indictment against the old feudalistic country organisations of Hungary- to him. When in September 1848 the Batthyány government resigned, and Eötvös decided to leave the country, Pulszky helped him to go abroad with a passport. During the first terror year in Hungary Eötvös remained in exile in Bavaria, while Pulszky helped to launch his novel in England. In 1850 Pulszky arranged with the publishers, Longmans and Green, to bring out *The village notary* in English[85] translated by Otto Wenckstern, and introduced by Pulszky himself. The long novel which describes the trials and tribulations of a small official cought in the cobweb of semi-feudal institutions has the additional attraction of a well-constructed detective novel. When it was first published in Hungarian,[86] Pulszky reviewed it,[87] welcoming the reformist political tendencies contained in it, but harshly criticising the author's use of the Hungarian language. It is not so surprising, therefore, that *The village notary* was not translated directly from the Hungarian, but its German translation[88] was used by the English translator. Pulszky's aim in presenting this novel to the

English public was twofold- beyond making a good turn for a friend. First he wanted the English[89] to have a well-drawn picture of *contemporary* life in Hungary and secondly he meant to introduce the name of József Eötvös as a politician.[90] Between the conservatism of Széchenyi and the republicanism of Kossuth there was Eötvös, the guiding light of a third political force, the liberal centralists in Hungary.

The rest of Francis Pulszky's literary contributions in the fifties, had a comparatively smaller significance, with the exception of *White, red, black* which we will discuss in connection with his visit to America, in a separate chapter. In 1850, the most prolific year of his literary career, Pulszky edited with notes and introduction a clear and well-constructed historical narrative of the Hungarian War by Max Schlesinger.[91] The author, as Pulszky tells us in his introduction, was a Hungarian by birth who resided in Berlin and whose work was a success in Germany. The translation into English was done by one of Pulszky's first friends in England, John Edward Taylor, who included his translation of Petöfi's *National Song*[92] in the first volume. The editor corrected errors in dates, and provided an introduction which put the Hungarian national movement in a European context. "Can it be supposed that nations will forget their past?"[93] Pulszky posed the question that kept the hope alive in the emigration.

When, years later, he, as an archaeologist and art-historian, was asked to contribute a chapter to an 'ethnological inquiry' on the indigenous races of the earth,[94] his argument is still conceived in the same spirit. His motto to the article *Iconographic researches on human races and their art* (p.87-202) is taken from a poem by the Hungarian poet Berzsenyi:[95] "Put the rude Scythian on the Tiber, and the son of great Rome on the Cimmerian coast; there the capitol will become a den, and here rises a new Rome." For Pulszky, using the medium of art history, wanted the reader to take a bird's eye view of the nations whose problems, like those of the Hungarians, in 1848, remained unsolved, and ask the question: "If they could be forced to forget their language and speak German, (if the Poles would merge into the Panslav family), would they become more useful to mankind?"[96] Can nations develop better under oppression or in freedom? There can only be one answer for Pulszky. All nations are entitled to know the truth and to choose between good and bad. So they are all entitled to freedom, to the management of their own affairs and to the pursuit of their own happiness.

Francis Pulszky's literary activities in England were an extension of his political work. Convinced as he was that his exile was only temporary, and that he will eventually return to Hungary, he developed certain themes which had their roots at home to grow to fuller proportions in the adopted language. His contribution as a translator,[97] essayist, philologist,[98] archaeologist,[99] range over a variety of subjects and his helpers merit part of the credit. His activities as a man of letters transmitting Hungarian folk-tales, literary works of value, historical and cultural information, left their marks on similar works by English and American writers who came into contact with him. Among them Matthew Arnold,[100] Francis Newman,[101] P.C. Headley,[102] Thomas Watts[103] and Charles Henningsen could be named.

The influence was reciprocal.

3. The Baroness von Beck affair.

In order to gain a new insight into a neglected but important aspect of Pulszky's character and his political methods dealing with weaker rivals, we ought to examine the case of Baroness von Beck.

The name of a certain Baroness von Beck twice appears in the Committee Minutes of the Association of the Hungarian Political Exiles in London, as a recipient of £3 monthly reliefs in March and April 1850. On the first occasion an explanation occurs beside her name: "Baroness von Beck who had carried out several missions in the service of the Hungarian National Government."[104]

The Baroness appeared in England at the wake of the Komorn capitulators who came to England via Hamburg in November 1849. In Hamburg she seemed to have been on good terms with Count Paul Eszterházy, the President of the Hungarian Association there, while in England she was often seen in the company of Captain Kászonyi, former secretary to Colonel Újházi, and Constantin Derra, a young man of "prepossessing appearance" as Charles Dickens was to style him in the Household Narratives.

In November 1850, Richard Bentley the London publisher who practically specialised in biographies, brought out a book of Personal adventures in the late Hungarian war[105] written by the Baroness von Beck, which soon rivalled Mrs. Pulszky's Diary in popularity. Narrated in vivid, dramatic prose, Mrs. Beck's adventures incorporated dangerous spy-missions in Kossuth's service, enthusiastic descriptions of the Hungarian Governor, who was depicted in the book as her personal friend, and an account of the events and personalities who had played important roles in the Vienna Revolution and in the Hungarian War. The work was dedicated "to Lord Dudley Coutts Stuart M.P., the Friend of Poland, the champion of the oppressed of all nations". The Daily News serialised a part of her book, which was described as a "spirit-stirring adventure" in the *Examiner*, written (according to the Morning Post) in a terse, simple, eloquent" style. The *Athenaeum* praised the combination of "her rank and personal daring". In the early spring of 1859 her book was again published in London, this time in an abridged German edition.[106] Although this edition was shorter than the English one, it contained a strongly-worded attack on Francis Pulszky's person and a criticism of his activities in the Vienna Revolution - where the authoress claimed to have been present - and his role among the Hungarian emigrants in London. The Baroness, who also claimed that her husband Baron von Beck had lost his life in the siege, thought that Pulszky did not deserve the high position he filled in London Society, as his conduct had been questionable in Vienna. She also criticised his private life and alleged that "Herr V. Pulszky weiss von dem ungerischen Kriege nichts; er kennt ihn nur vom Hörensagen, und aus den Zeitungen".[107]

Pulszky was forewarned of the attack about six weeks before the publication of the book. A man called, or using the nom de plume of 'Ferdinand de Carl' wrote to Pulszky on 16 January 1851[108] that unless he makes a generous pecuniary contribution to the authoress, he will be attacked in the German language edition of her work, all the more, as Pulszky had succeeded in 1850 to persuade the publisher of the English edition to suppress her criticism of his person. In his reply of 17 January 1851 Pulszky refused to be blackmailed and said that he knew how to deal with slanderers.[109]

The affair which started off as so many of the internecine squabbles of refugees, took a very dramatic turn at the end of August, which was reported widely in the English press. In the "Law and Crime" section of the September issue of the *Household Narrative*,[110] Charles Dickens reported that the Baroness, having been discovered to be an imposter, was arrested at the instance of a Society for the Succour of Hungarian

refugees together with a young man named Count Derra,[111] on the charge
of obtaining money on false pretences. "She was to have been brought
before the Birmingham magistrate on the 30th August; but when the
proceedings were about to commence, everyone was shocked by the
announcement that the woman was dead. She had just died in an ante-
room . . . It was proved that there was no such person in Hungary, during
the war, as Baroness von Beck; no officer of the name Von Beck was
killed at Vienna. The "Baroness" had issued prospectuses for another
work; and to obtain subscribers for this had been the ostensible object
of her visit to Birmingham. She had received much sympathy from persons
of station and full sources of information in London; and she met with
equal sympathy and very warm support in Birmingham; subscriptions
were promised for "the story of my life", and some were paid. Mr. George
Dawson took a great interest in the Hungarian lady; and through his
introduction she was, when unwell at a hotel, taken into the family
of a solicitor at Edgbaston. There the imposture became known, and
she and her secretary were arrested. Mr. Tyndale, the gentleman who
received the deceased into his house . . . had received about £15 or £16
as subscriptions for her new work . . . Mr. Paul Hajniz, formerly member
of the Hungarian Diet and Chief Commissioner of Police of Hungary
and Transylvania, deposed that the woman's name was Radicula; she
had been a subordinate paid spy to the Hungarians; she was an Austrian
woman of low birth . . . had no acquaintance with Kossuth, further
than she could claim from having seen him twice to receive directions.
There is a noble family in Hungary named Beck, but (the) deceased did
not belong to it. Derra in his defense stated . . . that he believed her to
be what she represented herself . . . and was innocent of any crime . . . the
magistrates discharged the young man . . . it appeared at the inquest,
that the sudden death of the woman had been caused by long-standing
disease of the heart."

Derra, however, was not content for having been discharged by the
magistrates, but -as soon as he was free - wanted to prove the innocence
of the deceased Baroness too. He collected as much documentary evidence
to disprove the charges as he could lay hands on and with the help of
Bentley published them in a pamphlet, entitled: *A refutation of the
charge of imposition and fraud, recently made at the police court at
Birmingham, against the Baroness von Beck*.[112] Derra introduced his

collection of documentary evidence with the complaint that the subsequent seizure of the Baroness' papers by the prosecution, have removed the most important means of proving that she was innocent. What remained were the testimonies of friends and acquaintances. Daniel von Kászonyi declared that he had met the Baroness in the Hungarian camp after the capture of Vienna, and she had been known under two names: Recidula and the Baroness von Beck. In January 1851 he "entered into an engagement with her to copy her autobiography."[113] The rest of Derra's 'evidences' are of lesser interest. They include a letter from Count Paul Eszterházy[114] addressing Wilhelmine as Baroness; a letter sent from Paris, on 12 August 1851, by Sabbas von Vukovics,[115] late Minister of Justice in the Hungarian Government who was glad that the Baroness had revealed an interest to promote the cause of Kossuth in London. Other letters of similar nature were included from two former officers of the Polish Legion in Hungary,[116] from two former colonels of the Hungarian army, and a letter from John Paget[117] who had ordered a copy of the Baroness' book and settled his bill.

There were two points in the case for the prosecution which Derra picked upon. First, Mr. Hajnik, their witness, stated at the trial that Derra had been estranged from his family. Derra published letters from his father, to disprove this statement, twice in the Times[118] and in his pamphlet too. Secondly, Toulmin Smith, the prosecutor stated in Birmingham that Bentley had sent two sheets of a proposed book by the Baroness to Pulszky who was reported to have stated that: "if it were better arranged, it would make an amusing book".[119] Derra said in his pamphlet that Pulszky stated that he had strong suspicions of her all along. If that was the case, why did not M. Pulszky mention his suspicions to Mr. Gilpin, who had promised to publish her new work? The reason is - concludes Derra - that a plan was concocted against her.

But Derra went even further to seek justice for himself. First he started proceedings against the plaintiffs, the magistrate, the prosecutor and the police at Birmingham and while the case was waiting for trial at the Warwickshire Assizes[120] he handed in a petition to the House of Lords[121] complaining of the conduct of the same people.

On 28 May 1852 Lord Beaumont presented Derra's petition to the House "with a view to granting him redress, and preventing such harsh exercise of magisterial authority for the future".[122] Lord Beaumont

recalled the short history of the case and its antecedents with obvious
sympathy for the deceased, who in his opinion was not an imposter.
Her name as Baroness von Beck might be regarded as an assumed name,
such as "Boz" or "Little", but it was her anme as an authoress. Lord
Beaumont had consulted a number of Hungarians on the matter and came
to the conclusion, that if the whole case had started by M. Pulszky having
been libelled in the poor woman's book he should have taken a different
course of action. As for M. Pulszky's friends, they acted with rashness
and ignorance.

A small debate ensued on the question. The Marquese of Salisbury
called the case a 'lame story'; the Earl of Aberdeen criticised him, the
Privy Seal, for his remark, and hoped that an inquiry would be instituted
into the conduct of the magistrates. The Lord Chancellor said that an
inquiry would be inopportune now, as there was an action pending.
Both the Earl of Carlisle and the Duke of Northumberland agreed. The
Earl of Ellesmere thought ill of the prostitution of our law for the
purposes of private malice and remarked that it was not a crime to assume
a title as Kossuth himself was not Governor General of Hungary as he
styled himself. Lord Campbell, the Marquess of Clanricarde, and the
Earl of Derby all thought that the matter would be inquired into at the
proper time. The Duke of Argyll thought it extraordinary that the prosecutor, Toulmin Smith, should still have the seized papers, but Lord
Truro answered that they might have included a list of subscribers. Lord
Beaumont summed up saying that it was his intention to recommend
the Secretary of State to make an inquiry into the case.

As far as Derra was concerned, an inquiry, which incidentally did not
take place, could not have helped him more than the decision of the
Warwickshire Assizes, in August 1852, who fully rehabilitated his honour
and ordered the prosecuting party of the first case to pay him £2,000
and to bear all costs of the lawsuit.

Meanwhile Toulmin Smith,[123] the prosecutor in Birmingham, and
Richard Bentley the publisher of the "Baroness" were fighting a battle
of the pen, which brought out new aspects of the affair. Toulmin Smith
was a good friend of Pulszky,[124] and he was an ardent defender of the
Hungarian cause. As a constitutional lawyer, he felt inspired in 1849
to write on the historical 'Parallels between . . . England and Hungary',
in which he compared the fundamental institutions of the two countries.

As one of the legal advisers to both Lord Dudley Stuart and the English Relief Committee for the Refugees, he had Pulszky's full confidence and was well equipped first to depose the imposter, and later to justify his actions.

He published two articles in the Daily News reaffirming the imposture in October 1851, and went as far as interviewing Kossuth at his arrival in England on his acquaintance of the pretended baroness. In his pamphlet, entitled "The facts of the case as to the pretended 'Baroness von Beck' " . . . published in 1852,[125] he quoted two excerpts from Kossuth's answeres, to show that the Baroness' claims were false, she was not a personal friend of the Hungarian Governor, she was an inferior spy who first sold her confidences to the Hungarians and later to the Austrians. The full document containing Kossuth's answers that came to light only in 1948,[126] corroborates the evidence for some of Toulmin Smith's points, but neither Kossuth nor anyone else has proved that Racidula, alias Baroness von Beck was an Austrian as well as a Hungarian spy.

Her importance as a Hungarian spy can be assessed on the strength of two sources. The Austrian ambassador in London, who kept a watchful eye on the activities of the emigrants, had asked for and received from Vienna the receipts of Racidula's payments from Kossuth's treasury.[127] The amounts were 1,000 frt, received on 11 March 1849 and 1,500 frt, received on 6 May 1849 by 'Wilhelmina Racidula', not really large sums for an important spy. Racidula's chief mission was the delivery of a letter in December from Kossuth to Stiles, American diplomatic agent in Vienna, whom Kossuth asked to mediate for a peace proposal between Hungary and Austria.

The Baroness described her meeting wiht Stiles in her book[128] very differently from the account given a year later by the American diplomat himself. Stiles in his work entitled "Austria in 1848-9"[129] talks of a very young lady in her twenties, who had produced the letter from a slate. In other words, it was not the middle-aged Racidula who had the letter with her but another person, called "Countess M.".

Toulmin Smith, who seems to have corresponded on the matter with Stiles, deduces that there were two spies on the mission, 'Countess M.' and her escort Racidula, and the latter, who became known as the self-styled Baroness von Beck in England had never met the American diplomat.

Richard Bentley's answer[130] to Toulmin Smith's *Facts* could only add one interesting but incidental piece of information on the affair. According to Bentley, Pulszky was misinformed on the Baroness having been an Austrian spy by a Hungarian emigrant, named Edward Szerdahelyi.[131] He had been an officer in the Hungarian army, and he became in London the Secretary of Colonel Nicholas Kiss,[132] who succeeded Pulszky as president of the Association of the Hungarian exiles. On 5 September 1851, Szerdahelyi wrote a letter to Pulszky[133] accusing the Baroness (posthumously as it were, since she died five days before), for spying for the Austrians.[134] The accusations, as Bentley pointed out, were never substantiated, and could well have been motivated by personal malice, as the Baroness, who had met Szerdahelyi in Hungary, depicted him in her book as a brainless character. Richard Bentley was convinced that the Baroness had been unjustly accused and harshly treated, and his view was shared by a considerable number of the Hungarian refugees.

Pulszky, who had never come openly to the forefront in this affair, and even later was to omit all references to the 'Baroness', had twice summed up his position privately, to his friends. When Kossuth was approaching the shores of England in October 1851, Pulszky wrote to him:[135] "An ugly affair has upset the press here; the so-called Baroness von Beck had been writing begging-letters all over the world and exploiting the Hungarian sympathy for herself. She had abased me as well as everybody else, and pretended to be your ladyfriend and more. Finally she said she had been employed as a secret agent by the English. Then an Englishman whom I had furnished with the documents, had brought her to Court and she died on the spot in fright. It was found amongst her papers that she had been involved in the main intrigues here."

Because of the publicity given to the late "Baroness" and her more fortunate secretary, one of Pulszky's closest English friends, Professor Newman, wished to be re-affirmed of Pulszky's blamelessness. The letter Pulszky wrote to Newman on 9 February 1853,[136] wished to reassure him: "My dear Newman, You know it has been my resolve not to notice the many calumnies of your press against me in the matter of the so-called Mrs. Von Beck. Nevertheless, at your instance, and to gratify you, I make the following distinct declarations, and give you authority to use them as and how you please. *She was arrested without my knowledge, without my having been consulted, and while I did not know it to be possible by English law*. How I behaved to her while I knew she was reviling me, but was not yet certain that she was an imposter, you can to some extent testify.

I am your friend." (Pulszky).

The question is, how far could Pulszky be believed?

An outside observer of the affair, J.F. Blackwell, the late British agent in Hungary, who did not lose contact with the Hungarian nationalists, now in emigration, commented on it in a memorandum, he wrote to Lord Palmerston in November 1851: "...I do happen to know that the plot against her was concocted in the house of Mr. F. Pulszky..."[137]

Blackwell may well have informed Palmerston correctly. Jealousy over her literary successes and anger provoked by the blackmailing letter written on her behalf seems to have activated Pulszky in his effort to defraud the Baroness. Although her death was an accident, and though she had indeed put forward extravagent claims as to her rank and import-ance, there can be little doubt that Pulszky dealt far too harshly with her, thus involuntarily exposing the darker side of his own character. He should have remembered that he himself had occasionally used the title of 'Count' in Society although his family had no title.

There remains a question unsolved. Was it the false Baroness herself, a sly but simple woman, who knew no French and distributed begging letters, who wrote the book of personal adventures, so well thought of by many critics? Since her personal papers were confiscated and have never emerged from the heritage of her prosecutor, we can only put forward a theory, supported by Toulmin Smith's references to an anony-mous diary,[138] that she had employed a ghost writer. This person is most likely to have been Daniel Kászonyi, who stated at the Birmingham trial that he was employed by the Baroness to copy her book. Later he became a prolific author of several works and in 1868 he published a four-volume history of the Hungarian war and its emigration[139] which included an account lamenting the fate and fortunes of the Baroness von Beck and attacking Francis Pulszky.[140]

Yet Pulszky's role as a spokesman for the Hungarian exile in England should be, on balance, assessed positively, despite the part he played in the Baroness von Beck affair. Though not recognised by everyone as such, he was still the central figure of the Hungarian emigration in London until Kossuth's arrival. He regarded his stay in England as transitory and earned his living with his pen. His literary accomplishments merited praise not only for himself and his wife, but for the Hungarian cultural and historical heritage he introduced through the medium of a judicious selection of literary and quasi-political works.

CHAPTER THREE

FOR KOSSUTH

1. For Kossuth's liberation.

Within a few days of Görgei's surrender, about 5,000 Hungarians, Poles and Italians had sought safety by crossing the Danube into Turkish territory. Among these refugees who crossed the frontier at Severin on 18 August, was Kossuth, soon followed by five cabinet ministers and some of the chief leaders of the Hungarian army. Of the Poles who had fought on the Hungarian side, the leaders were the old Napoleonic campaigner Dembinski, General Bem, chief of the Transylvanian campaign, Count Ladislas Zamoyski and General Wysoczki, joint chiefs of the Polish legion. The Italian legion was headed by Colonel Monti. They joined up with the Hungarians on the frontier and the three groups were united and uniformly treated by the Turks.

Turkey was a very logical, and perhaps the only reasonably safe choice of refuge for them. Both the Hungarians and the Poles had been seeking Turkish aid against the Russians, and were hoping to be of some use in a future political or military combination. The King of Sardinia had maintained a very active diplomatic relationship with the Porte, through his resident Ambassador, baron Tecco, in Constantinople.

In the beginning, the Turkish government pursued a friendly but wholly passive line towards the refugees: disarming them, granting them asylum, gathering them into a camp at Widdin, but guaranteeing nothing. The danger of a united Russian-Austrian confrontation was imminent and the attitude of the British and French governments was, or so it seemed, of benevolent neutrality only.

Already in December 1849, and before the change of military fortunes, the Austrians had assumed the likelihood of the Hungarian leaders escaping into Turkey[1] and had issued warrants for their seizure and surrender. The Russians were equally anxious to capture the Poles[2] and had considerably more power to give weight to their threats. On 4 September, Prince Michael Radzivil, Russian envoy in Constantinople, demanded the extradition of the refugees under the threat that 50,000 Russians were ready to march into Turkey at a word from the Czar.

These demands had an appearance of legality; the Austrian and Russian Prime Ministers, Schwarzenberg and Nesselrode, were able to base their demands for extradition upon certain definite treaty stipulations. Applying to Austrian subjects the Treaties of Belgrade (Art. XVIII) and Passarowicz (Art. XIV) guaranteed the right of jurisdiction for the Habsburg Monarch. As opposed to that the right of asylum under international law for political refugees had been in force since the turn of the century. After the French Revolution of 1789, the term "political crime" became universally known, and article 120 of the French Constitution of 1793, granting asylum to foreigners exiled from their native lands for their support of the cause of liberal institutions denied extradition for people of this description.[3] Britain embraced their principle with enthusiasm. The surrender of political refugees to Spain by the Governor of Gibraltar had annoyed the British Parliament in 1815. And Lord Castlereagh, the British Foreign Secretary had in 1816 called extradition the greatest abuse of law. In 1849 it was Palmerston's turn and also his test: whether to - and if so, how - adhere to this principle.

The first English advocate of the refugees in Turkey was Major F.W. Browne, who had been representing Kossuth in Constantinople with baron Splényi since the spring of 1849. In June Splényi was replaced by Count Gyula Andrássy. When in September Browne and Andrássy had learned of the threat of extradition they tried every means to avert the danger. While Andrássy alerted Teleki, and through him the French press, Browne immediately contacted Stratford Canning, the English Ambassador at the Porte and suggested he advise the Porte to protest against the Russian action. At the same time he also wrote to Pulszky:[4] "the vessel is wrecked and nothing remains to us, but to save the crew if we can. You can do a great deal in London. If Lord Palmerston gives the necessary instructions to Sir Stratford Canning he will surely protect those who take refuge in Turkey. Agitate it and quickly . . ."

Ideally, Palmerston would have liked to see a solution of the Austro-Hungarian question which would guarantee the re-establishing of the ancient constitution of Hungary with the improvements made in it in the previous year, such as the abolition of feudal service and the exemption of privileged classes from public burdens and a real and complete amnesty.[5] As it was not in his power to implement this wish he took up the cause of the Hungarian and Polish leaders in Turkey and within a few days of Kossuth's escape, he instructed his Ambassador in Vienna: "pray take an opportunity of representing privately and unofficially to Schwarzenberg . . . what a painful impression would be created throughout Europe . . . if any severities were used against Kossuth, Dembinski and Bem . . ."[6]

We know that both Pulszky and Teleki wanted to see him about the fate of Kossuth in September, but the likely inference from the date of the available documents is, that Palmerston had learnt of Kossuth's escape as soon as they did - if not earlier - and had already made up his mind to protect him. For it was the British Consul at Varna who supplied Kossuth with a false British passport, made out for 'James Bloomfield, English merchant' and much of the subsequent correspondence that was to pass between the refugees in Turkey and those in Britain went through British official channels unofficially. The real question was what would the British Government do in the face of a war-threat against Turkey, or as Nesselrode put it: "les graves conséquences qu'entrainerait un refus opposé à' la légitime réclamation de l'Emperor . . ."[7]

As so often in British diplomacy when humanitarianism could be profitably mingled with political interest supported by naval power, the solution presented itself. Stratford Canning, with the subsequent approval of Palmerston, wrote to Vice-Admiral Sir William Parker, Commander of the Mediterranean Fleet, requesting that a "part at least of H.M. Mediterranean Squadron might be available for any purposes of demonstration in the Archipelago."[8] The appearance of Parker's fleet in Becisa Bay in October was declared a naval exercise, and the same polite diplomatic language was used in connection with the sailing of Admiral Parseval's French Fleet, from Toulon to Smyrna.[9] The action taken by Great Britain was interpreted by Russia and Austria rightly: Palmerston showed force in supporting Turkey in her refusal to hand over the refugees.[10] They had to step down and change their policies from extradition to internment. After the Fleet had left the Dardanelles in the middle of November, the Austrian Ambassador handed over a list of the persons they wished to see interned. It included the names of the Hungarian chiefs together with Kossuth.[11]

While Turkey was waiting for an English move to support her growing resolution to protect the refugees, and the assurances were not forthcoming, her ministers had conceived a home-made guarantee of safeguard. Following a stormy debate of the Turkish Cabinet, Reshid, the Turkish Foreign Minister, offered to the refugees in September to take up the Muslim religion and so to become Turkish citizens,[12] over whom the Russians and Austrians could claim no jurisdiction. The offer was accompanied by a rumour, whose origin was traced back to an alleged letter by Gyula Andrássy to Kossuth. It spread like wildfire in the refugee camp that those who will not become Turks will be surrendered to the enemy.[13] Although Kossuth remonstrated with them, and simultaneously asked for Palmorston's support,[14] 74 Hungarian officers, and about 250 soldiers converted, together with roughly 100 Poles. Among the generals, Bem was the first one to adopt Muslim faith, followed by Kmetty and Stein. All soldiers retained their ranks or were given Turkish equivalent positions, full pay, and a promise to be enlisted in the Turkish regular army. In face of all these pressures and temptations—the refugees were badly paid at Widdin and often kept just over starvation level—the number of the converts was surprisingly small.

When the Porte was assured of Britain's help in the refugee question, her attitude changed, she became firmer and would not even listen to demands of extradition. But the Austrians, since they could not get Kossuth and the leaders, were ready with an alternative plan, and decided to reduce the number of the ordinary refugees. On 12 October an Austrian ship arrived at the port of Widdin, carrying General Hauslaab, who was entrusted to enlist every common soldier and low-ranking official wishing to return. Total amnesty for partaking in the 'rebellion' to be followed by conscription with pay in the Imperial army was promised and accepted by about 2,500 Hungarians, about 200 Italians and some Poles.[15] Kossuth made a speech in the camp, which quite fairly promised nothing more but emigration extending to an uncertain period of time for those who wished to remain; and indeed, only those remained—about 400 in number[16] who stayed out of political conviction or still feared the vengeance of the Austrians. The psychological reasons for the refugees' return, besides homesickness, and the hope of family reunions, were the willingness to exchange a condition of uncertainty to certainty, and the fear of an epidemic of gastric fever, which had already decimated their numbers in the camp.[17]

In the climate of general despair Kossuth's plans were alternating at the slightest change of his personal fortunes. Before investing Görgei with absolute power—not of his own choice but by the force of circumstances—he had dreamed of a last general offensive. "To crush Haynau with full force—then to transfer the war through Fiume and Austria to Italy and resuscitate again the freedom-fight of the nations beyond the frontiers."[18] After the lost battle of Temesvár when he decided to flee, he gave his word that "everyone may go, whenever he can." It was only in Widdin that he summed up his position, in the context of the general political situation, in a letter he wrote to Teleki and Pulszky on 12 September, and sent—via Andrássy—to London.

The letter arrived in London in November. There it was promptly copied, translated into German and sent to Wigand's publishing company by József Orosz. As this letter contained not only an insinuation that Hungary was betrayed by Görgei, which view was welcomed by the emigrants, but a surrender of hope for the independence of Hungary and a confession by Kossuth, that he had hoped for too much and lost, its uncensored publication[19] caused some alarm in Pulszky's circle. Orosz, who had belonged to his retinue, but had the letter published without Pulszky's knowledge, was stricken by remorse, and Pulszky himself tried to deny its authenticity.[20] But the letter had beneficial side-effects too. Teleki and Pulszky pressed for and were granted a further interview with Palmerston in November, when they were assured verbally of Kossuth's safety, and the press reports on Kossuth's communication kept the interest of the public and of the politicians alive. When Dudley Stuart, who was constantly informed by Pulszky, brought up the Kossuth question in February,[21] Palmerston's answer somewhat reassured Kossuth. Meanwhile, several factors contributed to Kossuth's regaining his confidence. He was well informed on the move of the English Fleet and its causes: Neale, the English Consul at Varna had kept regular contact with him through a messenger, three English travellers visited him in succession, bringing news and letters from outside, and over 400 Hungarians had shown their loyalty to him by refusing to return with Hauslaab.

Among his English visitors, Charles Frederick Henningsen was the first and proved the most useful and loyal of Kossuth's links with the outside world. Henningsen, a correspondent of the Daily News, was an authority on Russia. Having travelled inside that country, and written two works about it,[22] he was convinced that the Czar's influence in the Balkans and in Eastern Central Europe ought to be checked by England. He was an out and out liberal, who espoused the cause of equality and independence of smaller nations, but being conscious of the need for a strong state that would withstand Russian pressure in Europe, he advocated their federative alliance.

Henningsen arrived at Widdin sometime between the end of September and the 7 October. He introduced himself as 'Thompson' and spent several weeks with Kossuth.[23] At his first meeting with the ex-Governor he produced from the sole of his shoe a letter from Teleki and two from Pulszky, dating from 27 and 30 July.[24] At his outset from London in August he had been instructed by Pulszky to arrange for the shipment of a large quantity of arms through the Balkans into Hungary, but by the time he got to Turkey, the war was over. The presence and the influence of this Englishman seems to have poured new energies into the veins of Kossuth. Shaking off the dejected mood he devised new plans for the emigration. He wrote letters to Palmerston pleading for his intervention,[25] to Teleki and Pulszky requesting them to advocate his liberation. He even thought for a while that everything was not yet lost on the war front and asked Henningsen to deliver a message to the defenders of Komorn to hold out, and when he learned of the capitulation, new schemes for a future confederation kept his hopes alive.

Whereas Henningsen himself came back to London and met Pulszky there only in November, a long letter of his, describing his stay at Widdin, preceded his arrival. It came to be incorporated into the *Diary*[26] of Mrs. Pulszky, as it was written, in fulfillment of Henningsen's promise, to give Pulszky an account of the emigration in Turkey. Appearing in printed form in the book it had both news and propaganda value in London. For us, Henningsen's account has historical source value, particularly as we are able to contrast his reporting, with diaries kept and later published by two Hungarian emigrants, Egressy and Veress. Henningsen had rubbed shoulders with all the leaders of the emigration, and portrayed the life in Widdin, from the top, as it were. Gábor Egressy, the most renowned actor of his generation, who was enlisted as a major in the Hungarian war, looked upon events from a standpoint in the middle; while Sándor Veress, who had been a student, and was a lieutenant in the war, kept contact with the rank and file and described his experience as from below.

The description Henningsen gives of Kossuth, is that of the harassed hero, a man of great emotions and brilliant talents, but perhaps too soft a man for real leadership. It is, in its contours, the basic picture that numerous English, American, German, Italian and even Welsh biographers enlarged upon subsequently.[27] The differences amongst the late Hungarian Cabinet Ministers, and generals, Perczel, K. Batthyány, Szemere and Kossuth is noted and emphasised by Egressy but passed over by the Englishman. His comments on the national issue—one of the tragedies of the Hungarian war—are so diplomatic that the post-war attitude of the Serbs and Rumanians is said to be that of repentance towards the Hungarians. In other words, the political climate as he perceived it in the camp was favourable to a confederation-plan. Back in London he secretly discussed these plans and how they could be accommodated within the framework of the Turkish empire with Klapka, Teleki, Andrássy and Pulszky from the Hungarian side, with Prince Lubomirsky representing the Polish interests and Bălcesco, the Rumanians. With the co-operation of Dudley Stuart they were even received by Palmerston in January, but we have little knowledge as to what passed at this meeting.[28]

Egressy was of the opinion that the emigration was "Hungary in miniature".[29] Not only were all nationals and trades to be found here but all passions were represented too: pride, envy, hate, quarrels. "If we cannot quarrel with others we fight among ourselves." Veress understands only the tragedy, depicts the miseries and the small joys, but like the "everyman" of a medieval drama, he cannot detect the causes.

The next step in the international chess-game played by the powers with the fate of the refugees was the internment of Kossuth and fifteen other dangerous personalities of the late war to Kiutahia.[30] It is rather difficult to discern where the idea of removing Kossuth from Europe was hatched, since it might well have been Palmerston who first thought of it, as an alternative to extradition. Already on 11 October he wrote to Ponsonby: "indeed it was a mistake in the Turks not to have sent these refugees away or into the Interim".[31] Yet the opposite can also be argued from the documents: "What great harm could he do to Austria while in France or England? He would be a hero of half a dozen dinners in England . . . and he would soon sink into comparative obscurity . . . while so long as he is in a state of defence in Turkey he is a martyr and the object of never-ceasing interest".[32]

The facts are that while Russia and Austria were pressing for fifteen years of detention, the Porte would have gladly released Kossuth altogether, but the English and French Governments seemed to have preferred the detention of dangerous revolutionaries for at least a minimum period.

In November, the refugees were transferred to Sumla with the exception of the two Britons, Guyon and Longworth, who had served in the Hungarian army, and were freed. There the Austrians appeared to have engineered a last clandestine attempt to get hold of Kossuth. It came to Kossuth's notice that a party of fourteen suspicious characters hired by an Austrian agent, G. Jasmagy, were trying to get near him with evil intentions. One of Kossuth's officers, Rudolf Bárdy, heard of the approaching armed bandits, contacted first the Italian Consul, Tecco, then the Turkish authorities, who had the would-be assassins arrested. Baron Tacco was of the opinion that the Austrian aim behind the plot that had failed, was only to frighten Kossuth sufficiently in order to make him want to flee from Turkey, and the real task of Jasmagy was to arrest Kossuth in flight as soon as he was outside Turkish territory.

The internment of Kossuth to Kiutahia in February 1850 split up the Hungarian emigration in Turkey again into two groups. The Austrians insisted on the detention of the ex-Governor, his wife who had joined him in Widdin, K. Batthyány and his wife, the former war minister, Lázár Mészáros, the two Perczels, Maurice and Nicholas, Adolf Gyurman, the former editor of the Közlöny with his family, and János Szölössy, one of Kossuth's secretaries. Of the Poles, Dembinsky and Wysoczki, five other officers and their families, had to go with them. Another eighty Hungarians volunteered out of loyalty to go with Kossuth, but only thirty of them were taken.[33] The Hungarian and Polish officers who had become Muslim converts in Widdin were taken to Aleppo, with their own consent, as most of them had become Turkish soldiers. The rest of the emigration, still about 350 in number, but not deemed dangerous by any of the powers, was left behind in Sumla, and stayed together. At the end of June 1850, the Turkish authorities dispersed the camp in Sumla and granted freedom to the refugees. Characteristically, they asked the detained Kossuth's advice where they should go to. In his answer of 11 July, the ex-Governor advised those who wished to go away, to try Serbia or America, while he intimated to a few faithful followers, that he had some future plan with those who would settle temporarily in Turkey.

On 16 August 1850 the British Ambassador offered to have a few refugees transported to England upon their paying a per capita ship-fare[34] of 500 piasters. All in all, the Diaspora was complete by the autumn of 1850: about 150 of the Sumla emigrants dispersed in Turkey, sixty went to America, the remainder scattered between England, France, Germany, Serbia, Rumania—and a few returned to Hungary.

In Kiutahia Kossuth regained his full self-confidence. Being sure that his release was a matter of months and not years, he was preparing for a new role in politics he felt destined to play. He learned Turkish, and perfected his knowledge of English,[35] reading mainly Shakespeare and the Bible. He made contacts with agents from Hungary, preparing for the re-kindling of the flame, and he exchanged letters with Mazzini, chief of the exiled revolutionaries abroad, now domiciled in England. He kept Pulszky posted through the official route of the English and Turkish embassies and via the English travellers, David Urquhart the liberal politician, and Henningsen who had returned to Turkey again and by way of an American missionary, the Reverend H. Homes in Constantinople. Pulszky sent his answers either via Algernon Massingberd,[36] lieutenant in the Royal Houseguards, or the Italian embassy in Constantinople.

Kossuth's letters to Pulszky,[37] are anything but clear practical instructions as to what he wanted Pulszky to do for his release, or what plans he had for the emigration. It appears that Pulszky, in the beginning, had hoped that Kossuth, as soon as free, would help him to finance the emigration. Kossuth, on the other hand, was planning to use all his influence and rhetorical powers to collect money for a new war of Hungarian Independence. It is deducible from his obscure references that he anchored his hopes in a Russo-Turkish war, which was in his opinion bound to break out soon. Pulszky gave Kossuth to understand that his political plans were impracticable if he thought that Britain would support Turkey against Russia with armed force.[38] Meanwhile, Kossuth's ardent wish was to be free and Pulszky helped him with all means at his disposal.

In the January meeting with Palmerston, he was told by the British Foreign Secretary that Kossuth's internment was unavoidable since Sultan Abdul Medjid, had personally promised to keep Kossuth detained for at least a year. Pulszky's reaction was that of pessimism, and he never tried to appeal directly to Palmerston again, on Kossuth's behalf. In his letter to Kossuth,[39] he interpreted Palmerston's attitude saying that while the

Foreign Secretary had sympathised with him as a person, as an English politician, he could not and would not commit himself further. So Pulszky reverted to the same tactics of public pressure he had used before. In 1851 he managed to organise pro-Hungarian meetings, in Sheffield and in Manchester, and the Committees of these meetings sent petitions to Palmerston. His comments on these to Kossuth were that "Your popularity here is far too great and the ministers would not like to see you here."[40] The extent of this popularity could be measured by the number of memorials requesting the intervention of H.M. Government in favour of the Hungarian refugees detained in Turkey. A list, entitled *Louis Kossuth and others,* tabulating ninety-seven places, that included London, Leeds and Southampton, was drawn up on the fourth and ordered to be printed by the House of Commons on 7 and 8 August, 1851.[41]

Meanwhile, Dudley Stuart was urging Palmerston to present the official correspondence regarding the Hungarian refugees to the House,[42] and David Urquhart had asked the Foreign Secretary three times,[43] as to whether anything was done for the release of Kossuth. In neither case did Palmerston commit himself, although he must have known by May 1851, that the Sultan intended to release Kossuth on 1 September. Indeed, he himself offered secretly to the Porte to take the Hungarians to Malta in case no other power would provide transport.[44]

Pulszky was as sceptical about the Sultan's assurances to release Kossuth as he was about Palmerston's good will to act. So he had a different plan to get Kossuth out from Kiutahia.[45] In August 1849 a rich Polish emigrant, Xavier Branyiczki, one of Prince Czartoriczky's associates in Paris, lent 20,000 francs for the purposes of the Hungarian war. As the war had ended abruptly with Görgei's surrender, Teleki returned the money to Branyiczki. In the summer of 1851, when Henningsen had returned from his second visit to Kossuth—this time from Kiutahia—he was given the mission by Pulszky to return again to help Kossuth escape. Zähnsdorf, a Hungarian jeweller in London, and Lord Dudley Stuart bore part of the costs which included hiring men and horses at Kiutahia and a ship, which would be waiting for them in Constantinople.

The rest of the money, the same 20,000 francs, was again lent by Branyiczki, and given to Colonel Bikessy who delivered it to Pulszky in London.

As it happened, Kossuth's liberation came about in a different way, by the assistance of a neutral power: the United States of America.

Pulszky must have known something about the preparations for an American move in the question, for he was keeping contact with Lawrence, the American ambassador in London. On 29 June 1851 he reported to Kossuth in a letter:[46] "the present plan is to keep you there . . . then to transport you to America". Undoubtedly Kossuth was an embarrassment for the statesmen from Buol, the new Austrian Ambassador in England who feared he might come to London, through Napoleon III who would not want him in France, to the Turkish Sultan who was glad to get rid of him. The Gordian knot was cut by the American Senator, Foote, who proposed in the Senate that the United States Government should invite Kossuth and his followers to America and provide them with shelter. The American Senate agreed to send a warship to Asia, and on 1 September Kossuth was freed.

The American offer was not as gallant and spontaneous as it looked, for the American Government came to its decision after a joint request from England and France. Pulszky, commenting on it in his Memoirs wrote:[47] "It was a very clever step in the chess-game, when (America) paid the greatest respects to Kossuth, placing him on the same pedestal with Lafayette, who twenty-five years before had been jubilated by the Northern American Republic, as their guest and one time freedom-fighter; on the other hand it was the best service rendered to Austria and France to remove the alledgedly dangerous agitator from the European shores."

2. The reception of Kossuth in England.

When Buol, the new Austrian Ambassador learned from Palmerston's answer to Dudley Stuart's question[48] in the Commons, that Kossuth was to be released on 1 September, he anxiously sought the opportunity to sound Palmerston on the matter. When Palmerston received him in his country house at Broadlands, in the second half of September, Kossuth was already free, and declared his intention to visit England, before going to America. The apprehension of the Austrian Ambassador was shared by his Prussian and Russian colleagues alike, and the three diplomats together communicated their government's anxiety on the extreme danger, such revolutionary elements mean to the peace and security of Continental Europe.[49] The English Foreign Secretary tried to reassure the Ambassadors that the Government will not be influenced by a friendly public reception in any way. As long as aliens do not abuse the right of hospitality, Parliament will not permit the Government to proceed against them. Furthermore, since Kossuth had no financial means to equip an army or a fleet, he should not be thought dangerous when free. Buol's immediate reaction was to absent himself from London for the period of Kossuth's visit, while his Government resorted to petty reprisals. Magenis reported from Vienna that because of Palmerston's friendly attitude to Kossuth, the Austrians refused entry of British travellers into Hungary.[50]

The long-drawn diplomatic negotiations over the fate of Kossuth for once exasperated Pulszky - perhaps, partly, because he had no important role to play in his chief's liberation. The tone of his welcoming letter to Kossuth, written on 6 October from Southhampton, is full of impatience, and his important information is mingled with indignation on further intrigues which lay in Kossuth's way.[51] Pulszky complains that European diplomacy tries to keep Kossuth at sea (literally), to deflate the enthusiasm of the people. Every European refugee party - so Pulszky claims - tries to put Kossuth's name on its banner. Mazzini's European Central Committee includes the Rumanian Bratiano, an enemy of the Hungarians. He had more cheerful news about his English friends. Algernon Massingberd vacated his house in Eaton Place for Kossuth, and Henningsen set out to organise matters, that he may receive anyone he wishes, discreetly. A subscription is being prepared in his name. But alas, his voyage from France (Kossuth was in Marseilles on 2 October), will be the longest in memory, forecasts Pulszky. The interest of the powers is to let him spend as little time on European soil as possible. To have a chance of further discussions and to help Kossuth impress American public opinion, Pulszky will be ready after his English visit to accompany his friend across the Ocean.

The nearer Kossuth got to England the more Pulszky went out of his way to prove his loyalty and friendship. What bond held the two men previously together apart from the radical Magyar nationalism both had adhered to? Kossuth was a senior of Pulszky by twelve years, and like him a Protestant from Northern Hungary. Though Pulszky's family was by far the more prosperous, both men came from the middle strata of un-titled Hungarian nobility, and both their respective ancestors were of mixed Slav and Magyar stock. By profession they were lawyers, with the ambition to be legislators; Pulszky entered Parliament through the easy way of family connections, Kossuth had worked his way up, from being a reporter of the events, to a maker of them. They belonged to the most talented of the liberal opposition of the reform era; but while Pulszky, when he got himself into trouble, was whisked off to a foreign tour by his uncle, Kossuth welcomed the role of the martyr. Pulszky liked to be an *eminence grise* supporting a great man,[52] while Kossuth was of the charismatic leader mould. The best school for a would-be political leader in 1837, when Kossuth was first arrested, was imprisonment - the same as in our century: for it allows individual preparation and strengthens the sympathy of the community which awaits the liberation of the prisoner.

It was after Kossuth had served his first term in captivity and took up the editorship of *Pesti Hirlap*, that Pulszky joined him. Between 1841 and 1843 Pulszky wrote eight articles, six on important political topics,[53] in Kossuth's paper, and in 1847 he wrote a very flattering political character-study of Kossuth in the Allgemeine Zeitung.[54] When Kossuth got the position of Chancellor of the Exchequer in L. Batthyány's Government in April 1848 he chose Pulszky as Under-Secretary of Financial Affairs, and when, a month later we find Pulszky in the "Foreign Ministry", he performs his duties there as if he were Kossuth's confidential agent.

When, in September, the Government resigned and Kossuth emerged as the leader of the Committee of Defence - in fact, the country's leader - it was he again who sent Pulszky to Vienna to negotiate between Hungary and the revolutionaries there. Later, they rode together to the battlelines at Schwechat. And finally, in November and December 1848 Kossuth entrusted Pulszky with the task of arm and equipment supply to the army. Then Pulszky, to save his skin, deserted him - in the manner we have already described - although he did not desert the cause. As he practically owed his own political career to Kossuth, until his defection to England, we can very well understand his anxiety to face the first personal confrontation with Kossuth after a separation of three years, and his frustration at the delay.

Kossuth was taking his own course with the journey. His first seven days of freedom were spent by travelling from Kiutahia to the port of Gömlok,[55] where he was joined by the Mazzini's secret agents Lemmi and Beriggi, and some Hungarians who, like Kossuth's small entourage, wished to settle in America. In mid-September, the assigned American warship, the *Mississippi* called at Smyrna, where some of the refugees had stayed, and embarked at the harbour of La Spezia on 21 September. Colonel Monti, the leader of the Italian legion in Hungary and Kossuth's fellow captive at Widdin received him there, conveying a message from Mazzini for Kossuth to go through France. Four days later in the port of Marseilles Kossuth declared his intention of wanting to abandon the ship and proceed over land, via Paris, and eventually to London. The Prefect of the city sent a telegraphic message to Napoleon and after two days' delay the President's answer came, refusing permission for Kossuth to traverse French soil. In response, Kossuth gave a rousing republican speech to the people of Marseilles, adopting the motto of a French work-man who had previously swum to his ship to embrace him, with the words: "There are no obstacles to him who wills."[56] The Times reported the speech with the comment that, with this speech, M. Kossuth gave himself away: he was in fact no better than the revolutionaries conspiring in England, Mazzini, Ledru Rollin and their associates.

The next Port of call was Malaga then Gibraltar, where Kossuth left the American ship, taking only his family and a few others[57] with him, and promised his compatriots who stayed on the *Mississippi* and pro-ceeded to the States, that he will follow them shortly. After ten days' waiting in Gibraltar, on 15 October he boarded the British ship *Madrid*, which landed him in Southhampton on 23 October.

The reception of Kossuth in Southampton was prepared by Pulszky with the help of Joseph Andrews, the Mayor of the city, and Rodney Crosskey, the American consul.[58] The multitude was several thousand strong, the newspaper reporters were ready for a full coverage[59] of Kossuth's whole tour, and the politicians were over-bidding one another to get near the ex-Governor of Hungary. Pulszky claims that even Pal-merston invited Kossuth to Broadlands, through Lord Dudley Stuart, who was waiting in the port to deliver the Foreign Secretary's invitation. Pulszky, on the other hand, was carrying a letter of warning from Mazzini, who had learned of Palmerston's intentions, and tried to stop Kossuth meeting him. The Italian patriot-conspirator saw a trap in Palmerston's invitation, claiming that all the Foreign Secretary and the English aristocracy wanted was to *disarm* Kossuth, who - by associating with them - would lose his popular appeal to the masses. To deliver this message, Pulszky outwitted his good friend Lord Dudley Stuart, and went out to Kossuth's ship on a small boat. But Pulszky was carrying another warning as well. Richard Cobden, who was anxious to meet Kossuth, and indeed did so, next day, had sent a word to him via Pulszky not to take sides in English political life, and "not to attend any banquet where other people make speeches".[60] The advice was obviously not to include himself though, as Cobden, already on the second day of Kossuth's stay in England, made a speech following Kossuth, at a banquet in Winchester. The gist of it was that in international relations no nation should interfere with the internal affairs of any other. Cobden, like Mazzini, warned Kossuth to avoid Palmerston.

Lord Dudley Stuart appeared on Kossuth's ship soon after Pulszky, and accompanied the Hungarian leader all around England. Kossuth thanked him for Palmerston's invitation and asked him to convey a message that he,(Kossuth), cannot accept the Foreign Secretary's invitation before he spoke to the people of England who accept him as the delegate of the oppressed Hungarian nation. If Lord Palmerston would still like to receive him after such contact with the people, he would be honoured to oblige.[61] In what form Lord Dudley conveyed this message, if he conveyed it at all, we do not know. But he certainly made at least one further attempt to bring Palmerston and Kossuth together. On 29 October he asked the Foreign Secretary to dine at his home at any convenient day within the next fortnight, in order to meet Kossuth. Palmerston declined the offer.[62] Queen Victoria, alarmed by the possibility of severing ties with Austria, asked Lord Russell to stop Palmerston meeting Kossuth. When Lord Russell conveyed the Queen's wish, as his own, Palmerston's answer showed reluctance, but he complied.[63]

Political advice to Kossuth coming from Pulszky's other friends, was polarised on the question whether he ought or ought not to meet Lord Palmerston and Giuseppe Mazzini. Professor Newman belonged to the *Circle of the Friends of Italy* - one of the off-shoots of Mazzini's Italian Committee - so quite understandably, he argued against Palmerston and for Mazzini.[64] David Urquhart, who had visited Kossuth in Kiutahia at Pulszky's instigation, was now hoping to gain his support to his anti-Palmerston campaign, but at the same time was warning him against Mazzini too.[65] Evidently, in the eyes of their comtemporaries, Mazzini commanded as much respect in conspiratorial diplomacy as did Palmerston in official diplomacy.

Kossuth met Mazzini in London on 30 October.[66] They agreed to join forces for the liberation of Hungary and Italy. Synchronised revolts should be started in Lombardy, Venice and in Hungary, when they have suitably prepared the Italian and Hungarian elements of the Austrian army for it. Italy's final aim was unity and riddance of foreign occupation, Hungary's future perspectives - as Kossuth saw them - were independence and a republican system, with a Governor in charge. Kossuth and Mazzini differed on one important point. Mazzini believed the fight had to start immediately, following the presidential election in December, or in the spring of 1852 at the latest. Kossuth thought that a revolt had more chance of success if they waited until the outbreak of the Russian-Turkish war, which was bound to happen fairly soon.

Meanwhile the network of conflicting interests and intrigues around Kossuth's person had reached the rest of the exiles. Prince Czartoryski tried to persuade Dudley Stuart to keep the republican Poles away from Kossuth. The German emigrants were equally split: Marx and his associates 'the Communists' condemned Kossuth,[67] whereas the 'bougeois democrats' Karl Schurz and his organisation of German exiles sent a deputation to welcome him.[68] The Hungarians were divided into three groups. Two of his former cabinet ministers, Szemere and Batthyány were overtly against him. There were those who kept at a distance from him: Sabbas Vukovics, his former Minister of Justice, Miklós Jósika, the well-known novelist, and his personal friend, Teleki. The former plenipotentiary in Paris had disagreed with him - as reflected by the exchange of letters that passed through between Paris and Kiutahia[69] - on two scores: he would not accept Kossuth assuming dictatorial powers in any future combination, and his own federative plan for Hungary and for the surrounding states would be less Magyar centred than Kossuth's plan.

The third group of the Magyar emigrants, and this constituted the majority, turned to him loyally, in fact demanding his leadership. Czetz in Paris, Hajnik, Nicholas Kiss, Pulszky in London, Újházy and Wass in America, with them the scores of Magyars in diaspora were welcoming his release with enthusiasm, waiting for his word and ready to rally around him. And what is more, some of these people who identified Kossuth with the independence of Hungary, carried this belief to such religious fervour that they were to fight against overwhelming odds and endanger or sacrifice their life at the first opportunity. Kossuth's belief, that at the next outbreak of war, Hungary would be liberated, was taken as a true prophecy by such people as Fülöp Figyelmessy, János Matthäides and Mihály Piringer, who volunteered to go to Hungary, with secret missions from the ex-Governor, to organise revolutionary cells inside the country.

Whereas Kossuth appeared as an uncompromising republican to the people of Marseilles, a secret revolutionary conspirator to his fellow-exiles in London, he presented his case to the people of England as the defender of the constitutional liberties of Hungary. His public speeches reiterated almost exactly the same arguments Pulszky was using in his propaganda campaign in 1849, and in his literary ventures of the fifties. Some of his advisers were the same as Pulszky's, like Dudley Stuart who, similarly to Pulszky, followed him around England and was chairman of four meetings out of nine. Still, it is striking that the outline for some of the speeches might have been written by Pulszky himself.[70] His first speech in England, an expression of gratitude delivered to the multitude welcoming him at Southampton on 23 October, was a masterpiece of oratory disguised as an improvisation giving vent to pent up feelings. His second speech on the twenty-fifth, at the banquet given in his honour by Joseph Andrews in Winchester, moved the speaker himself, as well as some of his audience, to tears: Kossuth gave a summary of Hungarian history of the past decade, and at mentioning the circumstances of the Russian intervention "a burst of sympathy broke from the assembly".[71] The next public oration, on the twenty-seventh and in Southampton again, dealt with the idea of liberty, with special reference to England as the chief upholder of the virtue, as opposed to contemporary Austria wherefrom it was entirely lacking. On 30 October he spoke at the Guildhall in London, on 10 November in the Free Trade Hall in Manchester, and on 12 November at a public banquet in Birmingham,[72] in each case emphasising the special eminence of the town he happened to be in, and how this eminence was based on free municipal institutions - which was a key to free trade and prosperity. For parallel, Hungary had, in Kossuth's interpretation, a constitution which had created similar institutions.

These speeches freely incorporated the ideas of Toulmin Smith, the constitutional lawyer,[73] Richard Cobden, the apostle of free trade, and

Francis Pulszky, the propagandist, in dramatised and personalised form, but propagated nothing of a Mazzinian revolutionary. Even the speech at Copenhagen House, delivered on 3 November, on an invitation of a London Committee representing the Trade Unions, was not aimed at inciting the working classes, which Kossuth's conservative critics so greatly feared, but at the most, modestly justifying the dethronement of the House of Habsburg and vindicating the short-lived Hungarian republic. The two farewell perorations in the Hanover Square Rooms in London on 13 November, and in Southampton at the day of his departure, touched upon two themes which revealed Kossuth's political purpose, at least in general terms. He condemned the secrecy of diplomacy on high-power level (not among revolutionaries where he practised it himself), and advocated 'interference for non-interference', in other words, stopping Russia to deal with Turkey, as she had dealt with Hungary.

This was the essence of his message to the people of England, who came in greater multitudes to listen to him than to any other public orator in his century,[74] or to an Aldermaston march at its height in ours. Despite his moderation he made more enemies than friends among the leading parliamentarians: Russell, Disraeli and Gladstone condemned him outright as a 'Mazzinian'.[75]

But the strongest attacks came from the Times, whose editor, John Thaddeus Delane, was in Vienna meeting Schwarzenberg,[76] while Kossuth visited England. In his absence Henry Reed, the assistant editor, directed the paper's campaign against the Hungarian leader, who was, among other unsubstantiated charges, accused by them to have impounded the property of Count Jenő Zichy, a Hungarian aristocrat, executed by the Hungarians for high treason, during the War of Independence. The consistent attacks,[77] letters and reports of correspondents so perseveringly maligned Kossuth that Henningsen sprang to his defence with a pamphlet[78] which accused the Times of being in the pay of the Austrian Secret Police. Whatever their origins, the Times' attacks on Kossuth's personal conduct were fabrications as his honesty and high-mindedness regarding pecuniary affairs were without reproach.

At the end of his tour in England, he accepted the financial contributions offered to him as the fruits of nation-wide collection, not for his personal use, even then, but for the cause. We do not know the sum it amounted to, but we do know that he gave £200 to the Association

of the Hungarian Exiles, directly. He left Toulmin Smith in charge of
funds, who advanced another £500 to the London emigrants, which
Kossuth repaid him from America in December.[79] In January he sent
another £450 through Toulmin Smith to Nicholas Kiss, the *new* chairman
of the exiles in London. He was taking the *former* chairman, Pulszky,
as his closest adviser, to the United States.

3. With Kossuth in America.

> *"Only the grandchildren of giants*
> *Could perhaps still give us, life,*
> *And only the people of Washington,*
> *If willing, might give us relief."*[80]

The American steamboat 'Humboldt' left Southampton for New
York on 2 November 1851 with Kossuth, Pulszky, their wives, Lemmi,
Gyurmán, Ihász, Hajnik and a few Hungarian officers on board. The
Kossuth and Pulszky children were left behind at Pulszky's house in
London, entrusted to the care of Gyula Tanárky and József Karády,
an indication that the respective parents would not avail themselves
of the invitation to settle in the States. All of the other Hungarians,
with the exception of Colonel Ihász, Kossuth's most trusted personal
companion, intended to make a living in the New World, where about
800 Magyars, expatriated since 1848, had already found a home.[81]
During the thirteen days of crossing the Atlantic, Pulszky played
chess with Kossuth while Mrs. Pulszky was jotting down the life-story
of Mrs. Kossuth. The journey was made eventful by the repeated ap-
proaches of Lola Montez flirting with the ex-Governor. The dancer,
whose charms had so fatally influenced the politics of Bavaria, found
an opportunity to address Kossuth on the deck: "Please, General, the
next time you wage war with Austria, do give me a platoon of hussars!"
Before Kossuth could say anything, Pulszky promptly replied: "I am
sure, Miss, you would not be satisfied with less."[82] The brusqueness
and efficiency displayed, together with his quick-wittedness and ability
to improvise, were characteristics Pulszky needed in his new capacity
as closest personal adviser to Kossuth or, to use a twentieth-century
term, for a role he fulfilled: as a press secretary. Already on the second
day of their arrival in America, when Kossuth was unable to deliver

his first speech he had carefully prepared on the ship because the ovation
of the people of New York drowned his voice, Pulszky simply dictated
the speech to the assembled journalists. Later it was he who had visited
the editorial offices of the New York Semi-Weekly Herald and the New
York Tribune, dictating a political comment or an editorial if need be,
or - at least on two occasions - stood up when called upon to make a
political speech á la Kossuth.[83] Sometimes, as at Christmas 1851, Pulszky
stayed behind in New York, waiting for Mazzini's letter on the European
post, to telegraph the contents, if need be, to Kossuth at Philadelphia,
or - as in February 1852 - he went ahead of Kossuth to Cincinnati to
fix the programme of the reception with the local organisers. Typically
for him, who was always able to combine the pursuit of political ends
with making ends meet, his accompanying of Kossuth had also a private
aim: gathering material for a book on America to be published in England
by Trübner.[84]

As far as Kossuth was concerned, he first tried to pick up the loose
ends of diplomatic threads that had connected independent Hungary
with America. We shall remember, from the Baroness von Beck case,
that it was she and a certain Countess (Motesiczky?) who had delivered
Kossuth's request to the American chargé d'affaires, W.H. Stiles, in
Vienna to negotiate for an armistice with Austria. But in addition to
Stiles, who had adopted a cautious attitude, it was A. Dudley Mann,
the charge d'affaires of the United States in Paris, who had much more
faith in the success of the Hungarians, and was despatched by President
Taylor as a confidential agent in Hungary.[85] Mann reached Hungary
at the end of August but could not get in because the Hungarian army
had already capitulated. Almost simultaneously, an envoy of Kossuth's
Count Samuel Wass, after having called on Pulszky in London, reached
America and made a deal with a merchant for a shipment of arms to
Hungary. Independently of the deal, he was also received in the White
House as a private individual. In June 1849, Kossuth had also accredited
a merchant by the name of E.T. Damburghy, as an envoy extraordinary
to America.[86] Since Teleki and Pulszky had at that time planned to
send George Sumner - who had much better connections[87] - to the same
post, Pulszky bought Damburghy's credentials off him for £10. As it
happened, Damburghy had sold Pulszky the French version of his credentials only and proceeded to America to present the English ones. He
too, like Wass, was beaten by time.

From 12 January 1850 onwards, when Secretary of State, Clayton, instructed J.P. Marsh, the American Consul in Constantinople, that America would be glad to receive exiles, the Hungarian emigrants were helped by the United States' Consulates everywhere in Europe, and Kossuth himself was anxiously awaited by the American public. The Hungarian ex-Governor had not realised that their enthusiasm was not shared by President Filmore and Secretary of State, Webster. Before he embarked in England, he had sent a proclamation to the American people, explaining the historical causes of the revolution and describing the demands for a federation that would weld Hungarians and other neighbouring nations into a Union.[88] When, on 6 and 7 December, Kossuth was ceremoniously received by both Houses of Congress, Filmore expressed only his sympathies 'as an individual' and Webster said 'we shall rejoice to see our American model upon the Lower Danube . . .'[89] but neither of the politicians would go any further than that. Kossuth's speeches showed that he wanted material help, official declaration by the United States that Hungary had the right to independence and a promise that a second Russian intervention would not be regarded indifferently by the American government.[90] The American Government would not hear of official financial aid, and the strongest influential support the ex-Governor received was from former-President Tyler, who advocated the withdrawal of diplomatic intercourse with the 'aggressors', i.e. Russia.

The 'two patriots' as Kossuth and Pulszky were styled by American newsmen, toured the States for seven months, from New York,[91] through Philadelphia, Baltimore, Washington, Annapolis, Pensylvania, Pittsburgh, Cleveland, Cincinnati, New Orleans, collecting money for the Hungarian fund. The collection took the form of donations, contributions by Associations of Friends of Hungary, that sprung up everywhere, mushroom-like, and 'loans' Kossuth received against bonds from $5 to $200 he hoped to pay back on achieving Hungarian independence. Adopting a much bolder line than in England, Kossuth expounded that this forthcoming battle for independence would be between democracy and autocracy and that all European nations must unite against the tyranny of the Alliance. He advocated practical measures too: an American naval base in the Aegean, economic collaboration with Turkey and with the rest of the people in the Danubian basin.[92]

These were the political aims Kossuth publicised in America. Those he communicated privately to the Hungarian emigrants, namely to Nicholas Kiss in England, whose task it was to let the others know, were even more outspoken, more uncompromising and less 'federalistic' in spirit. He would have no transactions with the Habsburgs.[93] He would allow no territorial or other concessions to national groups in Transylvania. He wanted to establish the sovereignty of the people, to have no other but a republican form of government, universal suffrage, no centralisation. He wished to protect and preserve property, as laid down in the laws of 1848. His principles were 'republican democratic but neither socialistic nor communistic'.

We have to read between the lines in two of Pulszky's articles in defence of Kossuth's *person*, to recognise that he was in fact defending Kossuth's programme as well against strong public criticism by fellow exiles, K. Batthyány and B. Szemere. The wave of attacks started by the last 'Royal' Hungarian Foreign Minister, Prince Eszterházy's long letter to the *Times* in December,[94] which was first answered by Toulmin Smith in the *Morning Advertiser*.[95] Teleki had unsuccessfully tried to restrain the two former Kossuth Cabinet Ministers[96] who accused Kossuth in the *Times* of still assuming the title of 'Governor' and pursuing an irresponsible adventurer-policy in America.[97] The American press, mainly the *New York Herald* and the *New York Courier*, followed later by the National *Intelligencer* and the *North American Review* adopted the accusations and Pulszky perseived the danger that the former enthusiasm for the Hungarians cause migh dissipate overnight. His polemical articles, sharp, precise and able to save the Kossuth-image, appeared in *The Weekly Herald*[98] in January and in the *Semi-Weekly Tribune* in March. First, Pulszky disposed of the poor old Prince Eszterházy by claiming that all the former minister wanted was to earn good points with the Austrian Government by his attack on Kossuth. He reminded the Prince, in a semi-threatening manner, that he had once been his Under-Secretary of State and still had in his possession indiscriminating letters from him. Pulszky asserted that Kossuth was to be the leader of freedom's next battle on the Continent, and fearing the future, the Austrians induced the Prince to speak up. Batthyány and Szemere, on the other hand, spoke against Kossuth partly out of envy and spite, and partly out of their desire to show readiness to treat with Austria while Kossuth had been, and remained, uncompromisingly defiant. Pulszky concluded, that the people of Hungary "in every city, and in every village, and in every hamlet" were waiting for but one man to carry out his mission to liberate the country and it was Louis Kossuth.

How was this liberation to be achieved? Kossuth spent three-quarters of the 96,000 dollars he collected on armaments. First he bought 6,000 rifles from Gustavo Sacchi, and Italian merchant who was Mazzini's collaborator in America. Simultaneously, he dispatched Adriano Lemmi to Malta, to wait there - under the pretext of trading with wine - for a large consignment of arms and ammunition arriving in barrels from New York. Count Samuel Wass had revalidated his 1849 contract with the arms dealer, George Law, for 40,000 weapons and three warships to carry troops.[99]

Henningsen, who followed Kossuth to America, submitted a plan for the troops to be trained in San Domingo, for a future expedition. Mazzini who was disappointed in his earlier plans by the December coup d'etat of Louis Napoleon, suggested that such an expedition could be lead by Garibaldi. Lemmi, from Malta, could organise the discontents of Sicily, to spark off the rebellion when the expedition from America would reach Sicilian soil. Meanwhile, Pulszky was to translate and send off a proclamation of Kossuth's to the Croatians to ensure their neutrality. A revolt in Milan, to be organised partly by Mazzini's men and partly by Kossuth's agents Vetter and István Türr, would provide the transmitting wave of revolutions toward Hungary.[100] The revolutionary cells inside Hungary, organised by Kossuth's agent, József Makk, would immediately react and join forces with guerilla troops organised of Hungarian emigrants by Colonel Sándor Gál in Moldavia.

Pulszky had undoubtedly believed in the possibility that the revolution might succeed by the spring of 1853. His two letters written in May from Niagara Falls, and in June from New York, to Professor Newman, speak of his tentative preparations to end his exile.[101] But how far he was acquainted with the detailed plan, or a detailed plan of Kossuth - if we may talk in such terms of conspiratorial activities, the details of which only transpired in recent years - we may never know. He worked then, as perhaps all of Kossuth's followers did, trusting the politics of the leader, but at the same time safe-guarding himself from total involvement, and therefore - in the case of failure - from total loss of faith, of material means and of illusions. Literature was such a safeguard, and as before, the partnership with his wife proved most felicitous and profitable. The Pulszkys shared an attitude of elasticity, lacking from the typical emigrants, an openness towards future possibilities, which made them consider continuing life in America. He was offered a Chair of Modern History[102] in Cambridge, Massachusetts, which he was very tempted to accept. America is a place, he wrote to Newman, telescoping the conclusion of his forthcoming book - where the curse of Adam has become a blessing and every work is regarded honourable. And it was, at the time of this tempting offer, that he learned of his death sentence by the Austrian Military Court in Hungary. Later, on 4 July 1852, the newspapers reported that his execution for treason was carried out in effigy in Pest, his name being nailed on the gallows. And yet, he refused the Chair, came back from America on 26 July because, as he put it, he was[103] "still clinging to the homeland wherefrom he was exiled for ever".

The book *White, red, black* came out early in 1853 and was an instant success in England. The reviews[104] mainly praised its information value for future travellers in America, and its ease and elegance of style. The author's purpose was, as Mrs. Pulszky confessed to Newman, to lessen some of the prejudices current in England, against America. It was neither a description of Kossuth's journey, nor a political work espousing the merits of the cause, because these have been dealt with by Headley[105] and were to be tackled by Newman, both of whom relied on Pulszky for political information on Hungarian matters. The work described America, analysed its people, its problems and its institutions, with the 'causes' featuring in it as a constant term of reference but not the subject of the book. The narrative of the Pulszky's journey was composed of long quotations from Theresa's diary - she had proved herself as a diarist and the style especially suited her - while the analytical parts were written by the able pen of Francis. Although not a scholarly work, the parts written by Francis were based on primary and secondary historical sources such as population statistics and Bancroft's *History of America*,[106] and as it includes conversations with outstanding men of the period such as Emerson, Longfellow, Bryant, Houston, Godwin, Greeley and Dana, not recorded elsewhere; it is of undoubted value as social history.

The Pulszky's tour coincided with the primaries of the American elections in the spring of 1852. Both the Republicans and the Democrats made tentative proposals to Kossuth and Pulszky to win their support for the election campaign, but remembering Cobden's warning not to meddle with party politics, they both managed to keep out of it. Analysing the political system of America, Pulszky remained the interested but uninvolved "European observer", admiring the separation of powers, appraising the triumph of republican principles, and comparing the American constitutional achievement with that of England and France. The political issue of the day: 'abolitionism' versus 'patriarchalism', or the upkeep of the 'peculiar institution' confronted them as they visited the Southern states. Theresa, militantly, Francis Pulszky, diplomatically, countered the challenges, as he could not speak out openly against slavery without endangering Kossuth's appeal among the wealthy landowners in the South. He recalled in the book that on one occasion he[107] "told them, that I belong to a country where the landowners . . . converted their peasants into freeholders; . . . the Southerners were generally polite enough to drop the conversation; but in their countenances I saw that they thought, 'he did it', but now he is in exile."

Pulszky devoted the last chapter of the work to drawing a parallel between the American and the English character, which, in a way, was a summary of his social experiences after four years of exile spent in the two countries. In his opinion, the English were proud, xenophobic, reserved and conservative, the Americans more liberal with the new-comer, passionate and less reliable. He saw the chief dangers in England in a fruitless combination of pedantry with materialism, where good and evil was measured by pecuniary standards. English imperialism was just as untenable by liberal principles as the 'peculiar institution' in America: the former advocated two standards of liberty, one at home, the other in the colonies; the latter tolerated two standards within one country, one for the white man, the other for the coloured.

Motivated by closely similar political desires, neither Kossuth nor Pulszky were satisfied with the results. Kossuth in his rare moments of absolute realism foresaw that "the English will take our side only as much as they think it compatible with their interests"[108] and that the whole American tour might just remain no more but a 'political deed' without immediate consequences that might effect the fate of Hungary.

The money they had collected was not enough to finance any large-scale operation, no government in power showed any willingness to help, so the plans had to be fastened on to a revolutionary event, that might produce the expected chain-reaction.

Pulszky surrendered his individual approach to politics as soon as Kossuth appeared in England, gave up his own views on seeking aid for the emigrants and adopted Kossuth's attitude, that their duty was to turn the benefits of sympathy into armaments for a come-back. At the same time, Pulszky's personality asserted itself by finding a way to enrich his own experience and knowledge of the world. He excelled as an organiser and held his own as a writer. For the sake of these two roles he became closely acquainted with a new political system, with new types of social beliefs and moral philosophies which differed from those of Europe.

CHAPTER FOUR

TOWARDS THE CRIMEAN WAR

1. The rocket-affair and its background.

After the comparatively calm period that Kossuth and his associates had enjoyed since their return from America, in July 1852, the *Times* once more launched an attack against the Hungarian ex-Governor. On 15 April 1853 a long article appeared in its columns, reporting a *Seizure of arms of Kossuth*. The article claimed that Kossuth and his associates had abused the tolerant hospitality of England by carrying on conspiracies against other states. The writer - most probably Kossuth's implacable enemy, John Thaddeus Delane - urged the British Government to bring Kossuth and his adherents to the Court of Law. According to the *Times'* information, the Commissioner of Police, acting under the Secretary of State's warrant seized a large store of war materials on the previous day, in a house belonging to Kossuth, which "may be the stock in trade of a political incendiary, but certainly form no part of the household goods of a private gentleman". On the contrary, he must have had in view hostilities or insurrectionary movements of a very destructive character. If Kossuth came to this country for the purpose of levying war against foreign nations, and if he used his resources he may have had at his disposal to prepare means of destruction against Britain's neighbours, he violated the laws of England as well as the law of nations. Since this country was resolved to maintain its right of protection to foreigners the Government had a duty to keep them within the bounds of the law. If any plot was ever detected, the writer believed that Kossuth would be found to be engaged in it. The Editor reminded his readers that when many citizens thought M. Kossuth a person deserving all honour, and when Lord Dudley Stuart, Mr. Cobden and the Corporation of London took him to their hearts, the *Times* described him "as he is, as he will be yet more clearly proved to be. Guildhall is after all not very far from Old Bailey".

Having read the *Times* in the morning, Lord Dudley Stuart must have written to Kossuth immediately and had his note delivered by a messenger.

Kossuth's answer, discovered by the present writer in the Harrowby Archives, was sent from "Alpha Road, St. John's Wood" on the very same day:[1] "Mylord! In answer to your kind note I have the honour to say that all the malicious accusations in the "Times" of today about a house in my occupation having been searched, and a store of war materials belonging to me been discovered and seized are entirely unfounded.

Not only in no house in my occupation but also[2] nowhere else in England could have been any store of war materials belonging to me discovered and seized, from the simple reason, that I have no store of war material whatever in England.

But while I give this plain and flat denial to the alleged charge* I desire most explicitly to guard myself against the misconstruction, as if I wished to disavow my intentions of activ and eternal hostility to the lawless oppressor of my country, Francis Joseph of Austria.

No Mylord! I boldly claim the credit and the honor of these intentions. My life is, and will be devoted to the liberation of my country.

So God help me!

When the Congress of my nation, both Lords and Representatives of the people, elected me unanimously Governor of the realm of Hungary and all the millions of my people, County by County, City by City and town by town confirmed this election, I was called upon to swear that I will do all I can to maintain the rights, freedom and independence of my country. I swore that oath, before God the Almighty and my nation! - and thus the natural duties of a patriot became to me the sworn duties of a man, elected to the highest position in the Commonwealth for that very aim.

The fact of a foreign despot having in open violation of the laws of nations invaded my country, does not efface my oath, neither dispense me from the duties resulting therefrom, and from my being a man and a patriot, it rather increases these duties, by a sense of increased injustice.**

And therefore, I desire explicitly to be understood, that I do not disavow my hostility to the oppressors of my country, but rather avow openly my determination to free my country from them. To this my aim I shall and will devote all my life and all my activity, and to this activity I never will recognise any other limit, but *honor, morality and the laws of that country, where I happen to reside.*

From * to **: this passage is heavily crossed out in the letter.

And as it is not contrary to honor and morality to have stores of war materials to be used when required in the service of my country I declare that such I have; but I have them in such countries, where it is lawful for me to have them, even with those intentions, which I openly avow. But in England I have them not, because I have been told that some doubts may be entertained about the legality of such an act.

With this explanation I repeat no store of war material of mine could have been seized because I do not possess either directly or indirectly anything of the kind in this country.

I remain with high regards and particular consideration,

My Lord   Yours respectfully

Lord Dudley Coutts Stuart, M.P.   L. Kossuth."

On receiving Kossuth's letter, Dudley Stuart must have sent it on to Richard Cobden with a covering note, presumably commenting on the foreseeable effect its publication might produce, as we have the following reply from Cobden:[3]

103 Westbourne Terrace
23 Apl 1853

"My Dear Lord Dudley Stuart,

I say ditto to your remark that the enclosed "is very different from what I should have dictated" - Kossuth does not seem to me to attach much importance to the good or bad opinion of the English public. You and I on the contrary have been anxious that his fair name should not be tarnished by the British press. He is looking, and perhaps naturally, to what will be the effect of any thing he writes or says upon the course of events in Hungary or Austria. Hence the difficulty of our judging what his conduct ought to be in particular circumstances. Should the enclosed be published, it will undoubtedly be a great relief to the Times, for it will give that paper the opportunity of twisting out of its present dilemma. Is it quite impossible to get Kossuth to write two lines to you to say - "I pledge you my honor that I have no more connection with the establishment of Mr. Hale, & am no more responsible for its contents, than is your lordship or the speaker of your Honorable House of Parliament"?

I suppose the reason why Kossuth wishes to publish the fact of his having provided arms in other countries is that he would like to make the

Austrian government uneasy. But *to be forewarned is to be forearmed* & the thinking part of the world will doubt his discretion in publishing to the Austrians his preparations, & *humane* men will be inclined to say that he is provoking increased rigor towards his Hungarian brethren by thus alarming the Government of Vienna.

However I really do not feel that I can with any advantage interfere further in the matter.

Believe me truly yours,

R. Cobden."

Both Dudley Stuart, the advocate of Hungarian constitutional liberty, and Richard Cobden, the 'apostle of peace', whose house, as Pulszky said, was always open to the Hungarians,[4] must have felt deeply embarrassed by Kossuth's militant attitude, although he seemed to exonerate himself from the direct charges of storing arms in England. Their repeated warnings of Mazzini, and the restraint Kossuth had shown in the speeches of his first visit to England seemed to have evaporated, and Kossuth had shown himself as a revolutionary. Cobden seemed to have been particularly perturbed by Kossuth's belligerent tone. When they had made friends two years before, the peace-congresses Cobden had called into life were in favour of non-intervention and Kossuth was a victim of Russian intervention. Now, only a few months ago in January 1853 Cobden wrote an anti-war and anti-revolutionary pamphlet entitled *1793 and 1853 in three letters*. Although it was a success, it could do little to moderate the steadily mounting war-preparation, in which Kossuth seemed to have been taking his 'private' share. We know that Britain was the only country in Europe where, despite repeated requests for police surveillance, from Continental powers, the refugees could live unmolested, until they were found to break the law. As the English police would not oversee the activities of Kossuth and his followers, Austria had to find means to watch them. The Government in Vienna kept a ring of spies around the Kossuthites in England such as "Berndorf" an unidentified correspondent of Schwarzenberg, who sent his nom de plume letters from Pulszky's entourage, or István Varga,[5] who kept contacts with Kossuth's sisters in Hungary, or Mr. Loosey in America whose task had been to trace every step of the Hungarian colony there. "Berndorf" might also have been the informer of the *Times*.

The events of the last few months, as reported by the *Times* itself, had already exposed Kossuth to some extent as a 'conspirator'. On 10 February 1853 it was reported by submarine telegraph in the *Times* that "an attempt at insurrection took place at Milan on the sixth. It has been suppressed." It was also revealed that a proclamation from Mazzini to the Italians, and another one addressed by Kossuth to the Hungarian soldiers in Italy had been placarded in Milan, and the *Times* was even furnished with the text of the letter. As it in fact happened, Kossuth disclaimed the proclamation attributed to him, first through the pen of his friend and neighbour in Alpha Road, Captain Maine Reid,[6] and later himself, but he could not disprove his complicity. Their co-operation which had started in Kiutahia, and continued uninterrupted through Kossuth's first visit to England, and through his tour of America, was solemnly and publicly sealed by Kossuth himself in November 1852 in London.

Professor Francis Newman witnessed and reported Kossuth's address to the *Society of the Friends of Italy*, who called himself and Mazzini the 'two wings of one army'.[7] Newman judged the Milan report to have been "a deeply-planned inauguration of what was intended to be a national Italian movement...trusting to the collateral help of the Hungarians in Italy".[8]

The premature Milan insurrection was the last link in a tragical chain of recent conspiratorial failures for Kossuth. The revolutionary 'cell-system' of his agent János Makk, whose activities he had approved and promoted when he was still in Turkey, were discovered by the Austrian authorities. Many people were arrested and the ring-leaders were executed in Hungary. Of his other agents, sent from London in November 1851, Pataky-Piringer was also captured and shot in February 1853. István Türr, his agent in Milan who had acted on Mazzini's advice, instead of waiting for Kossuth's instructions, was captured by the Piedmontese and expelled from Italy. More unfortunate were the one hundred Hungarian soldiers serving in the Austrian army, who mutinied for Mazzini's word: they were court-martialled and sixteen of them were immediately executed.

Kossuth's conception, as we shall remember, was to organise an expedition from America which would join forces with Italian guerillas when the rebellion had broken out. On 15 February Kossuth sent Pulszky to America[9] with the instructions to represent the Hungarian cause to

General Pierce, the new democratic President of the United States. Representation, in other words, meant trying to obtain a loan for his European campaign.

Pulszky's second task would have been to help promote a direct steamship connection between Constantinople and New York. But as he tells us in his *Memoirs*,[10] he had carried out secret instructions as well, and these were the real goals of his journey. Pulszky was to contact Lieutenant Nelson, an officer of the warship *Mississippi*, who had become Kossuth's trusted friend, and through him, Colonel Picket who had promised to train the San Domingo expeditionary force. This would have been a Hungarian legion, composed of the hundreds of exiled Hungarian soldiers and their officers, working in America, who were to assemble under Pierce and wait for Kossuth's word to come over to Europe. Point 16 of Pulszky's secret instructions commanded him to tell the Hungarians that although Kossuth had meant to wait with the Italian revolution until the Turkish-Russian war had broken out, with Austria on the side of Russia, now that the Italian revolt sparked off, Kossuth was going to Italy immediately and inform the American Hungarians from there.

We know that the revolt started on 6 February and was suppressed on the same day. Furthermore, that the Times reported the event on 10th instant, yet on the fifteenth, the date of Pulszky's departure from Southampton, they must have been still hoping that the news of the revolt's failure was false. Kossuth's disclaimer of the manifesto was published on seventeenth instant and Pulszky informs us that he learned of the fiasco on the steamship *Humboldt*. "So my American journey (ibid. p. 119), lost its aim before I got there," he concluded.

Nonetheless, Pulszky proceeded to Washington and secured an interview with the President who, like his predecessor, Fillmore, assured him of his "personal sympathies". On 18 March Pulszky reported to Kossuth that it was impossible to interest the American Government in the Eastern Question as the official foreign policy does not regard events beyond Cuba with close interest. He could see no other way to interest the Americans in the question than to use the organ of the Democratic Press to keep the oriental crisis in the headlines.[11] Thus, from a personal point of view, his second American journey, lasting about two months, was not a failure. As before: when overt diplomacy was no longer possible and clandestine political action lost its efficacy he turned to journalism. In New York he looked up his old friend Horace Greeley, the editor of the New York Tribune, and got commissioned as the paper's European political correspondent.

Pulszky's first action was to take up the case of Kossuth in the New York Daily and answer the charges in the rocket-affair laid down by the Times. On 30 April[12] he reported that following the Times' allegations, the matter was alluded to in Parliament and led to a debate in which Kossuth was entirely exculpated.[13] The debate was opened by *Sir Joshua Walmsley*, enquiring what foundation there was for the report in the Times. *Lord Palmerston* answered that there was in a house near Rotherhithe, but not occupied by M. Kossuth, a quantity of war-like materials and gun-powder. A search warrant was issued and several thousands of war rockets were found. These were seized. Who they belonged to, the House would not expect him to say. No assurances respecting the political refugees had been given to any foreign power. The next speaker, *Mr. T. Duncombe*, said that the place was a rocket manufactory and that the whole statement with regard to M. Kossuth was a fabrication. Then *Lord Dudley Stuart* asserted that Kossuth himself denied all knowledge of the transaction.

On 2 May, Pulszky, signing himself as A.P.C. brought an ally of Kossuth's to the columns of the New York paper.[14] As he explained, Captain Maine Reid had twice written to the Times on Kossuth's behalf denying the ex-Governor's complicity in the affair, but the Times refrained from publishing his second, conclusive letter, which appears therefore in the New York Daily Tribune. Captain Maine Reid stated, that William Hale, son of the proprietor of the rocket-factory, had declared that Kossuth had nothing whatever to do with the undertaking and that the factory was a *bona fide* establishment carrying on a patent business.

The last sequel to the reportage of the affair was provided by the New York Tribune's other London correspondent, Karl Marx. On 14 May[15] Marx, who was, unlike Pulszky, not anxious to defend Kossuth, wrote that on 23 April proceedings were commenced against Mr. Hale, the proprietor of the Rotherhithe rocket manufactory. Hale could give no satisfactory answer as to where he had obtained the money for the manufacture of the rockets. He had employed foreign refugees, one of whom, Mr. Usener, had formerly been in the Hungarian army as Major of the Staff, and was recommended to Hale by Kossuth, with the following words: "I can recommend him to your employ to assist in making *our* rockets or your rockets." Mr. Usener, as a witness, could not remember which word was used by Kossuth. Marx concluded his article by saying that further explanations were needed from Kossuth.

But neither Kossuth nor Pulszky judged it expedient to provide further explanations, once the charge of complicity was dismissed by Lord Palmerston, who as Home Secretary stood firm against demands of foreign powers, and did not allow the refugees to be molested.[16]

Kossuth was certainly intransigent enough to interpret Cobden's maxim: "to be forewarned is to be forearmed" in his own way. We know that during the Hungarian war he had connections with the Hale establishment,[17] but it is fairly certain that none of his ammunition stores in the early fifties were kept in England. There was a store of arms in Switzerland, where General Klapka directed plans after he left England in 1851. Mazzini's arms which General Türr had access to in Italy, were seized by the Piedmontese. Lemmi kept some war materials for both Kossuth and Mazzini in Malta. The arms bought from Sacchi were stored in New York. But the best source of supply was two factories of arms and military equipment in the United States, one in Weaverston, the other in Morningsville, where the management was in the hands of Kossuth's agents.[18] It is very likely, but cannot be proved, since Pulszky does not give the full text of his second visit to America, that he carried specific orders addressed to the keepers of Kossuth's stock of arms in America.

Contrary to the wishes of Cobden, Kossuth was bent on provoking and alarming the Government of Vienna, and Pulszky, a more peace-loving and compromise-seeking man by nature, had to abide by him. To measure the change in Pulszky's own policy since his chairmanship of the Hungarian Association in 1851, we may point out that he was anxious then to get rid of arms the Hungarians had had abroad,[19] whereas in 1853, as he tells in a private letter to Newman,[20] he was ready to take up arms and use them.

2. Left out from the war.

When Pulszky came back from America, Kossuth acquainted him with a combination of plans which must have appeared to him as details of a great conception with a chance to succeed. Brushing aside Pulszky's unfavourable reception in the White House, Kossuth found some comfort in the co-operation of certain American individuals. Lieutenant Nelson visited him in England and he had not given up hope of an expedition, if only a ship could be bought. The young Americans on the left wing of the Democratic Party were pledged to support him. George Law, the arms dealer, had relied on his influence to sell arms and ships to the Turkish Government. The American Consul at Southampton, Rodney Croskey, Pulszky's close friend and Kossuth's confidante, had promised his diplomatic aid if he succeeded to the vacant consulship at Constantinople. With his help Kossuth had a memorandum conveyed to the American Government. The recommendations included the establishment of an American naval base in Turkish waters, the erection of a consulate in a Southern Danubian State, and a war loan for Turkey. Had some of these suggestions been accepted, and their conveyor, Croskey, appointed Consul in Constantinople, Pulszky would have gone with him to Turkey - this should be the interpretation of his 'belligerent' statement to Newman - as they were hardly listened to, he and Croskey stayed in England.

From being an active politician and a part-time journalist, whose writing had a primary aim of furthering a cause, Pulszky now became a full-time political commentator whose background as a former political agent and whose circle of friends equipped him to report on the current events shrewdly and faithfully. Yet not only did his Hungarian bias remain, but he himself remained a Kossuth man, a spokesman for *the general outline of his leader's politics*, anxiously waiting for the portends of war, and reporting events that Kossuth was involved with.

His letter in the New York Daily Tribune, dated London, 20 May,[21] posed the question that how much influence had Lord Palmerston, now Home Secretary, retained in foreign matters in the Government, whose watchword was peace at any price. He noted that the corollary of "Napoleonic socialism" the coronation of Napoleon, was to take place on 15 August, but this might bring a change in French foreign politics.

Reporting on Kossuth's movements, Pulszky adopted W.S. Landor's dedicatory motto to the ex-Governor: "Hungary is not dead: no, nor sleepeth". The anti-Habsburg tone of his next article[22] had risen out, naturally, from the description of a meeting of the *Society of the Friends of Italy* attended by Professor Newman and Kossuth, both of whom had emphasised that Hungary and Italy should be allied against the 'despots'.

The nature of these articles - political commentary in the form of long letters - allowed Pulszky to sprinkle the steady flow of political information with occasional news about artistic events and archaeological exhibitions, which were his private interests.[23] Thus, between reporting on the efforts of the Turkish nation to preserve peace and the endeavours of the Czar of Russia to foment war, he reported on exhibitions staged in London and even on the weather.

After a short and severe illness in July, when a 'lady correspondent' of the New York Tribune (perhaps Mrs. Pulszky), sent two contributions from London,[24] he resumed his commentaries in August. He reported on the mounting tension of war propaganda in London, and the active measures France was taking in preparation for war. He commented that "the secret societies are full of activity and the refugees in London and Jersey full of hope". His next article,[25] dated 5 August was entitled "war certain"; but reporting on the debate in Parliament two weeks later[26] that in England, the "peace at any price" policy still prevailed. " 'Mundus vult decipi' shouts Nesselrode, and 'Decipiatur ergo' is the answer of Lord Palmerston."[27]

From his own standpoint, his news for the Daily Tribune were partly auspicious and partly disappointing at the end of September.[28] Turkey was assembling troops on Russia's frontier (so the war, long-awaited, by the emigration, was imminent), and arrests and executions took place inside Hungary (as the conspirators were again discovered and the chances of a rising annulled).

The Turkish question had come under closer examination by Pulszky in August 1853. On 20 July he wrote in a private letter to Newman that he "had to write a paper on the present crisis of Turkey for the Eclectic Review".[29] A book published by David Urquhart - who became Kossuth's intermediary at the Porte in 1853, and remained so during the first stages of the war - provided Pulszky with the opportunity of writing a review article on the Eastern Question, in the August issue of the Eclectic Review.[30] The book itself, being very topical, vivid in style and somewhat prophetic in outlook immediately became a bestseller and within a month went into the third printing.[31] Pulszky's article is a skilfull fusion of Urquhart's main thesis, that Turkish rule in the East should still be preferred to Russian, with his own opinions - based on reports from Hungarian officers living in Asia Minor - that the Turkish soldier is far superior to the Russian. The crisis of 1853 is traced back to 1848 when, according to Pulszky, the Porte made the great mistake of allowing the Russians to use the Protectorates as bases for their military operations in Transylvania. This partiality was interpreted by the Russians as a sign of weakness, and only the tough line adopted by the Western Powers in 1849-50, stopped the Czar waging war on the Sultan over the refugee question. Since then, Russian tactics had been to foment unrest inside the Turkish Empire, and in territories under Turkish suzerainty, hence the revolt in Montenegro, and the Czar's claim to defend the Christian population of Bosnia.

Urquhart had clearly shown, Pulszky argued, by collecting evidence of Russian craft and diplomacy, that unless the Western Powers stepped in, the trade and resources of Moldavia, Wallachia and South Eastern Europe would be expoited by Russia. As war seemed inevitable, and Russia was armed to the teeth, the Western Powers had to aid Turkey without delay. "To make war, said Montecucculi, three things are required - money, and again money, and once more, money."[32] Pulszky advocated the war loan to the Sultan (a fact accomplished by secret diplomacy - Pulszky might not have known), as a first measure, and if it did not produce full results, he advocated the defence of Turkey for the protection of English trading interests.

A very different view of the situation was presented by Cobden, who still did not give up his efforts to moderate the war-fever. In a hitherto unpublished[33] letter to Lord Dudley Stuart, he recorded his reactions:

                                        Midhurst 27 Sept 1853

"Private

My dear Ld. D. Stuart,

You are the most scandalously ill-used gentleman of my acquaintance! Your good letter has been in my pocket many a day, whilst I was moving about at the sea-side, sometimes thinking of it when I had no check-book near, & then forgetting it when I had no such excuse. On my arrival here last night I found a letter from Kossuth in which he tells me that an electric telegraphic communication informs him that the first gun is fired in the East, & the purpose of his long letter seems to be to per-suade me that we ought now to fire into Austria! I really cannot agree to a war for any pretence afforded by the present state of the "Orient". No good to us or any body else would come of our joining the Crescent against the Cross. Your friends the Turks are past all saving - I don't deny that they are nearly as good Christians as the Russians - but they are decaying under the influence of a religion the laws of which are opposed to the laws of nations, & therefore they cannot be preserved. If your young friend the Sultan were to turn Christian, and sweep out the Eunuchs and w--s who infest his palace, take a decent young women from Germany for a wife & issue such a manifesto as would set Exeter Hall in a flame, he might preserve his European boundaries. But if not, not. You cannot preserve a Mahometan empire in Europe with a majority of Christian subjects. But I doubt whether Kossuth's information about a gun being fired is correct. I don't believe there will be any war. There is very likely to be an insurrection or a massacre of the Christians.

I enclose the £10–which you ought to have had long ago.

Believe me truly yours,

R. Cobden."

If Kossuth was more right about the outbreak of hostilities between Turkey and Russia than Cobden, it was only due to his being more speedily informed by his agents and not by his more realistic analysis of the situation. Both men entertained a separate illusion. Cobden's was a belief that international trade was furthered by peace-time conditions only and war itself was wrong and wicked, consequently - ignoring all signs to the contrary - he *hoped* and enunciated that war would not take place. Kossuth believed that Austria would be bound to help the 'Holy Alliance' and by a promise to reciprocate the help received from Russia in 1849, and would attack Turkey. Besides Urquhart, who was openly advocating his plans at the Porte, he sent secret Hungarian agents to Constantinople: Sándor Gál, Lórody and Bátorffy,[34] to organise the Hungarian emigrants into battle-troops and bombared the Sultan with memoranda to induce him to start a preventive war against Austria. He even worked out an operation-plan for the Turks; the left flank aided by the Hungarian emigrant troops, Gál's insurgents, the expedition force from America and General Klapka's regulars under a Turkish flag to attack in the direction of Vienna, and the right flank led by Schemyl Bey to attack Russia. Meanwhile, as Kossuth was eager to foresee and communicate to Persigny, France will have attacked Russia from the sea supported by her English ally.

We know from Newman, writing about Kossuth's secret preparations for the Crimean War thirty-five years later,[35] that he wanted quickly to collect £5,000 for a steamer on which he could raise the Hungarian flag and appear in Constantinople. Our inference is, that having failed to obtain an American loan, he wished to use the ship to transport troops and arms from America to Constantinople. Newman's advice was to send a circular to select, rich individuals who once "spoke vigorously on the side of Hungary".

In one of these letters, addressed to Adam Black, Kossuth, writing on 8 November 1853, spoke about the already commenced hostilities in the East which were bound to exert influence in their immediate neighbourhood. He continued: "I neither do foment nor execute it, what I desire is that should my nation spontaneously be led to some obvious resolution and call upon me to take my place. . . I should not from want of the necessary means to do good"[36] . . . Newman said, that Kossuth's letter informed him that all he managed to raise was about £400.

If Kossuth was far off the target in a part of his great plan which was fastened on to the Eastern War, his knowledge of the operation of secret diplomacy was equally amiss. Although Napoleon III had desired to break up the long-standing alliance of Russia, Prussia and Austria which had hemmed France in for forty years, and although she wanted to protect her special interest in the Levant, the Allies were determined to keep - where they understood to be - the balance and security of Europe. This required the checking of Russia's expansion, but it also required - as Palmerston had pointed out and was to repeat - the preservation of Austria. A war for Austria could have meant dismemberment, and nothing was further away from the intentions of the Viennese Government than to enter the war on the side of Russia. Indeed, the opposite was nearer the truth: as Pulszky vertured to *guess* in a private letter to Newman[37] there was "some plan about Italy, in order to bully Austria into active Alliance with the Western League". Turkey, for her part, took the most cautious measures to ensure the neutrality of Austria. Hungarian emigrants living outside Turkish territories were refused admission, and those within were prevented from forming a legion, lest they should provoke Austria. Those Hungarians who took part in the

Eastern War, were either fighting as individuals in Omar Pasha's army in the Caucasus, or were employed by the English as interpreters and traders in the Crimea from the spring of 1854 onwards.

By the time Her Majesty felt called upon "by the sympathies of Her People with right against wrong by a Desire to avert from Her Dominions most injurious consequences, and to save Europe from the Preponderance of a Power which has violated the faith of treaties. . .to take up arms in conjunction with the Emperor of the French"[38] both Kossuth and Pulszky were thoroughly disappointed in the war. The *form* of actions each had taken was similar, but the *content* was different. For Kossuth turned against the diplomacy of England with all his oratorical powers and was soon thundering against the *secret diplomacy* and the *meaningless war* in the lecture halls of London, Edinburgh, Glasgow, Nottingham and Newcastle; whereas Pulszky, imitating Kossuth's lecture tour went to Bangor, Conway, Leicester and Nottingham, Manchester and Highgate, to lecture on art and archaeology.[39] The switch for Pulszky to 'become a private citizen in pacific retirement' was much easier than for Kossuth, whom the Times and the Austrians would have liked to see as such.

Losing all hope in diplomacy, temporarily, Kossuth once again drew closer to Mazzini. In their principles they had always agreed: all rights emanated from God, but instead of despots, the will of the people was the ultimate authority in the matters of state. A republican form of government was the best guarantee for the happiness of the people and for the constant evolution of laws and duties.[40] The steps in the autumn of 1855 were to supplant the Holy Alliance of the Great Powers, that was broken up by the outbreak of the Crimean War, with the Holy Alliance of nations, claimed the *Manifesto of the republican party*, signed by Kossuth, Ledru Rollin and Mazzini.[41] The signatories claimed that with the fall of Sebastopol the moment had arrived for European democracy to constitute itself a powerful unity. They stated that the governments of Europe were divided among themselves, which provided a golden opportunity for the dismembered nationalities to regenerate, ally and arise united. Not only Hungary, Poland and Italy should take part in the splendid programme of organising themselves into republics, but other states could follow suit: Spain and Portugal could form an Iberian republic, a 'young' Scandinavia, a 'new' Illyria, an Alpine and an Oriental Confederacy could be born by harmonising the two leading ideas: Liberty and Association.

The *Manifesto of the republican party* belonged to the same idealistic dream world of wishful thinking which had brought forth the European Central Democratic Committee in 1851. The further away Kossuth got from those who held the actual power in their hand, Omar Pasha, Napoleon, and re-emerging Palmerston, the less chance he had to exert any influence on the course of events. It was Teleki, though he did not go along with Kossuth since the release of the latter, who at least knocked on the right door. In the spring of 1854, he submitted a memorandum to Lord Palmerston, arguing that the Western Powers will gain little and will eventually lose more by making a deal with 'decrepit' Austria. The Holy Alliance may have been broken by the Crimean War but England's policy towards Austria remained. Palmerston wrote, with his own hand, on the cover of Teleki's document: "This Memorandum is written with the resentful feelings of an exile, but the statement it contains as to the system of the Austrian Government and the feelings of the Hungarians are well worth consideration. The maintenance of the Austrian Empire is an object of first rate importance to Europe at large, and this statement points out internal dangers which threaten the unity of that Empire, and which notwithstanding Count Teleki's opinion to the contrary might surely be diminished if not averted entirely by an improved system of administrative government."[42]

Pulszky was also diffident of Mazzini's theoretical approach to European politics and had mistrusted Mazzini on practical grounds. Pulszky would ally himself with Mazzini for the sake of Kossuth in 1851, for the expressed purpose of furthering the cause of Hungarian independence, which might or might not bring in the triumph of liberal principles, and perhaps, but not necessarily, through the re-establishment of a republican government. But Pulszky trusted political ideas only on their merits of achieving immediate success.

This critical approach of Pulszky to Mazzini was already apparent in the late summer of 1849 when he wrote: "we have little confidence in French republicanism"[43] represented by Mazzini and his followers abroad, and he emphasised that the Hungarian insurrection was an act of self-defence and had "little to do with abstract principles or theories of government". During the Crimean War period, when his friend Newman welcomed Kossuth's return to Mazzini's way, he renewed his criticism of the Italian conspirator. In his view, Mazzini's plans and his compositions were 'clever', were motivated by noble sentiments but were lacking "any practical suggestions".[44] Pulszky mentioned only one further meeting with Mazzini in his *Memoirs*.[45] When future-President, James Buchanan, left his post as American Ambassador in London in 1855 he gave a farewell dinner, where Pulszky dined with the three signatories of the *Manifesto* in the company of other leading republican exiles in London: Worcel, Herzen, Orsini and Garibaldi.

The years that elapsed from the end of 1853 to the beginning of 1859 were to Pulszky a long period of waiting for an opportunity to enter politics again. Meanwhile, he continued to extend his personal relations, take his share in social activities, and find new ways to support a growing family. He corresponded with Dickens, often met Thackeray in aristocratic salons, contacted Landseer whose interest in art he shared, frequented the houses of the Horners and the Lyalls, and learned Sanscrit in his free time from Professor Goldstücker of University College. Although his excursion into the developing studium of Comparative Philology was unsuccessful, for he tried to find affinities between Hungarian and Sanscrit, he was recognised as a good amateur linguist, was elected a member of the Philological Society, and his opinion in word-etymologies was sought and acknowledged by the editors of the Oxford English Dictionary.[46]

His financial situation improved after 1856, when he sold his uncle's collection of ivories to the Liverpool Museum, and Mrs. Pulszky's parents, the Walters, were able to visit them in London, and offer occasional support. But he also completed smaller business transactions by collecting and selling ancient jewellery of artistic value and he claims in his *Memoirs* to have advised the acquisition department of the British Museum in these matters. On one occasion in 1857, when a post fell vacant in the Library of the British Museum Mrs. Pulszky, without her husband's knowledge, approached Lord Lansdowne, enquiring whether Pulszky would be able to get the position. "The old marquess bluntly answered"- Pulszky relates in his *Memoirs* - "that although aliens are not exempted from service, as the Principal Librarian is the Italian Panizzi; . . . they would not nominate anyone who still has prospects to return to his own country."[47]

Pulszky was prepared to bide his time until his chance came to return;
in due course he was nominated Principal Librarian - in the National
Library of his own country.

CHAPTER FIVE

TWO ENGLISH FRIENDS OF THE HUNGARIAN CAUSE

1. Lord Dudley Coutts Stuart.

Without influential friends Pulszky would have remained in a political vacuum, without advice on the modes of British political experience he would not have found the right words to communicate his message on the Hungarian cause. In the first respect, Lord Dudley Stuart helped him most, in the second, Professor Newman assisted him best. It is necessary, therefore, to examine the political contributions of these two men separately towards furthering the Hungarian cause as each of them interpreted the issues.

Lord Dudley Stuart, liberal politician and friend of Palmerston, is chiefly known as the advocate of the independence of Poland. His Hungarian connections are hardly remembered by anyone but the Hungarian historians of the Kossuth emigration and the descendants of his relatives. Yet this enthusiastic and important friend of oppressed European nationalities should still attract our attention since a good deal of his political activities were directed in supporting the cause of Hungary's independence, through his relations with her exiles.

Lord Dudley was in his mid-forties when he was first introduced to the struggle Hungary had been engaged in, by Count Ladislas Teleki in December 1848. From then onwards he followed the fortunes of Hungary till his death at the age of fifty-one.

Born in South Audley Street, London, on 11 January 1803, Lord Dudley was the eighth son of John Stuart, first Marquis of Bute (1744-1814), and the only son by his second wife, Frances, daughter of Thomas Coutts, banker. His father dying early, Lord Dudley's education was superintended by his mother, and it was from her words and example that he acquired his strong feelings of sympathy for the oppressed.[1] He was a member of Christ's College, Cambridge, and graduated M.A. in 1823. Impressed with admiration of the character of his uncle, Sir Francis Burdett, he stood for Arundel on liberal principles in 1830, and was returned without opposition. He was re-chosen for Arundel at the general elections of 1831, 1833 and 1835, but in 1837 was opposed by Lord Fitzalan's influence,· and defeated by 176 votes to 105. For ten years he had no seat in Parliament, but in 1847 Sir Charles Napier having retired he became one of the candidates for the borough of Marylebone and was returned at the head of the poll. He retained the seat to his death on 17 November 1854.

It was through Prince Adam Czartoryski's recommendations that Dudley Stuart became acquainted with Teleki. Czartoryski visited England in 1831. Lord Dudley was greatly interested in the account which the Polish statesman gave of the oppression exercised by Emperor Nicholas. The Prince had been the Foreign Minister of Czar Alexander I of Russia, but as one of the greatest landowners of Poland, he sided with his own countrymen in 1830 against the Czar and was invested by the nation with the dignity of the Chief of the National Government. Sentenced to death by the Czar, he did not cease, during thirty years of his life, as head of the Polish emigration, to urge the cabinets of Europe to acknowledge the rights of Poland guaranteed by them in the Treaty of Vienna.[2] Soon after Prince Adam's visit to England, many members of the late Polish army came to the British Isles too, and Lord Dudley was mainly instrumental in obtaining a vote of £10,000 for the relief of these Poles.[3] The grants made by the House of Commons were not sufficient to support all the victims of the Russian cruelty, but Lord Dudley was tireless in soliciting public subscriptions, by public entertainments, in replenishing the funds of the Literary Association of the Friends of Poland, of which he became President. He was associated with David Urquhart, Cutler Ferguson, Thomas Campbell and T.W. Beaumont, who shared his views about the danger of Russian aggression which was pronounced quixotic by many others.[4]

The first Russian intervention in Transylvania in the beginning of 1849 seemed to have given a warning to the British Foreign Secretary that Lord Dudley should be listened to while the second major attack of Russia on Hungary in the beginning of the summer, justified Lord Dudley even in the eyes of his earlier critics and made his counsel valuable to the Foreign Secretary.

His acquaintance with Pulszky[5] provided him with the key man who could transmit direct information from Hungarian sources, or who could evaluate news for him received from elsewhere, to be moulded into

addresses of public speeches, or speeches in the Parliament. But recipro-
cally he was the Magyars' main hope in London: he was their intermediary
link with the Cabinet on the one hand, and with the people of England
on the other. Just as he helped Pulszky in the spring of 1849 to contact
Palmerston, and later, in the summer of the same year brought Teleki
and Bikessy face to face with the Foreign Secretary, he was behind their
campaign of public meetings first to win support for their cause, and
later to enlist sympathy on their behalf. In this year alone, which was,
perhaps, the most active in his political career, he was associated with
three Hungarian Committees: in May, June and July he gave his support
to Pulszky's Hungarian Propaganda Committee, he was the moving spirit
behind the Parliamentary Relief Committee which was set up in July,
and in October he became one of the founder members of the Hungarian
Association.

From a Hungarian point of view, Stuart's most important role was
his parliamentary one. He belonged to Palmerston's party, but his views
on foreign policy sufficiently differed from those of the Foreign Secretary, to question him repeatedly in public speeches, thus to keep the
Hungarian issue alive. He drew a parallel between the English and the
ancient Hungarian constitution, emphasising that the latter was in danger
of total suppression. Answering the charges of a former speaker, Lord
Claude Hamilton, he said that recent legislation by the Hungarian Reform
Party and Ludwigh Kossuth not only had brought this constitution up
to date, but strengthened the positions of the Magyars so much, that
their country could offer great commercial advantages to England. As
we have seen, this was the line Pulszky and his circle put forward before
Görgei's surrender. Even more significant, that Dudley Stuart added the
unorthodox 'Kossuthian' suggestion: the true establishment of a bulwark
against Russia would be the reconstruction of Poland and Hungary.

Since Parliament went into the summer recess at the end of July,
the continuation of Dudley Stuart's exposition of the Hungarian cause
had to come half a year later, when circumstances had altered considerably. He put it this way in his next parliamentary speech on 7
February 1850: "the kingdom of Hungary had never been conquered -
it had always remained independent *de jure* and de *facto* until it was
put down by the power and treachery of Russia."[6] Dudley Stuart then
outlined the constitutional history of Hungary, particularly underlining

the issues raised in the preceding three hundred years. It was a sketch closely following the facts and arguments of Francis Pulszky's historical introduction to his wife's *Diary*.[7] He acknowledged his source of information by first holding up in his hand the MSS. of the *Diary*, and later by quoting from it at length, in an effort to denounce the Austrian police system set up in Hungary. His speech touched upon the most important Hungarian topics of the day: he condemned Batthyány's execution and cleared him of the Austrian charges of being implicated in the murder of Latour. (His lawyer, Sir Alexander Cockburn, had done the same for Pulszky). He expressed concern about the fate of Kossuth and his associates in Turkey and moved the motion "that there be laid before this House, copies of extracts of any correspondence between the British Government and the Embassies of Constantinople, St. Petersburg and Vienna".[8] Palmerston in his reply asked for time, and for allowing him to select such documents as may explain to the House the course which the Government had pursued. Only a feeble opposition came to Lord Dudley's well-planned, full-scale defence of Hungary from Lord Claude Hamilton - his habitual opponent - and from Disraeli, surprisingly ineloquent that day. Documents had their say, and Cockburn read out a list of people imprisoned and punished in Hungary, which had been prepared by Lord Dudley.[9]

Lord Dudley's stand in the Parliament, first on behalf of independent Hungary and later for the support of his victims was not made without cautious preparations. He took the chair of the public meetings with short but carefully composed texts in his hand.[10] He despatched a number of personal appeals to his fellow politicians, so when it came to a parliamentary speech, its well knitted arguments could organically grow out from the reactions of the people and from the responses of his colleagues. The most frequent testing grounds were the fund-raising campaigns where disappointments alternated with positive responses. "I think I shall want my name erased; not certainly because I do not sympathise with the Hungarians but because I do not know enough of their history," wrote the Marquess of Sligo from St. Albans, on 21 July 1849.[11] "I am really too ignorant of the merits of the Hungarian cause to join in," commented the Earl of Radnor in a letter sent from Grosvenor Street on 25 July 1849.[12] But on the other scale of the balance, Lord Alfred Denison wrote on 4 November 1849: "I most readily enclose a draft for £25 in aid of the gallant Hungarians as a testimony of my sympathy".[13] And one of the best co-operators in matters Hungarian, Richard Cobden, even urged him to do more: "I am trying to get some city people to help us in the Hungarian subscription. Could you induce Lord Robert Grosvenor or any of that stamp to give their name on the Committee".[14] His Polish contacts proved especially useful to Lord Dudley, for the Polish emigrants, sharing the fate of the Hungarians, were anxiously informing him about the refugees in Turkey. Count Zamoyski, the leader of the Polish emigrants there, wrote in a telegraphic style from Widdin: "We are here in a fine mess!"[15] A letter from Prince Czartoryski[16] informed him of the situation of Kossuth and Bem. One of Czartoryski's secretaries, Lieutenant Szulczewski, was anxiously warning him to help defend Kossuth's good name against the calumnies of the Times.[17]

The circumspection Lord Dudley displayed - after the danger of the extradition of the refugees was averted - in preparing the ground for his motion on 7 February 1850, was followed by his pursuance of the question, through several sessions of the Parliament. He was determined to see the diplomatic correspondence of the Government on the Hungarian refugees published, and he spared no effort. On 21 February 1851 he said in Parliament that during the last session he went to Lord Palmerston privately several times and asked him to produce the papers, and as they were still not published he would like to know the reasons for this extraordinary delay. Palmerston replied that Lord Dudley had a right to be angry with him and the papers would be in hand in an early day of the next week.[18] True to his word, Palmerston laid on the table of the Commons a selection of the "Correspondence respecting Refugees from Hungary within the Turkish Dominions", on 28 February 1851.[19] Yet it dealt with matters from 25 August 1849 to 8 April 1850 only. Lord Dudley was anxious to see the rest as well. He wrote to Palmerston on 3 January 1852:[20] "It has long appeared to me that, in justice to you as well as. . . to all concerned, there ought to be laid on the table of the House of Commons a sequel to that *Blue Book* on the affairs of Hungary and on the prisoners of Kiutajah. . ." Palmerston replied on 10 January 1852:[21] "I think that a selection of papers might without public inconvenience give to them the course pursued by the Government in 1850 and 1851 on the subject of the Hungarian refugees who had been detained in Turkey. The only real difficulty in making the selection would be that of . . . how urgently and frequently we pressed the matter on the Turkish Government, without at the same time showing (sic) the apparent hesitation of the Porte."

Having received the green signal, Dudley Stuart moved the motion on 21 April 1852. The Derby Government had recently come into office, with Disraeli as Chancellor of the Exchequer, and his was the last word in the parliamentary debate which saw both Lord John Russell and Viscount Palmerston supporting the motion for completing the publication of the documents. Only one aspect of the question remained obscure: Palmerston claimed that he was not really able to say in what degree the American Government contributed to produce the result of the refugees' release.[22] The motion was agreed to, and the *Further correspondence respecting the Refugees from Hungary within the Turkish Dominions*[23] . . . was presented to Parliament. It dealt with the diplomatic correspondence of the affair from 4 May 1850 to 17 October 1851.

Dudley Stuart also prevailed in his efforts to safeguard the essential material and moral maintenance of the Hungarian refugees in England. After the Relief Committee was dissolved on 18 March 1852 he secured a grant of £1,000 from the Treasury,[24] for eighty-three exiles wishing to emigrate to America. Those who remained and continued to take part in exile politics were exposed to the threats of Austria. On 1 April 1852, two series of papers had been laid upon the table of the House upon the insistence of Austria and France respecting the residence in England of certain foreign refugees and measures were demanded from the English Government to procure their punishment.[25] Dudley Stuart was perhaps his most eloquent best in refuting such demands and springing to the defence of the weak. The Austrians - he argued - had power and bayonets in their hands; Kossuth, their adversary, had only one weapon: liberty of speech. He did not believe that the Austrians had much to fear from the conspiratorial activities of "some persons forming themselves into a society for promoting liberal principles". But he produced his trump-card when he dealt with the indignation of Napoleon, who was represented in London by Count Walewski: "Not long ago Count Walewski was himself nothing more than a Polish refugee in this country . . . and now he came forward with a list of Polish and other refugees, and called upon the English Government to belie all its antecedents, by introducing some alien Bill." Dudley Stuart's last parliamentary interventions, on behalf of the Hungarians, and especially Kossuth (exposed after the Milan insurrection and charged with storing weapons in England), on 1 March 1853 and 15 March 1853 respectively, brought repeated assurances from Palmerston that these refugees were safe in England.

In his relations with the Hungarian refugees, Lord Dudley Stuart displayed a greater diversity of attitudes and elasticity of action than in Parliament. While the war of independence was still being fought he transmitted the offers of arms-dealers to Pulszky,[26] whom he treated as an aristocratic patron would treat a near equal. He invited Pulszky to his salon, introduced him to a variety of people, from David Urquhart to Prince Carl von Braunschweig, helped him to pursue his political ends by means of social contacts, but had enough tact never to offer him direct financial aid. Their co-operation was the closest at the time of Pulszky's visits to Palmerston in the spring and summer of 1849 but as we have seen, Dudley Stuart also took part in the Pulszky-Henningsen plan to help Kossuth escape.

Dudley Stuart stood on a different footing with Kossuth. In the beginning, he saw Kossuth as the personification of the Hungarian national movement, a constitutionalist, like himself, and even a *royalist* forced only by circumstances to de-throne the Habsburgs. His impressions at the reception of Kossuth in Southampton in 1851 and during their subsequent tour of England were deep enough to evoke lasting personal admiration for the man, and on the basis of Kossuth's speeches in England, he even believed that they shared the same political convictions. In 1852 he came to be disappointed in Kossuth's politics on two accounts; as Nicholas Kiss reported it to the ex-Governor, who was touring the United States at the time.[27] Dudley Stuart had clearly felt a little resentment ever since Kossuth's polite refusal to meet Palmerston, which grew into a grievance as the ex-Governor's policies turned decidedly republican in America. He wrote to him repeatedly,[28] and Kossuth did not answer. Secondly, Lord Dudley could not really condone Kossuth's choice to spend his funds on arms instead of giving more help to his fellow exiles. This lurked behind the disagreement revealed in 1852 between Joshua Toulmin Smith, who Kossuth had entrusted to look after his funds in England, and Lord Dudley Stuart who continued to act on behalf of the Relief Committee. In 1849 the two English politicians co-operated with one another on successive errands to help the Hungarian cause. Their relations were the closest, at the establishment of the *Hungarian Association* - not described by previous historians - which was founded in the second week of October 1849 "to collect accurate information, and to diffuse it".[29] A couple of weeks earlier on 27 September 1849 Dudley Stuart had requested T.W. Beaumont to be president,[30] but as we do not find his name on the list among the members, he must have declined the invitation. Among those who accepted we find the names of Pulszky's personal friends, names of the former members of the "Propaganda" and the "Relief" Committees and that of J. Toulmin Smith as Honorary Secretary. We have no knowledge of how long this Association operated.

Lord Dudley's disagreement over Kossuth's 'relief-policy' led to the dissolution of the Committee for the relief of the Hungarian refugees. On 15 February 1852 he informed Count Paul Eszterházy, who was at that time elected chairman of the Association of the Hungarian Political Exiles, that the Committee had fulfilled its purpose in the past by relieving the wants of the refugees in England, and successfully helping the majority to proceed to the United States, but now since Kossuth made it known that the refugees required no more assistance, it decided to dissolve.[31] It was characteristic of Lord Dudley, the "good Lord Dudley Stuart" as Count Teleki had called him, that he was still anxious to secure the £1,000 parliamentary grant for the last group of Hungarians who wished to emigrate to America and even added to it another £100 which he had collected privately.

Dudley Stuart's efforts on behalf of the Hungarians were closely watched by the Austrian officials stationed in London. At the time of the second Russian intervention, Ambassador Buol complained to Palmerston that letters had been found from Dudley Stuart in the captured bureau of General Bem.[32] Later his successor, Buol, and after he absented himself, Kübeck, the chargé d'affaires, took particular pains to describe Lord Dudley's moves before and during Kossuth's first visit to London. Buol wrote to Schwarzenberg on 11 October 1851: "Lord Dudley Stuart dont les journaux annoncent l'arrivée à Broadlands chez Lord Palmerston y attend sans doute l'arrivée de Kossuth à Southampton pour aller le complimenter."[33] On 24 October Kübeck wrote to Schwarzenberg about the preparations to receive Kossuth in London, and commented: "Les discours prononcés en cette recesion par Sir de Lacy Evans[34] et par Lord Dudley Stuart ont été dignes de ces avocats de toutes les causes de désordre en Europe."[35] On 12 November he reported on the ball Lord Dudley organised for the benefit of the refugees: "Dans la soirée, le bal Hongrois - Polonais au Guildhall attirera sans doute, outre les personnes adonnées à ces causes révolutionnaires, bon nombre de curieux puisque la présence de Kossuth doit célébrer cette fete scandaleuse. Lord Dudley Stuart a addressé une longue lettre à Monsieur le Comte Walewsky pour l'engager d'accorder son patronnage à cette oeuvre de charité. . . L'ambassadeur vient de décliner toute participation. . ."[36]

Thus, he who was known as the advocate of the independence of Poland, earned the honour to be named among the advocates of all the disorders in Europe by his adversaries, on account of his efforts for the Hungarians. But at the same time he also earned the frequently-expressed gratitude of the Hungarian exiles, recorded in the Minutes of their Association, in their letters to the Daily News, and to one another, and most explicitly in Pulszky's *Memoirs*. Pulszky remembered him as the most unselfist political friend Hungary has ever had in England. He acted, we may add, always true to his family motto: "Causas non fata sequor".

2. Francis W. Newman.

Francis W. Newman belonged to the circle of liberal intellectuals who lent their pen in the service of the Hungarian cause and helped the work of the Hungarian Propaganda Committee late in the spring of 1849. Long after the events, Newman recalled that he had met Pulszky for the first time at one of the meetings of the London Hungarian Committee,[37] and that Pulszky became his chief political instructor over the years. The close friendship that developed between the two men ensured that Newman was always correctly informed about Hungarian politics, a fact well illustrated by their unpublished correspondence,[38] kept in the Hungarian National Library, and by Newman's chief publications, regarding the Hungarian question in the fifties. Although their friendship and correspondence lasted from 1849 until their death in the same year, 1897, we wish to concentrate here on the years from 1849 to 1853, which was Newman's most active time from a Hungarian point of view. We shall conclude this chapter with a sketch of Newman's relations with Pulszky in the fifties.

Francis Newman, the youngest son of John Newman, banker, was born in London in ·1805.[39] He was thus Pulszky's senior by nine years - as he remarked in one of his letters - and four years younger than his more famous brother, Cardinal John Henry Newman. Pulszky drew a parallel between the careers of the two brothers in his *Memoirs*. Both of them were educated at Oxford where Francis took a double-first in Classics and Mathematics in 1826. But whereas John Henry, partaking in the 'Oxford Movement' became a theoretical theologian, Francis chose the thorny path to test and propagate the faith and set out on a missionary tour to Asia.[40] When (after having converted no-one in two years), he returned from the East in 1833, he himself gave signs of conversion from doctrinal anglicanism to a very broadly based theism. His career as a teacher started in 1834 when he became classical tutor in the Bristol College, continued in Manchester New College, where he was appointed professor of classical literature in 1840, and finished at University College, London, where he held the Chair of Latin from 1846 to his retirement in 1863. So during his 'Hungarian period' Francis Newman was also an active University College man, already interested in a variety of subjects, ranging from religion, history, mathematics to classical literature and moral philosophy to which politics and education were added lately. In 1848 he was elected the first principal of University Hall, but later he disagreed with the governing body about a matter relating to the construction of the building and resigned before the opening in October 1849.[41] He could not have foreseen his resignation for Pulszky relates in his *Memoirs* that Newman invited him to deliver a public oration at the opening ceremony, and coached him perfecting his pronunciation: "I was in the belief that I had mastered the English words well, when a German writer, Dr. Oppenheimer, came up to me after my speech and praised me how well I spoke; he said that he visited Parliament every day to learn better English, listened to Peel, Cobden, Disraeli but could never understand them perfectly, whereas he understood me as if I were speaking in German. I felt apprehensive as I saw that I was rather far from perfect English pronunciation."

Newman served on the Hungarian Committee from 1849 to its dissolution in 1852. His most important contribution to the work of this committee appears to have been the composition of a paper issued in November 1849 by the committee and reprinted in Newman's

'Reminiscences'.[42] This paper brings out an aggregate of opinions from these friends of the Hungarian cause[43] and shows the united front they were able to present regarding Hungary. It was drawn up - like the demands of the Hungarian Nation on 15 March 1848 - in twelve points. The first of these points explained the electoral basis of the Hungarian kingship in the past and how it was changed into a hereditary one by the Habsburgs. The second sketched the attempts of the Habsburgs to overthrow the Hungarian constitution and the triumph of the latter as codified in Article 10/1790-1791. (Hungary with her appanages is a free kingdom, etc.). The third point dealt with the internal reforms carried out by successive Hungarian Diets from 1825 onwards (privileges, taxation, tenure, religious toleration), and with the programme of progress (free trade, free press, education, industrialisation) which the Austrian Cabinet cut short after the war. Point four explained how Austria used to rely on the Upper House of the Hungarian Parliament to extinguish Bills undesirable to her. Point five described the constitutional changes that came to pass as results of the March revolution (disintegration of the conservative party, independent Hungarian Government), and referred to the ensuing struggle to maintain independence in face of the Court in Vienna. The sixth point was devoted to an exposition of unconstitutional actions by Vienna (declaring Jellashich a rebel than reinstating him, dissolving the Diet). Point seven focused on the plot which brought about the abdication of Ferdinand and the succession of Francis Joseph. Point eight explained how the succession of a monarch, not recognised by the Parliament, and the publication of a new constitution (4 March 1849 by Count Stadion), for fusing down Hungary into a part of the Austrian Empire, provoked the Hungarians to reject both. Point nine dwelt on the righteousness of armed resistance by Hungary. Points ten and eleven purported that the calling in of the Russians by Francis Joseph brought about the dethronement of the House of Habsburg and the investiture of L. Kossuth as Governor of Hungary.[44] Point twelve laid down that the overthrow of Hungarian law affected the English crown too since it undermined the confidence of the people in princes. The aristocracy of England was concerned by the loss of constitutional rights possessed by the Hungarian aristocracy, and the *commonalty* was concerned by the loss of liberties of a noble nation, particularly as this was brought about by Russian intervention in Hungary.

Work on the Hungarian Committee brought the friendship of Joshua Toulmin Smith to Newman, who was introduced to him by John Edward Taylor.[45] Both men were enthusiastic *decentralisers*, champions of local government and of constitutional freedom, though Newman, partly due to the influence of Mazzini and Kossuth, was more lenient towards republicanism than Toulmin Smith. We noted in the previous section that Newman belonged to the Hungarian Association whose secretary was Toulmin Smith. They combined to welcome Kossuth in Southampton in October 1851 and to offer help and advice to the ex-Governor composing his speeches in England. Later, the differences of opinion emerging between Lord Dudley Stuart and Toulmin Smith caused a coolness between friends, and their correspondence came to an end when, in 1852, Newman sided with Lord Dudley over the refugee relief question.

Kossuth's first visit to England animated Newman to great activity[46] for his Hungarian protegees and a number of suggestions sprang forth from his pen. As an individual member of the Hungarian Committee he was invited by the Mayor of Southampton to take part in the reception organised for Kossuth. He took great care in advising Pulszky - the chief organiser - on the smallest details, from the price of food to the type of banner to be used.[47]

Following the immediate progress of the cause with anxiety, he noted in a letter written to Pulszky on 11 November 1851 that (on the suggestion of Mazzini), the Society of Friends of Italy wished "to transform itself into a society for Italy and Hungary".[48] Newman thought that vigorous and immediate action was needed for Hungary who had a rightful Governor, and possibly powerful friends in America, whereas the Council of friends of Italy (of whom he was one) were far too insignificant to head such a league. Newman enclosed a paper entitled "Respectful suggestions" to his letter asking Pulszky to convey it to Kossuth. These suggestions included a request to Kossuth to address the English who had manifested sympathy with Hungary (Kossuth acted accordingly), and an idea to form a *League of Liberty* between the members of the free peoples to resist the conspiracy of despots. It was a decidedly Mazzinian type of suggestion, on the lines of the *European Central Democratic Committee,* and was not used. When, four years later in 1855, Kossuth, Mazzini and Ledru Rollin issued their *Republican*

Manifesto, a similar but much bolder and less practical document, Newman privately criticised Kossuth for associating with Ledru Rollin whom he never trusted.

But more interesting were his "Brief notes to Kossuth" included with the previous suggestions, so that Kossuth may study them en route to America, and then build them into his speeches. In these notes Newman argued that the destruction of unjust international law - for he was convinced that it was the application of such a law that crushed the Hungarians - may come from America. In his opinion English ministries superstitiously conformed to the letter of International Law and as for English reformers, such as Hume, Cobden, Bright, Walmsley, they were singularly incompetent to deal with any European question. Concerning Kossuth's direct actions, Newman wrote that he had the right to raise armaments on neutral soil, such as the United States. When he returned to England, he could issue notes, which would be freely accepted by the people of England up to the value of S5 apiece . . .

At the same time as he submitted his *Respectful suggestions* to Kossuth, Newman asked Mrs. Pulszky to cut out the press-reports of Kossuth's speeches on the American tour and send them back to him in England. The material Mrs. Pulszky collected was the basis of Francis Newman's selection of Kossuth's speeches which appeared in 1853. Kossuth made over five hundred speeches in America; Newman put forty-eight of these in condensed form in his book. He added extracts from three other speeches of Kossuth, delivered in England, published a stylistically corrected version of the *Hungarian Declaration of Independence*[49] and attached three appendices from the press controversy over Kossuth. Newman obtained Kossuth's written approval of stylistic changes so he felt at liberty cutting short "what was temporary interest and condensed what was too amplified".[50] Pulszky arranged for the book's publication at Trübner & Co., and corrected the proofs as well.[51] In his preface, Newman touched upon three subjects: he interpreted Kossuth's republicanism as a product of a time in his nation's history "when all sympathy with royal power was gone out of the nation's heart". (P. viii). He explained Kossuth's wavering attitude toward Italy in the summer of 1848 as an effort to keep the Pragmatic Sanction.[52] And lastly, he maintained that Kossuth's trip to America was *not* a failure, as America may yet act decisively. The main topics found in the selection: the

Secrets of diplomacy, the legitimacy of *Hungarian independence, Nationalities, Democracy, Russia* and the *Balance of power* bear witness to the fact that Kossuth had listened to some of the "respectful suggestions".

In the autumn of the same year, Newman published a pamphlet, designed to support the Hungarian cause by a ferocious attack on the House of Habsburg.[53] It appears that Newman was particularly upset by the failure of the Milan insurrection and Austria's repressive measures in Italy on the one hand, and by her insistence on the 'surveillance' of Italian and Hungarian refugees in England on the other. Writing in the Eclectic Review on the "Society of friends of Italy" he congratulated the Aberdeen ministry on not having listened to the insolent demands of Austria, and expressed his trust in the collateral help Hungarians would continue to offer in Italy.[54] In the preface of the tract of the *Crimes of Austria* - as Pulszky was to call it - Newman confessed to have been motivated by the 'recent events' to expose the crimes of the oppressors. He claimed to have done no original research but a faithful statement of broad facts. His sources were Coxe's *House of Austria,*[55] Robertson's *Charles V*[56] and Grattan's *History of the Netherlands*[57] for the historical part of the work, and well digested information from Pulszky, Kossuth, Tanárky, Vukovics and Teleki on the treatment of contemporary events. The booklet was divided into seventeen chapters, the first and the last ones dealing with general aspects of the subject, while in the rest the extent of the Habsburgs' treachery was examined in relation to each country or people they subjugated. Newman's thesis was propounded in the first chapter; in his opinion, neither religion nor philosophy had succeeded in carrying private morality into public life. All great empires had been born in crime. But the Habsburgs had an extraordinary number of offences on their conscience: the crime which history charged against the House of Austria was not merely that they had waged unjust and cruel wars against foreigners - this was a common guilt - but that having been freely accepted to protect the laws and liberties of a large number of nations, they had in every instance played the part of a guardian who murdered his ward.

The twelfth chapter dealt with the crimes of the Habsburgs in Hungary; the reader was given a full list of them: protracted non-residence of the king in Hungary, appointment of foreigners to civil and military offices, introduction of foreign troops, making of public treaties, declaring war without the leave of the Diet, neglecting to summon the Diet, oppression of the Protestants - each and every crime was the violation of the Constitution.[58]

In the conclusion of the tract, Newman posed the question that "what was all this to England?" (p. 55). He gave the answer himself by breaking down the question into four parts, and administering a strong criticism of British foreign policy as regards what had been done as opposed to what might have been done. He thought that by signing the treaty of Vienna Britain had given her assent to worse despotism than Napoleon's and had disabled herself for supporting European liberty and law. This had determined Britain's foreign policy in general, but even so some mistakes should have been avoided.

Britain had an observer at the Hungarian Diet in 1847, J.W. Blackwell, whose despatches should have been published. The public would have understood then the cause of Hungary in time. In the following year Palmerston might have sent a special envoy to the Hungarian Diet to readjust the broken treaty between Austria and Hungary. Later, the British Government might have acknowledged independent Hungary provisionally, which would have brought similar recognitions from France and the United States. This would have forced Austria to peace and the Russian intervention might have been avoided. Newman thought that the attitude of the British aristocracy was to be blamed to a great extent for the neglect of these necessary actions and warned that if the aristocracy continued to play into the hands of despotism, republicanism might conquer here. As far as Europe was concerned, the scale had already tipped: to feel hostility to republicanism was "to feel hostility to freedom".

Pulszky received the products of Newman's pen in 1853 enthusiastically.[59] He reviewed the *Select speeches of Kossuth* in the November 1853 issue of the Eclectic Review[60] and "requested the Examiner to notice the *Crimes of Austria*". It had a short but good notice in the Eclectic Review.[61]

In addition to the theoretical and moral support he gave to the Hungarians, Newman aided the Magyar refugees financially through the Relief Committee and even after its dissolution. He thought for a while - as Nicholas Kiss reported to Kossuth on 12 March 1852 - that he might be able to reconstruct the Committee on new lines.[62] In the beginning he succeeded to persuade others to contribute to the Hungarian cause, later he gave or lent money himself, as generously as he could. He wrote to Pulszky on 9 May 1850:[63] "I send you a cheque of eleven pounds for the Hungarian Committee. Of this £5 is from Henry A. Wedgwood, Esquire - £3 from Charles Darwin, Esquire - the remaining £3 is from myself." On 9 April 1852 Richard Gelich, a major in the Hungarian army, reported to Kossuth that he had received relief from Professor Newman.[64] On 28 May 1852 Kiss notified Kossuth that he had sent an agent to the Balkans with £100 out of which £60 had been given to him by Professor Newman.[65] On 30 July 1852 Kiss noted on his monthly account of the Hungarian fund a loan of £80 from Newman.[66] This was repaid to him by Kossuth. Lord Dudley Stuart appealed to Newman - as to a former member of the Committee - on 7 September 1853[67] to help repay a debt of £100. In 1851, Zähnsdorf, a jeweller of Hungarian extraction, had lent the above sum to the Committee, which he badly wanted back two years later. Nine members of the former Committee, Newman and Lord Dudley amongst them, put up the money for him.

But Newman frequently helped out the Pulszkys with smaller or larger sums of money since Pulszky would have been too proud to accept gifts, even from his own prosperous father and mother-in-law. When the Pulszkys came back from America in the summer of 1852, Newman offered to share his abode at Park Village and accommedate them all until they managed to find a suitable house. Pulszky thanked him for the offer but did not accept it.[68] In the next year, having got a part of his inheritance after the death of his uncle, Gábor Fejérváry, he bought his own place in London, and proudly announced to Newman: "Please direct your next letter to 13 St. Albans Villas, *Highgate Rise*, we are leaving our old uncomfortable lodgings (34, St. Petersburgh Place, Bayswater), tommorrow."[69] In 1854 Pulszky again got into small financial difficulties before he was able to sell his collection of ivories. On two occasions Newman stated his willingness to lend him £50 and £100 respectively, and having done so, helped Pulszky to earn another eighty guineas by arranging for a contract of four lectures to be delivered at Conway.[70]

The Pulszkys would have had no financial difficulties in exile had they been able to draw the income of their estate in Szécsény, Northern

Hungary. As the land was in Mrs. Pulszky's name it was not confiscated but was subjected to a long litigation, ending only in 1865 when Mrs. Pulszky finally got back the estate. Meanwhile - and certainly from 1859 onwards - they were able to draw money on it, and Newman offered to lend £300 or £400 himself in the year of the Austro-Italian war.[71] It is not on record whether they took this offer.

During the summer months the Pulszkys regularly rented a villa at Ventnor, Isle of Wight. The weather was sunny, the company congenial, for Kossuth and his family and Tanárky often went with them, and they met other friends and acquaintances at Ventnor; Herzen and even Palmerston. Pulszky, in his letters from the summers of 1854 and 1855, describes the attractions of the place and their delights at botanicising, geologicising,[72] with such obvious enjoyment that the Newmans, who usually spent their holiday in Bangor, went to Ventnor instead in 1856. Years later, Newman wrote nostalgically to his friend:[73] "I think I once before wrote to you from Ventnor, a place which necessarily reminds me of you, your excellent wife, and Kossuth. I inhabit a house erected by the side of a field where Kossuth, Tanárki and others played *pat-ball* with a huge 'football', as we should call it." But Ventnor was also a place where they could read undisturbed, such books as Bunsen's 'Christianity and Mankind' or Macaulay's speeches which Pulszky much enjoyed, or French-Arabic and English-Arabic dictionaries with which Newman occupied his restless mind.

Exchange of opinion was always the strongest bond between the friends; as anxious as Newman was to 'learn' politics from Pulszky - and he imparted information willingly - so keen was Pulszky to have his literary style in English corrected by Newman. As a good professor, he carefully read Pulszky's historical introduction to his wife's *Diary* in manuscript and corrected all the un-English phrases and terminology;[74] he also went through the narrative itself and was able to forecast confidently to Mrs. Pulszky: "the book will produce a great effect".[75]

In Pulszky's eyes, Newman was a great authority on religion, with a very critical, undogmatic cast of mind, and a pioneer spirit, similar to his own. Whether reading Buckle or Renan, the Trinitarian Christians of the Reformed Church, or trying to give guidance to his children in matters of faith, Pulszky turned to Newman for advice.[76] It was not so readily forthcoming. It was as if he who wrote the *Phrases of faith*[77] or *the natural history of the soul*[78] would show the signs of reluctance confronted with a fellow-doubter but go on besieging those with discussions, whose faith was stronger than his own.

Though never discussed in detail before, Francis Newman's Hungarian connections were better known in this country than those of Dudley Stuart. His interest in Hungarian affairs was noted by his contemporaries.[79] A recent essayist in *Comparative Intellectual biography* argued,[80] that Newman was attracted to the Hungarian question and to the Hungarians on moral grounds. He had always been, throughout his life, a champion of minority causes: anti-tobacconist, anti-alcoholist, anti-church, pro-women's rights, pro-vegetarian. Yet we should not forget that his anti-slavery inclinations, his support of the Italian cause, his hatred of despotism and his avowal of national constitutions were popular issues in the first half of the eighteen-fifties. Whether the Hungarian question is judged among the minor causes or not, it had a major part in Newman's intellectual make-up. The political opinions voiced in the *Crimes of the Habsburgs*, had their roots in the *Appeal to the Middle Classes* published in 1848.[81] But likewise, the suggestions communicated to Kossuth were developed in the *Deliberations before war*[82] and in the *Ethics of war*[83] incorporating the moral lessons which Newman learned from his friends and wished others to teach. In his last return to the Hungarian question,[84] in the *Reminiscences of the two patriots* in 1888, Professor Newman paid a tribute for a lasting intellectual stimulation to Kossuth and Pulszky. And his was "the mind of one of the most remarkable men in the nineteenth century".[85]

CHAPTER SIX

THE 1859 WAR

1. The preparations and the war.

After a long political incubation which followed the Crimean War period, the year 1859 started auspiciously for the Hungarian exiles. The Emperor Napoleon III in his New Year's greetings to Hübner, the Austrian Ambassador in Paris, expressed his sorrow over the gradual estrangement between France and Austria. For Kossuth and Pulszky the writing was on the wall: the estrangement would lead to hostilities and the war would present an opportunity of participation for the emigration that might result in the liberation of Hungary. In fact, they were trying to interpret the signs that showed up before. In 1857 Pulszky learnt from Mazzini, that a significant letter Orsini wrote from prison after his attempted regicide,[1] was authentic: repenting, the conspirator called on the youth of Italy to refrain from similar deeds. It suggested that the conspirator learned something in prison he had not known before. Soon Mazzini divulged the secret to Kossuth of a meeting between Napoleon and Cavour at Plombieres - a spa in the Pyrenees - where the two statesmen laid down the terms of a covert Franco-Italian alliance. In the event of defeating Austria in a future war, Lombardy and Venice would be ceded to Piedmont while Nizza and Savoya would be attached to France.

Further news came from France via Nicholas Kiss, who had moved to Paris and married the sister of Thouvenel, Napoleon's advisor on foreign policy and future foreign minister. The alliance was an extension of an already existing bond that had survived from the Crimean League, an expression of Napoleon's gratitude for services rendered, to the House of Savoy. The bond was further strengthened by Prince Napoleon's betrothal to Princess Clotilda, daughter of Victor Emmanuel, and its significance was discussed between Newman and his Hungarian friends in 1858.[2] The Emperor's nephew, who was the strongest exponent of the war party in France, had several meetings with two leaders of the Hungarian emigration: Klapka and Teleki.

Differences of opinion had arisen in the past among the leaders of the Hungarian exiles, mainly about the leadership of Kossuth, but now a united political stand was needed. This was put to Klapka by Cavour, who as a representative of a Swiss bank, visited him in Turin. Cavour, knowing Kossuth's immense political appeal among the Hungarian masses was anxious to get the password from him, and Napoleon, still keenly remembering the Marseilles incident, was bent on reconciling him and enlisting his support. It was clear before the allies that in a war with Austria a proclamation issued by Kossuth to the Hungarian soldiers fighting on the Austrian side could make them desert their ranks. So, first Klapka came to Kossuth in January 1859, then Teleki wrote to him a conciliatory letter from Paris[3] in the hope that the three of them would soon be able to join forces, and thus united, put the case of Hungary before the allies.

Gyula Tanárky, Pulszky's personal secretary, recorded in his diary some noticeable hesitation[4] on the part of Pulszky to enter into the political arena again. But as soon as his mind was made up - he witnessed the call of secret messengers from Hungary, and the return of stray sheep, like former Minister Vukovics and General Vetter to Kossuth's flock - he threw himself wholeheartedly into political life again. On 24 April 1859 he started a *Notebook*, where he recorded his daily activities. This remained unpublished to the present day.[5]

The *Notebook* opens with communications from Alexander Herzen and Charles Vogt. Herzen was the most influential member of the Russian emigration in London, a good friend to both Kossuth and Pulszky. Vogt used to be a member of the Frankfurt parliament, then emigrated to Switzerland where he became a member of the Swiss parliament. Both Herzen and Vogt were devout liberals and therefore enemies of all forms of despotism Russian, Austrian as well as French. But Herzen declared his willingness to help the Hungarians through his contacts such as Vogt, who was anti-Habsburg to the extent that he declared his sympathies with Napoleon. Kossuth instructed Pulszky to rally the German emigrants for an anti-Austrian demonstration where Vogt's line of argument could be put to them, who thought that the dissolution of the Habsburg monarchy was in the true interest of all Germans. Pulszky visited the German emigrants one after another without success. Bucher[6] was of the opinion that the Austrians must not be weakened since they were Germans.

Charles Blind declared that he hated Napoleon who, in his view, wanted eventually to conquer the Rhineland, more than he hated the Austrians. Professor Goldstücker of University College[7] said he was strictly neutral and could support neither the Austrians nor Napoleon.

The tactics Kossuth adopted were to alienate Austria from her friends. This emerged more clearly when he met both Teleki and Klapka in London and was preparing to go to Napoleon with a proposition to exert his influence in ensuring the neutrality of Britain in the event of war. He wrote to Pulszky on 2 May 1859:[8] "Teleki and Klapka arrived today claiming, that in the name of the Emperor...the Prince (Jerome Napoleon) had asked them to come and invite me to go over (to Paris) and confer with the ruler...I shall see whether they will insist on such details which only pretend the acceptance of my principles and simulate agreement between us." Kossuth rightly guessed that Napoleon would try to persuade him to issue a proclamation to the people of Hungary to revolt against Austria.

Before their departure, Pulszky met Klapka, Teleki and Kossuth.[9] On 7 May 1859 he recorded the receipt of a letter informing him that the meeting had taken place. Next day, Pulszky saw the three Hungarian leaders back in London and recorded Kossuth's interviews with Prince Napoleon, which took place on 5 May 1859 and with the Emperor on the following day, as told by Kossuth on 8 May 1859.[10] On the night of 6 May the Hungarian National Directory was formed by Klapka, Teleki and Kossuth, for the liberation of Hungary. As President, Kossuth wanted guarantees from Napoleon to equip a French expeditionary force which would land on the Dalmatian coast and march on Hungary, before he would be prepared to send a proclamation into the country. Napoleon gave no firm promise, but granted money for propaganda purposes, for arms, and for the organisation of a Hungarian legion. They were in complete agreement as regards Britain. Kossuth promised that as soon as he was back in London he would start a campaign advocating British neutrality.

Pulszky had already tested the ground. On 30 April he contacted Charles Gilpin an admirer of Kossuth and a supporter of the Hungarian cause. Gilpin was a publisher, and a member of Parliament for Northampton in Cobden's party, with well-established connections with the Manchester group of liberals on the one hand, and with Palmerston's

Whigs on the other. He promised his support to Pulszky if and when Kossuth wanted a public meeting. On the night of 8 May Pulszky visited Grant, the editor of the Morning Advertiser, enquiring how well disposed the British newspapers were to the idea of neutrality. Grant promised his support and so did Walker, the editor of the Daily News.

Pulszky and Kossuth considered that Napoleon could count on the throne, but not on the Derby Government well known for their support of Austria. Since the end of March, Lord Augustus Loftus, the British Ambassador at Vienna, made proposal after proposal for the great powers to disarm simultaneously.[11] As they were of no avail there was mounting fear of British mobilisation in support of Austria. These were partly dispelled by the Queen's announcement of strict neutrality on 12 May but the general feeling was that the Tory Government could not be trusted. Elections were held on 20 May resulting in the return of 302 Tory, 263 Whig and 90 independent Cobdenite members. It was obvious that when Parliament reassembled on the last day of May the vote of the Cobdenites would decided the fate of the Government.

Kossuth and Pulszky concentrated their propaganda efforts for the ten days between the election and the reassembly of Parliament. As in the past, the organisation was left to Pulszky. He went to Bradford on 12 May and spoke to the Mayor. Next day he moved on the Manchester, while Kossuth himself made arrangements with the municipal authorities in London with the help of Gilpin. Pulszky's entry in the *Notebook* on 18 May reads as follows: "News confirming that in Bradford, Glasgow, Manchester everything is all right, meetings on 24, 25, 27 May . . ." The first meeting was held at the London Tavern on 20 May. The Lord Mayor was in the chair, Kossuth, Pulszky, Gilpin, White (M.P. for Plymouth), Nicholay, Newman and the Rev. Newman Hall took part. A resolution was passed that "England would not under any circumstances whatever violate the principles of non-intervention."[12] "A nice meeting" put Pulszky in his *Notebook* at the conclusion of the day. The next day Seward, American senator, an old friend and supporter of the Hungarian cause since 1852, called on him at Highgate Rise. The meeting at Manchester Free-Trade Hall held on 24 May was reported quite favourably in the Times of the following day, and the next two meetings in Bradford and in Glasgow had similar receptions.[13]

The favourable reports in the Times, which had been notoriously anti-Kossuth in the past, may have been due to two factors: a genuine support for neutrality, and the influence of Hungarians, such as Ede Horn and F. Éber, who were employed as correspondents at the time of the outbreak of Austro-French hostilities. Occasional letters were also published by other Hungarians, notably by Béla Széchenyi (István Széchenyi's stepson), who as a visitor to London wrote an objective assessment of the Hungarian situation in the 28 June issue of the Times.

It would be difficult to decide whether Kossuth in fact had a modest and indirect share in the eventual overthrow of the Tory Government, as claimed by some Hungarian historians,[14] or he just happened to support a policy which won the day on 11 June 1859. Cobden was away in America and in his absence Kossuth did not speak to Bright, the deputy leader of the decisive voters. As his own recollections testify[15] he repeatedly conferred on the matter of tactics with Gilpin who was in constant communication with Bright. Gilpin was selected to be an intermediary between Palmerston and Bright on the night of the victory he wrote to Kossuth: "Nothing could possibly be more unequivocal than the answer they *all* give . . . that no. insurrection in Hungary could justify or even excuse the intervention of England."[16] Gilpin's next letter to Kossuth, announcing his own appointment by Palmerston as Secretary of the Poor Law Board in the new government, which incidentally included another friend of the Hungarians, Milner Gibson, did not find the ex-Governor in London. The battle of Magenta on 4 June brought a flood of Hungarian deserters from the Austrian army to the Franco-Italian camp. On 14 June the first battalion of the Hungarian Legion was formed in Aqui. On 16 June Kossuth left London for Italy. As President of the Hungarian National Directory[17] he left instructions to Pulszky, consisting of five points:[18]

1. Pulszky was nominated the representative in Britain of the *Directory* with the primary task of keeping a close watch on the changes in the Government's foreign policy and reporting to the *Directory* thereon.

2. Pulszky was to maintain contacts with the friends of Hungary in Britain with a view to holding further meetings when necessary.

3. He was to continue his contacts with the newspapers.

4. He was to make a contract over certain printing machines for the eventual production of paper money.

5. He was to deal with Kossuth's correspondence in his absence.

On 20 June Gilpin assured Pulszky of Palmerston's firmness in the question of neutrality, and quoted the Prime Minister: "That I shall go in the European Crisis as far, as Mr. Gilpin." Pulszky renewed his contacts with Lord Lansdowne and recoreded the gist of his exchange of letters with the Marquess in his *Notebook*. On 4 July Lord Lansdowne wrote: "Let us hope that the present crisis will give us a better Austria, but an Austria Europe requires." On 5 July Pulszky replied: "A better Austria is impossible. . . yet a country is needed in the East, whose centre is not Vienna but Pest."

The newspapers Pulszky continued to keep contact with were the American New York Tribune, the Morning Advertiser and the Daily News. He sent his weekly letters from London to the Tribune, receiving ten dollars apiece, which remained the basis of his income. He paid frequent visits to the editorial offices of the Morning Advertiser. He relates in his *Memoirs*[19] that on one occasion Grant, the Editor, said to him excitedly, that he must have been misleading him about the feelings of the Hungarians in Austria, as the Field-Marshal of the Austrian army was a Hungarian aristocrat, Count Ferenc Gyulay. "I was slightly annoyed and answered in jest, that an Englishman could understand neither the stupidity of the Viennese nor the patriotism of a Hungarian. The Field Marshal will outdo even Brutus, and relinquishing his fame and military honour will let himself be beaten by the French army. As it happened, in three days' time, the news of the battle of Magenta reached London, and duly the Morning Advertiser extolled Hungarian patriotism, which recalled the legends of ancient Rome."

The signature "A Hungarian", well-known ten years before, appeared again in the columns of the Daily News. On 2 July, in an article entitled "The Austrian Empire"[20] Pulszky analysed the motto of the Austrian monarchs: "Den vereinigten Kräften" and concluded that the days of "divide et impera" ended for Austria, as it was near dissolution. It would turn to the misfortune of this country, Pulszky thought, to consider Austria a political necessity. The support of Britain could only delay her fall. Next day Pulszky published extracts of a long letter[21] from Kossuth, describing his reception in Italy. The letter was sent from Parma on 27 June 1859, three days after the victory of the allies at Solferino. Before the battle Klapka and Kossuth issued proclamations to the Hungarian soldiers in the Austrian army to desert their ranks, and come over to the allied camp where a Hungarian legion was being organised to fight for the liberation of Hungary. The Austrian defeat was partly due to the success of these proclamations; over three thousand Hungarian soldiers and officers surrendered their arms and came over. Soon the Hungarian legion counted over four thousand men. General Klapka was named commander of this small army and he recruited his officers from the Hungarian exiles coming from different parts of the world. A contingent from Britain was led by Colonel Mogyoródy. Colonel Ihász became the leader of the first battalion. From Turkey came István Türr, Lajos Tüköry and many others who, in 1850, had become Muslims and had been serving since in the Turkish army, like József Kiss, and Károly Eberhardt (Abdurman effendi).[22]

Kossuth met Prince Napoleon again, this time at the French headquarters. He adamantly refused to issue a proclamation for rebellion *inside* Hungary, before a French army would embark on the Dalmatian coast. On 3 July Kossuth and Napoleon III met at Valeggio.[23] Kossuth went there, perhaps slightly overstating his role in the victory of the neutrality party in England and claimed that a French diversion into Hungary would not change Palmerston's attitude to the war. A letter from Pulszky, dated 24 June 1859, who had consulted R. Monckton Milnes, Under-Secretary of State for Foreign Affairs, contained a warning though: "they want here to pacify at any price and are afraid of the Hungarian diversion".[24] But Napoleon knew even more of the British attitude. He received Kossuth with a telegram from the British Foreign Minister, Lord John Russell, in which Russell confirmed the British Declaration of Neutrality but warned the Emperor "with special regard to the trip of the Hungarian statesman published by the press",[25] that his support of the Hungarian independence struggle would provoke the Germans. The Emperor spoke of his fears of a possible Prussian and Bavarian action on the side of Austria which might compel him to make peace with Austria. Otherwise he was firmly decided to make Hungary independent.

Although it was 'no go' for a French expeditionary force, Kossuth's hopes were kept alive and he also derived encouragement from a shipment of French arms to the Balkans, a deal arranged between Klapka and Prince Cuza, ruler of the recently united principalities of Moldavia and Wallachia. So he sent instructions to Pulszky about ordering cloth and 5,000 boots for the Hungarian Legion stationed in Italy, and reminded him about drawing．up a contract for a banknote-press. Kossuth's idea was that in the event of liberating the country from Austrian rule, he should issue new banknotes - as he did in 1849 - as the only legal tender acceptable in independent Hungary.

Meanwhile, Pulszky was acting according to his instructions. He jotted down in his *Notebook* that he conferred at least twice a week with Professor Newman, who reflected on the attitude of the French Emperor: "It was one thing for him to wish to see Hungarians on their own responsibility move revolt, and another to let Europe see that he did it: for the latter would enable his enemies everywhere to allege that he is seeking war for war's sake."[26] He paid almost daily visits to the Sardinian and French Embassies in London to get passports for more Hungarian exiles who wished to join the legion in Italy. He extended his newspaper contacts to the Manchester Examiner and to the Times,[27] informing them of Kossuth's journey, with the unsought result - was we have seen above - that Lord Russell was to refer to it in his message to Napoleon III. When he received Kossuth's instructions about the boots and clothing for the army, he went to Bradford to order the goods. Before he set off he called at the Sardinian Embassy, where he learned that French troops occupied Lussin Piccolo near Fiume. "I started to believe . . . that it will be Fiume next, and here, on Hungarian land they will set the Hungarian tricolour flying, and issue the proclamation which will involve Hungary into the war. With these hopes I travelled to Bradford, where, after a few hours of my arrival I learned the news of the armistice, which soon ended the war. I went back to London immediately . . . our hopes evaporated again, at at time when it seemed they were about to be fulfilled."[28]

On 11 July 1859, Francis Joseph and Napoleon III met at Villafranca. The terms of peace soon transpired. On 18 July 1859 Kossuth wrote to Pulszky from Aix-les-Bains, Savois.[29] He described how Napoleon sent him a message on 14 July saying that his hand was forced to make peace with Austria. Kossuth rushed to Turin on a call from Cavour. Cavour told him of his resignation: "I feel dishonoured. How could I sign a peace which makes my king a confederate with the Austrians and with the Pope? Which gives back Tuscany and Modena to the Princes who had escaped? Never! . . . Mais ca ne sera pas. Cette paix ne s'executera pas. Moi je me ferai conspirateur, revolutionnaire s'il le faut."[30] Kossuth on his part, stipulated that those soldiers of the Hungarian Legion who wished to go back to Hungary should be free and able to do so. He insisted on a guarantee of total amnesty for these soldiers to be included in the final peace treaty. This was promised by Cavour, communicated to Napoleon, and accepted without qualms by Francis Joseph, still afraid of a revolt in Hungary and desirous to make conciliatory gestures.

The Legion was disbanded. Kossuth travelled to Switzerland where he was joined by his wife and children. Teleki went to Zürich where he kept a watch on the peace conference to see if the guarantees for the Hungarian soldiers were kept. Klapka left Turin and occupied himself with finding employment for the exiles who did not want to return to Hungary. He entered into long negotiations about the fate of the weapons stored by Prince Cuza. The Hungarian National Directory still existed, anchoring their hopes in the future, when and if Cavour would return to power.

2. A sequel to the war.

The abrupt conclusion of the war brought no tangible advancement to the Hungarian cause and only half-solutions to Italy. Austria was still standing in the way of Hungary's independence and constitutional freedom and Italy's unification by holding on to Venice, which made the representatives of both causes, the Hungarian political exiles, and the Italian politicians, conspirators and guerilla fighters, natural allies. The stir created in the wake of military engagements had not subsided with their cessation and Toscana, Parma and Modena did not want to have their old princes back despite the arrangements of Villafranca. They planned to place themselves under the administration of Piedmont, and formed a military alliance with one another under the leadership of Garibaldi to prevent a possible Austrian intervention. Luigi Carlo Farini gradually extended his dictatorial powers to the whole of middle-Italy, thereby preparing the accession to Piedmont.[31]

The majority of the Hungarian Legion was returning to Hungary. Many took London addresses with them to send reports back of the situation at home. Others decided either to emigrate to America, or to take up their civilian occupations again, which they had given up for the sake of the war in various parts of the world. A third group, decided to stay in the Piedmontese army. Their commander, Gergely Bethlen, emembered the Italian legion of Alessandro Monti in 1849 and formed a similar contingent called the "Hussars of Piacenza". Their numbers rapidly swelled, and with Italian recruits the little army reached 750.[32]

The last notes in Pulszky's *Notebook* at the end of July show his awareness of the minute plans of the emigrant officers who assigned their future in joining the above-mentioned groups. He himself took the bad turn of events to heart. Although his secretary, Tanárky, put down in his own diary that Pulszky received the news phlegmatically, we know from his *Memoirs* and from his correspondence with Newman, that he was only showing a brave face, but in fact broke down and fell ill. He had packed his family and went to cure himself in Ventnor.

At the end of August Kossuth sent him a letter from Switzerland. He had been staying there, meeting some former Hungarian politicians on a visit from the homeland, and from their description of the lack of political life, the measure of passive resistance and general discontent inside the country, he surmised that the key of the situation: to conspire and then to act decisively, was still in the hand of the emigration.[33] Kossuth had 100,000 francs severance pay from Napoleon which he put to the best use. On 24 September he came back to England with the conception to keep the Hungarian question alive by a press campaign organised on an international scale. Pulszky was mobilised again. The role assigned to him by Kossuth was to restart his supply of articles to the English newspapers, but at the same time using some of the material for Continental papers as planned and allocated by a Hungarian exile press bureau in Brussels. The bureau was set up and directed by Miklós Jósika, a former politician, and one of Hungary's leading novelists, the founder of the Hungarian historical novel. Jósika had been a member of the Transylvanian Parliament and during the War of Independence he was a member of Kossuth's National Defence Committee (Honvédelmi Bizottmány), and the President of the Court of Grace (Kegyelmi Tanács), in Arad. In the autumn of 1849 he escaped to Hamburg but later he moved to Brussels, where he successfully combined his literary and political activities with manufacturing and selling lace to the end of his days in 1865.[34] The Brussels Bureau launched its campaign on 1 November 1859 based on material received from Hungary in the form of private letters. The Austrian spy-system made the organisers cautious, which explains why Pulszky's own secretary, Tanárky, who was engaged on copying some of the material learnt of the 'organisational secret' only on 31 December 1859. He wrote in his diary on that day: "this propaganda, which is continuing on Hungary, Europe-wide was initiated by Kossuth and maintained mainly, one could almost say exclusively, by four people: *Horn* in the French papers and revues, *Szarvady* in the French and German papers, *János Ludvigh* in the Belgian newspapers and *Pulszky* in the English papers. Now an elegant, diplomatic-sounding letter is needed in the National Zeitung of Berlin; Pulszky is writing it."[35] In England the Morning Advertiser, the Morning Herald, the Standard, the Daily News and the Times were supplied with articles. The "letters from Pest" that appeared in the columns of the Times were sent by Ede Horn, the newspaper's correspondent in Paris. Pulszky's main topics were the freedom of the Protestant church in Hungary, which had recently been curtailed by the Austrian administration, and Hungary's internal situation as dealt with in an anonymous exchange of pamphlets. Pulszky's attention was called to the tract *Ein Blick auf den anonymen Rückblick*[36] by Professor Goldstücker, and he soon divined that the author of the pungent satirical condemnation of Bach's regime in Hungary was Count István Széchenyi, who had given his MSS. to Béla Széchenyi to print it in London. On 8 December 1859, Pulszky wrote in the *Daily News*, and again on 20 December 1859 and on 7 February 1860, naming his article as letters from Pest, without, of course, revealing that part of the information was transmitted by the Brussels Bureau. Pulszky had translated, and on 24 December 1859 published a letter of Gergely Bethlen's in the *Expresse*, which contained an account of the new Hungarian fighting battalion in Italy. On 4 January and 13 March 1860, Pulszky wrote in the *Volkszeitung* ridiculing an Austrian charge that Hungarian propaganda is directed against German culture.

Meanwhile, the events in Italy progressed further towards unification. La Marmora was succeeded by Cavour as Prime Minister on 20 January 1860. His diplomatic skill bore its first fruits when, on 11-12 March, Tuscany, Emilia and Romagna voted by plebiscite to unite with Piedmont and consequently, the *Parliament of Middle and Northern Italy* could start their first session on 2 April.[37] Cavour also gave his silent consent to some of Garibaldi's plans which began to materialise: with the help of Mazzini's *Societa Nazionale* Garibaldi carried out his expedition against Naples in May and his conquest of Sicily in July. It seemed as if Kossuth's

conception of 1852, which would have started with a Garibaldian expedition, was taking shape after all. His agents attained his positions in
Garibaldi's army. F. Éber, the Times' correspondent and Lajos Tükőry
were colonels, and István Türr became a general and the military governor
of Naples. If Austria persevered in holding on to Venice and kept up the
threat of war against Piedmont, Cavour would be persuaded to back up
the Hungarian revolutionary movement openly and join forces with
Garibaldi, who would land with his followers on the Dalmatian coast.

Cavour responded positively to the renewal of the alliance between
Piedmont and the Hungarian National Directory. He held out the prospects of a new supply of arms and money to the Hungarian exiles and
wanted a representative of the Directory to be stationed in Turin. Teleki
and Klapka came to London in February 1860 to discuss the matter
with Kossuth. It emerged from these talks as a suggestion that Pulszky
should go to Turin as the representative of the Directory. We learn from
Tanárky's Diary that Pulszky was at first very hesitant to accept this
post.[38] On 11 February he went to lunch at Lord Lansdowne's, who
sounded pessimistic about Austria's chances to survive yet another crisis.
Mrs. Pulszky was urging him to go because of domestic considerations:
their modest income derived from journalism would be more adequate
in cheap Turin than in expensive London. In mid-March Pulszky agreed
to go and at the end of the month he acquired a British passport. Cavour
now requested from Kossuth, via Bixio and Szarvady, that the representative should appear in Turin soon. Kossuth's letter of credence for Pulszky
was issued on 3 April 1860, on the day of Pulszky's departure:

"Since M. Bixio transmitted to me Your Excellency's permission to
send a firm, intelligent and most trustworthy man to Your Excellency's
person, who would be entitled to accept such propositions that will be
expedient and would transmit my respectful requests to Your Excellency,
I chose for this purpose the carrier of this present letter: M. Francis
Pulszky, who used to be Under-Secretary of State for Foreign Affairs
in Hungary, and subsequently my Government's agent in England. He is
a sincere, discreet man, who serves the cause of my heart's concern with
devotion, and who is one of the most honest men I have, enjoying my
deepest trust."[39]

But before Pulszky went to present his excellent recommendations,
he needed a cover which should facilitate his movements in Turin, and

that his absence from London should not be conspicuous. He went to Walker, the editor of the Daily News, and volunteered to be his *unpaid* correspondent, as the paper had already had a correspondent in Turin, Count Mamiani, one of Cavour's ministers. At first Walker was unwilling to fall in with Pulszky's plan, but when Pulszky threatened to repeat his offer to the Morning Advertiser, he agreed. Pulszky wrote in his *Memoirs*: "I left Britain . . . with the intention not to return to live there any more, and that my family will follow me to Italy as soon as I will have become familiar with the circumstances there. -It was difficult for me to part from London, where in eleven years I nearly became acclimatised, where I met so much kindness and where everybody treated me and my family as if we were not aliens but old friends."[40]

Pulszky's stay in Britain had come to an end on 3 April 1860 when he left London for Turin. He returned to London only once on 6 July 1860 when he came to collect his family and stayed here for two weeks. His house, 13, St. Alban's Villas, which was sold soon afterwards, stood until it was bombed in the Second World War. His post as representative of the *Directory* in England was given to Sabbas Vukovics. Tanárky, his secretary, followed him to Italy in December 1860.

Although Pulszky exchanged his habitation in April 1860 we need to follow up his actions to examine the causes that finally induced him to change the politics he pursued in England and part with Kossuth in January 1861. In Turin, Pulszky was kindly received by Cavour and worked on the preparations of a secret shipment of arms to the Balkans and a conference between the Piedmontese politicians and the *Directory*, which was to take place in September 1860. He soon built up his contacts in Italy which boosted his position as a newspaper correspondent as well as a political agent: he made the acquaintacne of the English and American Ambassadors, of Garibaldi and of the Piedmontese politicians, and even of the king who granted him an audience in July 1860. The conference on 11 September 1860 was the last success of the Kossuth emigration. On that day Piedmont drew up an agreement to supply 50,000 small fire-arms and two batteries of guns for the purpose of the emigration and to transport them to the Principalities. They promised to give 300,000 francs to organise revolutionary agitation in Hungary and in Transylvania, and 200,000 francs to print banknotes in England for the eventual change of power in Hungary. Pulszky conveyed 100,000 francs into the hands of György Komáromy, the leader of the Revolutionary Committee in Hungary. Kossuth received a similar amount and started to have the banknotes printed by the firm of William Day in London.

But when the revolutionary fervour was at its height, and Piedmont armed to the teeth, Vienna suddenly changed her tactics. The war-threat against Italy was exchanged with conciliatory gestures, and the promulgation of a new constitution in Hungary eased up the revolutionary tension. The October Concessions (Októberi Diploma) opened the channels of a political life inside Hungary again, and although they brought but half-measures, they deprived the Hungarian emigration of its strongest claim that it alone was representing constitutional Hungary. Moreover, it appeared to be a triumph of Ferenc Deák's policies, who always refrained from hostile attitudes to Austria, and advocated reconciliation with the Habsburgs on the basis of the 1848 laws. Five days after the publication of the Concessions, on 27 October 1860, Pulszky commented on it in a private letter to Newman: "It must have cost a great sacrifice to Francis Joseph to yield to the rebel Hungarians, and to wipe out, as far as he could, twelve years of his reign . . . ".[41] Pulszky went on explaining to Newman that although the people at home could not trust the word of Francis Joseph, the change freed the Hungarians from the imperial police, from the foreign officialcy, from arbitrary arrests and public life and elections were possible again.

Although only Bertalan Szemere welcomed the change openly among the public figures of the emigration, it was soon obvious that a thaw started, which the others, and particularly Pulszky, could not ignore. The troubles of the *Directory* started at the end of November when Cavour told Pulszky that the arms sent to the East were seized by the Turkish authorities at Galac. A face-saving operation ensued in the course of which Cavour and Pulszky jointly persuaded István Türr to take the blame for the shipment of arms in the name of Garibaldi, and English ships brought part of the cargo back to Genoa. Cavour showed signs of being tired of the Hungarian exiles. In December 1860 László Teleki of the triumvirs of the *Directory* was arrested in Dresden, conveyed to the Austrian authorities, who transported him back to Hungary and released him there, under a binding promise that he would cease to conspire against the House of Habsburg.[42] This was the end of the Hungarian National Directory *de facto* and *de jure* since Cavour, using the affair as a convenient pretext, treated the remaining members as if they were discredited by it. Throughout November and December 1860 Kossuth was anxiously pleading for the rest of the money which the September agreement ensured for the revolutionary organisation. Pulszky's repeated remonstrations with Cavour were in vain: the Prime Minister finally dismissed him stating that he could not give out any more money for Hungary and the revolutionary organisation might as well be disbanded inside the country.[43] This was enough for Pulszky. On 8 January 1860 he resigned as Kossuth's representative.

The parting between Kossuth and Pulszky[44] was not only brought about by their difficult political assessment of the changed political situation, but also by the subjective reactions to a role they thought they could fulfill in the future. In his letter of resignation, Pulszky sketched two alternatives to Kossuth, the politcs of emigration might take. They could join Deák's party and help the complete restoration of the constitution, or they could go along with Garibaldi alone, discounting Cavour, and land on the Dalmatian coast with an expeditionary force hoping that the nation would rise to regain its independence. It did not take long for him to realise, that the second alternative favoured also by Klapka, attrative as it may have seemed, was completely unrealistic. On 27 February 1861 he visited Garibaldi at Caprera and sounded him about at landing. The leader of the *Thousand* said he would not go to liberate anyone without an invitation; which meant a fire of guns - otherwise, an inner revolt. Then in March 1861 it looked as if the road of the first alternative would open for him personally. Szécsény, the constituency of his, or to be more precise, of his wife's estate, offered a mandate for him, for the new Parliament to be opened in the autumn.[45] Pulszky published his willingness of acceptance in the Hungarian Press[46] and only the denial of a free pass, by the Hungarian chancellor, made him postpone his decision by five years.

Kossuth's decision in 1861 to refuse all notions of reconciliation with the Austrians was his final one, as he adhered to it until the end of his life. While Pulszky could see himself as a future member of parliament at Deák's side, Kossuth preferred the role of an outside critic, whose only weapon left was his own protesting voice against Austrian rule, whatever form it might take in the future. Years later he was still agitating for and outside intervention, when no-one else believed in it or expected any good results from it. Pulszky's personal assessment of his own position had always included an element of very realistic economic calculations: if his or only his wife's estates were restored in Hungary he could be a wealthy landlord again, a part-time scholar and a part-time archaeologist, whose absorbing interest in politics might remain but for whom this would not be a way of life any more.

We have described Pulszky's political activities in England and their short sequel in Italy in the context of the aspirations of the exiles of independent Hungary, the Kossuth emigration. The main issues of his political stand were his fight for the restoration of the Hungarian constitutional freedoms, and the re-establishment of Hungary as an independent political state. Since Hungary had enjoyed constitutional privileges as a separate kingdom, and later as a separate country, though as a separate state she only existed for a short spell in 1849,[47] the claims which were stated as inseparables by the Kossuth emigration, were proved to be separable by a compromise solution. Because the emigration insisted on all the claims, when other voices of the nation were muted or strangled, it became possible for the nation to achieve some of the claims. The political work of Pulszky in Britain should be assessed by showing his rate of success or failure in carrying out the actual tasks he set himself. He failed to achieve the maximal claim: the recognition of Hungary by Britain, but he successfully carried out the smaller tasks: set up a propaganda machinery, whereby he reiterated the rest of the claims for eleven years. We have tried to survey and partly to evaluate his contributions in the pattern of events that governed the political and personal fortunes of the Hungarian emigration. In the course of this survey attention was drawn to the roles Pulszky had played in England in the service of a cause, and to the variety of methods he adopted. This included the examination of plans worked out by Kossuth where Pulszky's contribution had been solely to facilitate their execution, surrendering his own political personality to Kossuth. There was after all some truth in the general criticism of Pulszky's political career, voiced by one of his parliamentary opponents, after his return to Hungary, that Pulszky had always followed a great leader: first Deák, then Kossuth, then Garibaldi and finally Deák again. He was, above all, an eminet organiser, who possessed the quality of awakening the interest and even the enthusiasm in others with similar political creed and rallied them behind the cause he represented. The extent of his personal influence was evident in the work of Hungarian and hungarophile associations in Britain, and in the opinions which two of their leading members, Lord Dudley Stuart and Francis W. Newman expressed. Naturally, this worked both ways: Pulszky was eager to learn form his circle of friends, advisers and well-wishers, and his stay in Britain made him one of the most anglicised of Hungarian politicians. When confronted with a choice, a compromise was always closer to his nature than a heroic stand, a quality he admired in others. Empirical in his methods, practical in his outlook, Pulszky never really trusted political theories. He adhered instinctively to the principles of nationalism, and for practical purposes courted even with the ideas of federalism, but without really believing in them.

The essence of his political activities in England was a threefold contribution to the Hungarian cause: he helped to form an active front of protests against the suppression of Magyar constitutional life; he belonged to those who most effectively spoke up for the conquered nation when its voice was dumbed; he closely assisted those who kept the Hungarian question in evidence among the problems of the world which should be solved in the future.

EPILOGUE

Nationalism and the federative plans

In the whole wide world
There is no place for you other than this;
Whether the hand of Fate bless or smite you,
Here you must live, here you must die.[1]

In this, our concluding chapter, we shall give an account of the federative plans that co-existed as alternatives with other projects that had been drawn up to solve the Hungarian problem on more directly nationalistic lines in our period. It should be noted that Pulszky, whose political activities have been the subject of our thesis, played a secondary and a reluctant role, in all discussions concerning a federation, as he was a political empiricist and held orthodox nationalistic views. A very advanced type of nationalism and a good deal of political idealism was needed to stretch the doctrine of mid-nineteenth century nationalism to accommodate any federative plans.

The gist of the doctrine was that the human race consisted of nations whose criteria and characteristics could be defined. A state was lawful if it expressed the sovereignty of the nation.[2] To the adherents of this doctrine, and we count the orthodox nationalists of the re-awakening nations of Europe amongst them, not only was the nation the focus of their political loyalty, but it was exclusively so. The claim to political power became the programme of each individual nation within the multi-national states such as Austria and Turkey with the ultimate goal of complete independence in directing their internal as well as their external affairs.[3] Few thought that the size of their country, and the number of their nation's population, should be a matter of serious computation, to safeguard their projected freedom against the aggression of great powers.

In the opinion of foreign observers, such as Paget, Quin[4] and particularly Blackwell, Hungary seemed to have had the best start on the road of national independence in the eighteen-forties. Hungary possessed an ancient constitution, which was more than a collection of privileges and had been upheld for centuries, she engaged on a course of great internal reforms, and her crownlands covered the largest territories. As for population, Blackwell furnished Ponsonby with statistics showing the relative predominance of Magyars to the rest of the races inhabiting Hungary.[5] Out of a total of fifteen million inhabitants - this covered Transylvania also, which rejoined Hungary in 1848 - there were five and a half million Magyars to five million Slavs and four and a half million people belonging to other races. Blackwell repeatedly argued that the multi-national Habsburg Empire, because it took little or no account of the various national aspirations, would sooner or later break up into its constituent elements and would most probably be replaced by a federation of Central and Eastern European States. The Magyars were the most likely nation to establish themselves at the head of such a federation as they were in the geographical centre and they were the most advanced politically.

Some Hungarian historians argue that[6] Blackwell borrowed these ideas from Louis Batthyány's circle of *advanced* nationalists.[7] Others, like Sproxton, contend that Blackwell's starting point was the Palmerstonian balance of power policy, and he hatched the federation idea to satisfy its needs. As the two are compatible both might well be true separately, but further points should be added. Batthyány must certainly have been aware of an earlier instance when the federation idea occurred in Hungarian history - mentioned incidentally by Pulszky in the introduction to his wife's *Diary*[8] - when Gábor Bethlen tried to organise a federal alliance of neighbouring states in the Danube basin in the beginning of the seventeenth century. Blackwell, on his part, might have known about Mazzini's plan of a European federation, published in the eighteen thirties, whose final object was to have been the weakening of Austria in the interest of Italian unification. It is interesting to note at this juncture that Mazzini, who was the foremost theoretician of nationalism, and who formulated one of the basic tenets of the doctrine, *that power was only legitimate if it belonged to the nation,*[9] was also the advocate of supra-national political systems, consisting of freely associating smaller nations.

Blackwell, whose proposals were directed to his superiors, was certainly over-impressed by the strength of the Hungarian radicals displayed in the Diet of Pressburg, without being able to assess the true scope of orthodox Magyar nationalism, the real feelings of the national minorities, and the limited aspirations of the neighbouring nations. Until very recently,[10] no attention was called to the fact that the famous Article X of 1790/91 of the Magyar Parliament, which laid down that Hungary was an independent county - regnum independens - had its Transylvanian and Croatian equivalents, each insisting on the very same privileges.[11] Given the case of similar constitutional developments it would have been reasonable to expect that the national minorities, the Serbs and Croatians for instance, would feel the pull of their own nationals more than the magnetism of Magyar nationalism. Moreover, Magyar nationalism asserted itself by an ever-increasing insistence on the use of the Magyar language and on the claims of exclusive territorial rights to the so-called crownlands of St. Stephen. Pulszky in his press debate with Leo Thun[12] likened the position of the Slovenian minority in Hungary to that of the Welsh minority in Britain. He argued that it was as unreasonable for the Croats to insist on the official use of their language in Hungary as it would have been for the Welsh to make the same claims for their language in Britain. The best choice for them would be to Magyarise: if they persisted in their separatist claims, such as national autonomy, they should emigrate. The Slav reaction was typical: Kollar paid poetic justice to Pulszky, by casting him together with other Magyar nationalists, to the Panslav Hell, in his great epic poem, *Slavy Deéra*.[13]

Likewise the Rumanian nationalists were quick to answer the St. Stephen story with a mythical Daco-Rumanian theory, designed to counter the claims of the Magyars to Transylvania, with an even more ancient claim going back to the Roman conquest. What hope was there that these fighting nationalists would make truce, recognise the common danger threatening them all, and direct their divergent paths to pave a road of communal affairs?

It is no accident that the first Hungarian politician adopting the idea of a federation was one of the most progressive thinkers, László Teleki, who was viewing the situation from outside, as Ambassador in France. He wrote to Kossuth from Paris in May 1849, when the Hungarian arms were victorious over the Austrians, and when it seemed a possibility that they might even take Vienna. Teleki thought that this moment of victory was the most suitable time to behave magnanimously towards the nationalities, forget St. Stephen territorial claims, grant every possible municipal, administrative and linguistic freedom to the minorities and lay down the foundation of a future Danubian Confederation. He considered that the Confederation itself might have an inner circle, comprising Rumania, Hungary, Serbia, Bulgaria and an outer circle that would include Bohemia, Moravia and Poland. Teleki most certainly had read a Frech pamphlet[14] published in the previous autumn, which advocated a confederation under the protectorate of the Porte, and was aware of the plans of Prince Czartoryski who supported a similar scheme with free Poland as the focal point. It happened actually a few days later on 19 May, that Czartoryski's agents succeeded in calling together the first conference to discuss the idea of a confederation at the Hotel Lambert in Paris. Polish, Rumanian and Czech exile politicians took part in the conference, beside the three Hungarians, Szarvady, Teleki and Pulszky. In fact the Rumanians had already taken the matter one step further: in September 1848, A.G. Golescu met Bastide, the French Foreign Minister, and proposed a confederation of Rumania, Hungary and Croatia to stand in the place of the collapsing Austrian Empire.

Pulszky, whose orthodox nationalism had not changed since his pronouncements in 1843, did everything in his power to frustrate the talks at Hotel Lambert, and even thirty years later[15] wrote derisively of the vain efforts of László Teleki, who would have agreed to the 'dismemberment' of Hungary. Kossuth would never have allowed Transylvania to part from Hungary, commented Pulszky, knowing fully well that a great deal of Kossuth's mass-appeal in the Hungary of the forties was based on his orthodox nationalist propaganda expounded in the press organ: Pesti Hirlap.

Yet it took only two months, and the Russian intervention, for Kossuth's Foreign Minister to consider the idea of a federation and instruct Pulszky to approach Palmerston with a proposal.[16] It was a similar one that had been propounded by Desprez, which would have assigned a leading role to the Porte. But when Pulszky received these instructions it was already too late to do anything.

A year later, and independently from the Kossuth emigration, József Eötvös approached the problems of the nationalities and a federation from a different angle. In a pamphlet written by him in emigration, but published in Pest,[17] he espoused the theory that the Danubian peoples, interdependent as they were, could only withstand the tide from the East if they rallied in a federation under the same monarch. It was so far the first theoretical attempt to accommodate federative principles with a monarchical system, in fact, an improved system of the very same Habsburg Monarchy.

Kossuth's approach to the problem was republican when he came to reconsider his whole position in Turkish internment in 1850-51. There Henningsen's visit and his initiative gave rise to the occasion of an ad hoc conference, which the interned Kossuth called together to discuss the position in Eastern Europe, following the Russian intervention and the Habsburg restoration. Besides Kossuth and Henningsen, Kázmér Batthyány, three Poles, Zamoyski, Bystrzonowski and Koscielski, and Italian, Monti, and a Serbian liberal minister, Gerasanin, took part in the discussion.[18] Alexander Karagyorgyevics, Prince of the Serbian principality, discreetly supported the proceedings. Henningsen informed Lord Dudley Stuart and Cobden, who lent a sympathetic ear to Kossuth's new proposals, and Lord Dudley was even instrumental in arranging a private reception of East European politicians by Palmerston, on 1 January 1850. Andrássy, Teleki, Pulszky, Klapka, Bălcesco and Prince Lubomirski, Czartoryski's representative, put the case of a federation before Palmerston. The reaction of the English Foreign Minister was that the plan was interesting but impracticable, as its realisation would provoke a war.[19] Undaunted, Kossuth worked out a detailed plan in Kiutahia, which he sent to Teleki on 15 June 1850.[20]

The plan was certainly the most advanced and most democratic up to that date and showed that its author became a progressive nationalist. Kossuth started off his argument with an attack on one of the basic principles of the doctrine: "jede Nationalität ist im Stadte gleich-berichtigt" and declared it to be "just a beautiful dream". He also came to re-define what the criteria of a nation was: Not the language, but the communalty of interests, its past, the rights and duties, but mainly the communalty of a people's institutions.[21]

Kossuth laid down three points, which he called the basic roots of the federation. Smaller nations can only maintain their separate political existence if they federate; this should safeguard their own interests as well as that of the rest of Europe against the supremacy of Russia; the House of Habsburg cannot fulfill this dual role.

Kossuth's federation would still have its geographical centre in Hungary, like Blackwell's, and would comprise those countries whose defensive gravitation would not lie elsewhere. This could mean that the Germans - i.e. Austrians - might, the Rumanians and the smaller Slavonic nations must federate with Hungary, unless they want to be absorbed into Russia, under the umbrella of Panslavism. The Confederation, provisionally called *Federation of North-Eastern Free States*, should guarantee the freedom of nationalities within each state. There were fourteen organisational principles laid down by the ex-Governor, covering the internal as well as the external set up. 1. Every state will enjoy internal interdependence; 2. National autonomy; 3. Serbia and Moldavia would act in conjunction with the Porte; 4. The objects of the confederation were: a) common defence, b) duty-free trade within, c) common diplomacy; 5. Federal council would govern the confederation; 6. Its members would be elected by the legislative assembly of each state; 7. Each state would bear the burden of taxation according to the size of the country and the size of its population; 8. The decisions of the federal government (elected by the Council) would be binding to all states; 9. Each state would have a minister of federal affairs; 10. Ambassadors would be nominated by the federal government; 11. It would have absolute power to wage war or contract peace; 12. The federal government would reside in Hungary, but not where the Hungarian Government would be; 13. The Council would elect a president for a year; 14. The federal statutes would go through a revision in every twenty-five years.

As regards the internal organisation of Hungary and Transylvania - Kossuth took it for granted that Transylvania would stay with Hungary, the solution suggested would be the same as in the Declaration of Independence, but with more concessions in respect of the language problem. Still, the language of legislation and the official language of the Government would remain Hungarian.

Kossuth's plan earned the violent disapproval of the orthodox Rumanian nationalists, but was also criticised by the progressives who soon made a different plan.[22] Their projected centre was Daco-Rumania, to be united with Transylvania and the Banat, and federated with Croatia, Serbia and Hungary. Prince Czartoryski criticised Kossuth's plan from a Polish point of view; he secretly recommended the dismemberment of Hungary for the benefit of her Slavonic neighbours, and the establishment of a federation with ill-concealed Polish supremacy. It seemed that, even if a power-vacuum had come to pass, which was the pre-requisite condition for all confederation plans, the individual small nations would still not have been able to agree among themselves.[23]

Despite his optimism that the differences between the small nations could be overcome, Kossuth knew that the main snags were the so-called historical claims, and the various national grievances. The policies of the Hungarian National Directory were, therefore, from the outset laden with promises of further concessions to the nationalities, to gain the co-operation of the surrounding nations, when the next opportunity presented itself to renew the negotiations of a federal alliance, in 1859-60. In a memorandum submitted to the Turin Government on 15 September 1860[24] the *Directory* laid down the principles of a projected reorgan-isation, which included a re-orientation of views on the language ques-tion - the most sensitive point of the nationalities. The *Directory* proposed that in a New Hungary each community could decide which language they wanted to use. The countries would have the right to choose any language of administration they wished for, and their representatives could retain that even in parliament. The laws would be promulgated in all languages spoken in the country, and the nationalities could set up clubs, schools, institutions and religious organisations under their own leaders and priests without the least interference of the state. Whether it would have been an acceptable first step to pacify all internal dif-ferences, and whether the surrounding nations would have followed suit in treating their minorities in the same way, thus preparing the ground for a federative alliance, and later on, a federation, was not put to the test until half a century later.

Meanwhile, in 1862[25] Kossuth published his last plan of a *Danubian Confederation*. It was an indirect answer to the concessions, known as the *October Diploma*, issued by the Austrians in 1861, which to some extent repaired the channels of a political life inside the country, and split the emigration abroad. Kossuth saw the dangers of a compromise more clearly than any of the other politicians: in terms of the future, "dualism" would mean propping up a shaky monarchy, maintaining the same short-sighted course of orthodox nationalism that characterised Hungarian public opinion, and furthering the rift with the surrounding nations. Kossuth launched his plan with a desperate plea: "I ask all our

Magyar, Slavonic and Rumanian brothers to cast a veil on the past and
shake hands with one another . . . rising all for one, and one for all, on the
ancient Swiss example . . . ".[26] The plan replenished all the points of the
1851 Kiutahia project, but went even further with concessions than the
Turin memorandum. It offered a choice to the inhabitants of Transylvania
to decide by general vote whether their country should be one with
Hungary[27] - thus foregoing all "historical" and all nationalist claims to
territory, and advocating the methods of liberal democracy. This was
equally evident in the rest of his proposals, which put an end to all
"primacy" claims by Hungary, even on geographical grounds, and recommended a rotational system for the seats of the authorities in the confederation.

Yet this theoretically most attractive plan did not account for the
political realities of its day. It met with a wholesale condemnation of
most newly emerging political forces in Hungary, entrenched in the old
nationalists traditions from which Kossuth had at last freed himself.
Pulszky, still living in Italy, did not take part in its rejection at the time,
but expressed his opinion in his *Memoirs*, calling it impractical and not
even desirable as a dream.

By way of summary we may conclude that all efforts to establish
a federation in the period from the late forties to the early sixties had
failed on two fronts. First, they failed on account of a nationalism,
which even in its best form could not act as a cohesive force. It looked
as if the individual countries concerned still had a long way to go on a road
of frustrated independence and political self-development before they
would be ready to federate. But the plans could not succeed in the given
international situation either. Weak as it was, the Habsburg Monarchy
survived all cataclysms and the rest of the great powers did not wish to
replace it with a more democratic federation of Danubian States.

Those who put their trust in the future, hope that nationalism, in its
highest and most advanced form, might yet act as a cohesive force in the
Danubian basin. This will only be possible when the cultural bond will be
generally accepted as a distinguishing factor of nationality, in preference
to the dubious biological factors of blood and race. Active individual
participation is necessary if the nation is to be more than a cobweb of

mere linguistic and ethnical ties and develop into a living spiritual unit. In Renan's famous phrase, a nation is nothing but a choice, a plebiscite of every day. "Such a conception of nationality is not necessarily conducive to antagonism and hatred. On the contrary, it may permit the possibility of reconciling national differences with the complexity of human civilisation."[28]

APPENDICES

APPENDIX 1

Palmerston to Ponsonby,[1] *F.O.*
2 August 1849

"My dear Ponsonby,

I send you some Instructions about Hungary which you will no doubt execute with your usual zeal and judgement. -You will of course at first find Schwarzenberg and his Colleagues male and female, Counts, Archdukes and Archduchess, adverse to any negotiation with the Hungarians; and his Russian allies will naturally try to persuade him from anything but settling matters by fire and sword, the Bullet and the (. . .) But I think if you urge perseveringly but calmly the reasoning of one Despatch the Austrian Gvt. must soon see how much the true interests of the Austrian Empire would be consulted by an accomodation with Hungary. The real question at issue now is whether Hungary shall be incorporated in Stadion's aggregate constitution, or whether it shall retain its ancient separate constitution with such improvement as have been or may be hereafter made in it, in the regular legal way. I say that this I take to be the real question at issue, because I cannot suppose that the Austr. Govt. can seriously contemplate the establishment of arbitrary power in Hungary, in the event of their being successful, and because I am convinced of what has been said to me by the Hungarians now in London that notwithstanding all that has been said and done, the Hungarians should submit to the Emperor if they were assured of the maintenance of their separate nationality, upon the former footing, under the Emperor as King of Hungary. It seems to me that it would be perfect madness on the part of the Austrian Govt. to continue the war for the difference between the old Hungarian Constitution and Stadion's scheme. . . . because it is very probable that for other reasons and on account of other difficulties, Stadion's scheme will be given up. But mainly because I cannot conceive that any rational man or woman can imagine that any advantage that would arise to Aust. by ignoring Stadion's plan in preference to the old constitution could counterbalance a truth fact (sic) of the evil which will accrue to Austria from the most complete success on Hungary by aid of a Russian army. In the first place the war if continued will devastate and ruin for years the whole of that fertile country naturally full . . . of resources of every kind and which ought to be a foundation of strength to Austria; next even if the Aust. Govt. after victory should have resource to its usual barbarous system of wholesale confiscation, and should plunder all the Hungarian aristocracy, and endeavour to exterminate the Magyar nobility as a race they would . . . entirely fail. They would only engrave more deeply on the heart of every Hungarian eternal hatred of the Aust. name, and sow a crop of future insurrections of which they would reap a plentiful harvest. The new proprietors, if Germans, would be murdered one after the other and if Hungarians would be animated by the same national antipathy which led the former owners . . .

But the indignation of Europe would rise up in judgement against such a barbarous imitation of the policy of the middle ages. Anyhow all that Austria could hope to accomplish by vengeance after victory, would be reduce Hungary to impotence, that is to say to paralize her own right even for a century to come; whereas by making a friendly arrangement with Hungary Austria would reoccupy her former position as a first rate power. Every week that the war continues is one may say a nail in Austria's coffin: She's playing a game of right hand against left, with this difference that whichever side loses she is the sufferer while the winnings go to the officious neighbour. I will suppose for the moment that which I don't believe that Austria is to receive no payment either in money or territory for the great and expensive military exertions that she is making. But will she derive no advantage from this war? Or is it not an obvious interest to Russia to cripple Austria? not to extinguish her but to cripple, and to render her dependent upon Russia for help and unable to oppose . . . Russia? Why of course it is; it must be so by every rule of reasoning; and is not what is now going on, directly tending to such a result? What could Russia wish for better than to be allowed to send her army then to ravage and lay waste to one third of the Austrian Empire; to destroy politically and militarily a third of the population of that Empire and to transform them from faithful and useful subjects into revengeful and implacable enemies? Why now the Russian govt. must secretly laugh, and with what bitter and scornful derision, at the imbecility of a Govt. which rather than make peace on reasonable terms with a third part of its own dominions prefers to give up that third to be the theatre of an exterminating war! This is supposing that the only compensation to be given to Russia is the slaughter of Austr. & Hung. subjects, the devastation of Hung. and the long to come impoverishment of the Austrian Empire: but when of course the work of destruction is done, the Emperor will send in his Bill "for laying your territory to waste, and for killing and wounding on one side and the other one or two thousand of your subjects" and that bill will have to be paid either in money or in territory. Let us not then be deterred by the ill humour and bad temper of unstatesmanlike men, or by the blind and ignorant and . . . passions of violent women, from giving and pampering upon the Austrian Govt. advice which is founded upon reason and which is conducive to the true interests of Austria. The people you will have to talk to on these matters will begin by saying that this is an Austrian conern with which we have no business to meddle, that they do not want our advice, and can manage their own affairs and they will bring the changes upon many such commonplace assertions. But the answer is that this is not a domestic affair between the Emperor and his subjects. It is a war between nation and nation which by the magnitude of its scale has become a European transaction; and which if it was not such by its own nature and circumstances has been rendered such by the Aust. Govt. themselves from the moment that they called on the Russian army to assist them. You must not therefore allow them to put you off with the stale pretences about non influence, and you may say, moreover that the feeling in England is becoming so strong and general upon this matter that it is impossible for the Brit. Govt. to avoid making every endeavour in its power to persuade the contending parties to come to an amicable arrangement. Schwarzenberg is of course the person with whom you must communicate officially, but seek an opportunity of talking also to Bach, and to Schmerling . . . and to anybody else who may have influence in these matters. I have seen and talked much to several of the Hungarians now in London, and am convinced that even Kossuth would come to reasonable terms. Any of the Hungarians now here would willingly be useful as organs of communication if it were wished, but probably Blackwell who knows Kossuth personally would be the best person to be employed to sound him; and I am told by the Hungarians here that the

Aust. Govt. are disposed to make peace upon fair and reasonable terms, the best way of taking the first step for that purpose would be to make a communication to Kossuth himself. Blackwell might be able to do that will less appearance of committing the Aust. Govt. than if an Austrian were sent, and he might be relied upon for executing his commission with exactness. I send you a Despatch desiring you to (confine?) into reports which have reached us; my object is that the fact of you being instructed to make inquiries for the information of your own Govt. may act as some check upon the Austrians.

I am afraid that great atrocities have been committed by their officers and troops; I have even heard that women have been tried by Court Martial and have been sentenced as a punishment for political offences to be given up to the soldiers. What a depth of degradation and depravity must a nation have been brought down to when any men belonging to it, can have been guilty of such unexampled & infamous baseness. The people of Vienna will say, as they did about the atrocities perpetrated in Galicia, that nothing of the kind had happened, and that all these stories are calumnies invented by their enemies but unfortunately we know from (unsuspicious?) evidence too much of their proceedings in Civil wars, to make us very ready to give credit to their denials.

Yours Sincerely,
(signed) Palmerston."

I shall tomorrow read to Colloredo my Despatch to be given to Schwarzenberg.

To the Vis ct Ponsonby.

APPENDIX 2

Pulszky to Toulmin Smith,[1] *(London),*
19 October 1849.

8 Spring Street
Cambridge Terrace
19 October

"My dear Sir

Your kind offer of your house for Kossuth did show me anew how kindhearted you are, I am sure he will be much more consoled by such kindness, than by the beautiful words of L. Palmerston, contradicted always by the acts of the ministry. -Your letter of the 17 reached me yesterday morning, I feel Lord D. Stuart is not the man for opposing L. Palmerston. Next *Tuesday* in all cases it is necessary to meet again, would you be kind enough to be surely at your chambers at three o'clock, Lord Nugent will be present and I also, we cannot leave the suffering in the way they are. Some new executions took place at Pest, Csányi one of Kossuth's ministers, and B. Jeszenák Lord Lieutenant of the county of Nyitra, a rich nobleman were hanged, a catholic clergyman shot.-

Mrs. Pulszky is very sorry that she cannot have this and next week the pleasure to visit Highgate, she is too much occupied with the publication of a Diary concerning the hungarian war.

Prey present our compliments to Mrs. T. Smith and believe me

Yours
truly
Signed/F. Pulszky."

APPENDIX 3

Exchange of letters between Dudley Stuart[1] and Lord Palmerston
29 October 1851 - 30 October 1851.

6 Stratford Place, Oxford
Wednesday night Oct. 29th 1851

"My dear Lord Palmerston
   It has occured to me that it would be a good way for you to see Kossuth for you to meet him at dinner at my house if you feel no objection to it, & would do me that honor - if you are disposed to this be kind enough to inform me when you are likely to be in town, and what days would best suit you-
   Kossuth will leave England on the 13th or 14th Nov. at Latest.
   Believe me, my Dear Lord Palmerston, Yours truly,
                                        Signed/Dudley Coutts Stuart."

. . . . . . 30 Oct. 1851
"My dear Dudley Stuart
   I am out of town and shall not be in town again except for a few hours in a morning till the latter end of next week; I shall therefore not be able to have the pleasure of dining with you.
                                        Yours sincerely,
                                        Signed/Palmerston."

APPENDIX 4

Hungarian Association,[1] Highgate, near London
October 1849

(Proof.)

HUNGARIAN ASSOCIATION

For some time past a number of Gentlemen in London have been associated together, under the name of the "London Hungarian Committee," whose object has been to collect accurate information, and to diffuse it where they have had opportunity.

It is no less important, under existing circumstances, than it was during the struggle of arms, that such information should be collected and diffused. The character of the struggle itself, and of the Hungarian nation, makes it certain that the present cessation of that struggle is no settlement of it; but that it must speedily be renewed. The interests of England are in every way concerned with the issue.

It is proposed, therefore, for a number of Gentlemen to remain united, under the name of the "Hungarian Association," with the following definite objects:-

As a private Association - not pretending to intrude itself in any public shape - to collect and circulate all the information in its power with respect to the events of the last two years in Hungary; as well as with respect to the historical associations bearing upon them, and the constitutional and social relations which they have affected: further than this, to collect together and to circulate in an available form, all the *Official Documents* which have, during that time, been issued, either (1) by the Hungarian nation, or any of its leaders, or (2) by the Austrian Cabinet, or any of those who have been openly or secretly acting on its behalf.

To be able to accomplish these objects, it is necessary to invite the assistance of those who have already taken any interest in Hungarian affairs, or who feel that the welfare of England is intimately bound up with the maintenance of the independence and free institutions of other nations, and therefore that an accurate knowledge of the facts is indispensable.

The names of those who have already united in this Association are given below, and will be a guarantee for the careful application of all funds which may be entrusted to them. Subscriptions are requested to be transmitted to   or to the Honorary Secretary. Each subscription will be duly acknowledged, and the subscriber will receive at least one copy of every document issued by the Association.

It is particularly requested that every one intending to subscribe will do so with as little delay as possible, as what the Association will be able to accomplish must *depend entirely* upon the extent to which this Circular shall meet with a response.

J. Toulmin Smith
Honorary Secretary

Highgate, near London, October 1849.

Members of the Hungarian Association

Lord Dudley Coutts Stuart, M.P.
Richard Taylor, ESQ.
George Crawshay, ESQ.
Francis W. Newman, ESQ.
William Bonham Donne, ESQ.

William Lloyd Birkbeck, ESQ.
Thomas C. Banfield, ESQ.
Joshua Toulmin Smith, ESQ.
John Edward Taylor, ESQ.
David Jennings Vipan, ESQ.

BIBLIOGRAPHY*

I. 1. List of archives and libraries, with collections used.

Bibliothéque publique et universitaire Geneva: MSS. Bruns.
Birmingham Public Library: Toulmin Smith Collection. British Museum:
   Dept. of MSS. Add. MSS. 28,511; Dept. of Printed Books; Dept.
   of Newspapers.
Harrowby Archives, Sandon Hall, Stafford: Harrowby MSS. Vol. XXIV,
   XXV, XXVI, XXVII, XXVIII, 451, 453, 1062, Cracow Xerox Volume.
Magyar Tudományos Akadémia: Blackwell MSS.
National Library of Scotland: Adam Black MSS.
National Register of Archives: Palmerston Papers. Correspondence;
   Memoranda.
Országos Levéltár, Budapest: Kossuth Hagyaték; Vörös Collection. (i.e.
   Vörös Antal gyűjteménye.).
Országos Széchényi Könyvtár, Budapest: Dept. of MSS. Pulszky Col-
   lection; E.MSS.; Vol. 287; Quart. Hung. 2501, 2506.
Public Record Office: Home Office Documents. (H.O. 1,45); Foreign
   Office Documents. (F.O. 7. 363-5, 567-8).
University College London Library: Brougham Collection.
University of London Library.

I. 2. List of annuals, newspapers and periodicals.
(Those containing primary material are italicised).

ABAUJ-KASSAI KÖZLÖNY, 1878. ACCOUNTS AND REPORTS, 1851.
A HON, 1868. *ALLEANZA, 1862. ALLGEMEINE ZEITUNG, 1847.*

---

*This bibliography includes all primary and secondary sources quoted or referred
to in this volume, excepting references to poems quoted, and material used by
Pulszky, Mrs. Pulszky and Newman as their sources. These are elucidated only in
the footnotes at the appropriate places. Articles in periodicals, etc. are listed together with the rest of the material either in the primary or in the secondary
sources category. The titles of the periodicals, etc. are capitalized.

BUDAPESTI SZEMLE, 1936-7. BURKE'S PEERAGE, 1967. *CHRISTIAN REFORMER, 1853. THE COURIER, 1852. The ECLECTIC REVIEW, 1851-1854. DAILY NEWS, 1849-1851; 1853-1854; 1857; 1859-1860. The EDINBURGH REVIEW, 1849-1852.* ERDÉLYI MUZEUM, 1912. *The EXAMINER, 1849-1853. FRASER'S MAGAZINE, 1850-1853.* FŐVÁROSI LAPOK, 1881. *GENTLEMAN'S MAGAZINE, 1855.* HÁBORUS FELELŐSSÉG, Vol. 1. *ILLUSTRATED LONDON NEWS, 1843, 1849, 1851. HANSARD'S PARLIAMENTARY DEBATES,* Third Series. Vol. 103, 105, 107, 114, 116-118, 120, 125. *The WEEKLY HERALD, 1852. The HOUSEHOLD NARRATIVE, September 1851.* HUNGARIAN QUARTERLY, 1936-1942. INQUIRER, 1897. *IRODAL-MTŐRTÉNETI KŐZLEMÉNYEK, 1917.* IRODALMI UJSÁG, 1964-68. *JOURNAL OF THE HOUSE OF LORDS, Vol. 84. KŐZLŐNY, 1848. LONDON UNIVERSITY MAGAZINE, 1859.* MAGYAR KŐNYV-SZEMLE, 1889-1890. *MAGYAR SZÉPIRODALMI SZEMLE, 1847. MAGYARORSZÁG, 1861. MORNING ADVERTISER, 1851. MORNING POST, 1853. The NATIONAL INTELLIGENCER, 1852.* NEMZET, *1884.* NEW HUNGARIAN QUARTERLY, 1968. *The NORTH AMER-ICAN REVIEW, 1852.* NEMZETI UJSÁG, 1935. *NEW YORK HERALD, 1851. NEW YORK Daily TIMES, 1851. NEW YORK Daily TRIBUNE, 1853-1859. PESTI HIRLAP, 1843, 1847.* RIVISTA STORICA ITALIANA, 1964. *SOUTH EASTERN AFFAIRS: Materials relative to the history of Central Europe and the Balcan penninsula, 1938-1940.* The SLAVONIC AND EAST EUROPEAN REVIEW, 1930-1931, 1950, 1960-1966. *The TIMES, 1849-1860.* TIMES LITERARY SUPPLEMENT, 1968. *TRANS-ACTIONS OF THE PHILOLOGICAL SOCIETY, 1859.* The semi-weekly TRIBUNE, 1852. *UNION, 1851. VIERTELJAHRSCHRIFT AUS UND FÜR UNGARN, 1843.* WHO'S WHO, 1967.

II. PRIMARY SOURCES.

1. Manuscripts.

ALIEN ACT: Suggested repeal, 1860. P.R.O. H.O. 1. O.S. 7063.

Minutes of the ASSOCIATION OF THE HUNGARIAN POLITICAL EXILES IN LONDON, 1850. O. SZ.K. 2506 Quart. Hung.

BIRKBECK to PULSZKY, 20 July 1849. O.SZ.K. Pulszky Coll.

BLACKWELL to PALMERSTON, 7 November 1851. N.R.A. P.P. GC/BL/5.

BLACKWELL, J.A. Missions, I-VI. M.T.A. Blackwell MSS.

COBDEN to DUDLEY STUART, 23 October 1849. Harrowby MSS. Vol. XXV. P. 120-2.

COBDEN to DUDLEY STUART, 23 April 1849. Harrowby MSS. 4th Ser. Vol. 1062. P.313-4.

CRAWSHAY, G. to DUDLEY STUART, 3 September 1849. Harrowby MSS.; Vol. XXV. P. 164-5.

CZARTORYSKI to DUDLEY STUART, 3 September 1849. Harrowby MSS. Vol. XXV. P. 217-8.

DENISON, Lord A. to DUDLEY STUART, 4 November 1849. Harrowby MSS. Vol. XXV. P. 231-2.

DUDLEY STUART. Noble people of Hungary . . . an address, 30 July 1849. Harrowby MSS. Vol. XXVIII. P. 337.

DUDLEY STUART to BEAUMONT, T.W., 27 September 1849. Harrowby MSS. Vol. XXVIII. P. 1.

DUDLEY STUART to ESZTERHÁZY, 15 February 1852. O.SZ.K. Pulszky Coll.

DUDLEY STUART to NEWMAN, 7 September 1853. O.SZ.K. Pulszky Coll.

DUDLEY STUART to PALMERSTON, 16 April 1850. N.R.A. P.P. GC/ST/140-3.

DUDLEY STUART to PALMERSTON, 21 April 1850. N.R.A. P.P. GC/ST/141/1.

DUDLEY STUART to PALMERSTON, 18 May 1850. Copy. Harrowby MSS. Vol. 453. Section 13. P. 154-6.

Exchange of letters between DUDLEY STUART and PALMERSTON, 29 October 1851 - 30 October 1851. Harrowby MSS. Vol. 453. Unpublished sources, section 13, P. 219-21. (See: Appendix 3.).

DUDLEY STUART to LORD PALMERSTON, 3 January 1852. Copy. Harrowby MSS. Vol. 453. Section 13. P. 224.

DUDLEY STUART to PULSZKY, 9 March 1849; 10 March 1849. O.SZ.K. Pulszky Coll.

EXECUTIONS AND PUNISHMENTS, 1849. Harrowby MSS. Vol. XXVIII. P. 338-9.

HORNER, S. Escape of Mr. Pulszky taken from memory of his relation . . . by Miss Susan Horner. O.SZ.K. E.MSS. Quarto 5.

HUNGARY LIST OF MEMORIALS, (1849). Copy. Harrowby MSS. Vol. 453. f.214, 216.

HUNGARY MEMORANDA, 1849. N.R.A. P.P. MM/HU/1.

HUNGARY MEMORANDA, 3 September 1849. N.R.A. P.P. MM/HU/2.

HUNGARY MEMORANDA, 24 November 1849. N.R.A. P.P. MM/HU/3.

KOSSUTH to BLACK, Adam. National Library of Scotland. Adam Black MSS. 3713.

KOSSUTH to DUDLEY STUART, 15 April 1853. Harrowby MSS. 4th Series. Vol. 1062. P. 305-6.

KOSSUTH to PULSZKY, 26 February 1849. O.L. Vörös Collection. No. 1351/b.

LOFTUS to MALMESBURY, 29 March 1859. P.R.O. F.O. 7. 568.

MALMESBURY to BUOL, 28 March 1859. P.R.O. F.O. 7. 567.

MAZZINI: loan for purchase of arms. Report. P.R.O. H.O. 45.3272.

METROPOLITAN POLICE OFFICE to WADDINGTON, Home Office. Report. P.R.O. H.O. 45. O.S. 3518.

NESSELRODE MEMORANDA, 1849. Copy. N.R.A. P.P. GC/NE/2.

NUGENT, Lord to DUDLEY STUART, 12 August 1849. Harrowby MSS. Vol. XXVI P. 207-10.

NEWMAN to PULSZKY, 1849; 1850; 9 May 1850: 1 November 1850; September 1851; 18 October 1851; "Beck affair" 1852; October 1853; 1854; 1 January 1854; 28 August 1854; 2 December 1854; 24 January 1855; 25 August 1855; 1 September 1855; 16 September, 22 September 1856; 5 October 1857; 9 October 1857; 26 July 1858; 24 December 1858; 1859; 28 June 1859; 12 July 1859; 23 July 1859; 28 July 1859; 8 August 1859; 15 December 1859; 1860; 5 October 1860; 22 December 1868; 1887; O.SZ.K. - U.C.L.

NEWMAN to Mrs. PULSZKY, 9 January 1850. O.SZ.K. - U.C.L.

PALMERSTON to DUDLEY STUART, 21 May 1850. Copy. Harrowby MSS. Vol. 453. Section 13. P. 157-9.

PALMERSTON to DUDLEY STUART, 21 May 1850. Copy. N.R.A. P.P. GC/ST/146.

PALMERSTON to DUDLEY STUART, 10 January 1852. Copy. Harrowby MSS. Vol. 453. Section 13. P. 227.

PALMERSTON to MAGENIS, 2 July 1849. P.R.O. F.O. 7. 364.

PALMERSTON to PONSONBY, 21 January 1849. Copy. N.R.A. P.P. GC/PO/825/1.

PALMERSTON to PONSONBY, 20 March 1849. P.R.O. F.O. 7. 363.

PALMERSTON to PONSONBY, 28 March 1849. Copy. N.R.A. P.P. GC/PO/829.

PALMERSTON to PONSONBY, 4 April 1849. Copy. N.R.A. P.P. GC/PO/830.

PALMERSTON to PONSONBY, 1 August 1849. Draft. P.R.O. F.O. 7. 364. (cf. N.R.A. P.P. GC/PO/432.)

PALMERSTON to PONSONBY. F.O. 2 August 1849. N.R.A. P.P. GC/PO/833/1-3. (See: Appendix 1.) (cf. Draft 104. P.R.O. F.O. 7. 364.)

PALMERSTON to PONSONBY, 22 August 1849. N.R.A. P.P. GC/PO/834.

PALMERSTON to PONSONBY, 25 August 1849. Copy. N.R.A. P.P. GC/PO/835.

PALMERSTON to PONSONBY, 31 August 1849. Draft 119. P.R.O. F.O. 7. 364.

PALMERSTON to PONSONBY, 4 September 1849. Draft 121. P.R.O. F.O. 7. 364.

PALMERSTON to PONSONBY, 9 September 1849. Copy. N.R.A. P.P. GC/PO/836/2.

PALMERSTON to PONSONBY, 22 September 1849. Draft 132. P.R.O. F.O. 7. 364.

PALMERSTON to PONSONBY, 6 October 1849. Copy. N.R.A. P.P. GC/PO/837. (cf. Draft 142. P.R.O. F.O. 7. 364.)

PALMERSTON to PONSONBY, 11 October 1849. Copy. N.R.A. P.P. GC/PO/838.

PALMERSTON to PONSONBY, 19 October 1849. N.R.A. P.P. GC/PO/839/3.

PALMERSTON to PONSONBY, 20 October 1849. Draft 152. P.R.O. F.O. 7. 364.

PALMERSTON to PONSONBY, 23 October 1849. Copy. N.R.A. P.P. GC/PO/840.

PALMERSTON to PONSONBY, 24 October 1849. Copy. N.R.A. P.P. GC/PO/841.

PALMERSTON to PONSONBY, 6 November 1849. Draft 164. P.R.O. F.O. 7. 364.

PALMERSTON to PONSONBY, 30 November 1849. Copy. N.R.A. P.P. GC/PO/843.

PALMERSTON to WESTMORLAND, 5 April 1851. H.O. 45. O.S. 3518.

PONSONBY to PALMERSTON, 1 May 1848. N.R.A. P.P. GC/PO/569.

PONSONBY to PALMERSTON, 18 October 1848. N.R.A. P.P. GC/PO/538/2.

PONSONBY to PALMERSTON, 10 December 1848. N.R.A. P.P. GC/ PO/588/1.

PONSONBY to PALMERSTON, 7 January 1849. P.R.O. F.O. 7. 365.

PULSZKY to CHARLES II Braunschweig. Bibliotheque publique et universitaire Geneve. MSS. Bruns. 35.

PULSZKY to FORSTER. London,/undated/. Myers Catalogue, No. 6. Spring 1967.

PULSZKY to KOSSUTH, 30 July 1850; 6 October 1851. O.L. K.H.

PULSZKY to NEWMAN. 28 May 1852; 20 October 1852; "House," "The Crimes of Austria", "Correcting Proofs" (1853); February 1853; 9 February 1853; Summer 1853; Spring 1854; 18 July 1859; (1860); 9 July 1862; 24 October 1866. O.SZ.K. - U.C.L.

PULSZKY to BIRKBECK, 22 May 1849. Copy. Harrowby MSS. Cracow Xerox Volume.

PULSZKY to TOULMIN SMITH, 9 October 1849. B.P.L. Toulmin Smith Collection, Item 133/1.

PULSZKY to TOULMIN SMITH, /London/, 19 October 1849. B.P.L. Toulmin Smith Collection, 7215, Item 133/2. (See: Appendix 2).

PULSZKY to VIPAN, 10 June 1849. O.SZ.K. Pulszky Coll.

PULSZKY'S MSS. Notebook, 24 April 1859 - 29 July 1859. O.SZ.K. Quart. Hung. 2501.

PULSZKY, T. (Extracts from unpublished Diary.) O.SZ.K. MSS. 287. Oct. Germ. vol. 19. (Transcript communicated by Mrs. D. Forgács.)

RADNOR, Earl to DUDLEY STUART, 25 July 1849. Harrowby MSS. Vol. XXVI. P. 221-2.

RUSSIA MEMORANDA, /War against Russia/ 28 March 1854. Draft. N.R.A. P.P. MM/RU/20.

SLIGO, Lord to DUDLEY STUART, 21 July 1849. Harrowby MSS. Vol. XXVI. P. 282-3.

SZÉCHENYI to Lord BROUGHAM, 11 June 1836. U.C.L. Brougham Collection, 39.964.

SZULCZEWSKI, C. to DUDLEY STUART, 4 January 1850. Harrowby MSS. Vol. XXVII. P. 65-6.

TELEKI MEMORANDA /by L. Teleki with Palmerston's comments./ 1 May 1855. N.R.A. P.P. MM/AU/2.

TELEKI to BROWNE, 26 February 1849. O.L. Vörös Collection, No. 1951/a.

TOULMIN SMITH to DUDLEY STUART, 17 October 1849. B.P.L. Toulmin Smith Collection, 7215, Item 132.

TURKEY MEMORANDA, 1849. N.R.A. P.P. MM/TU/38-40.

VIPAN to PULSZKY, 3 May 1849; 6 May 1849; 14 May 1849; 8 June 1849; 11 July 1849; 16 July 1849. O.SZ.K. Pulszky Coll.

ZAMOYSKI, Count L. to DUDLEY STUART, Harrowby MSS. Vol. XXVII. P. 312-7.

II. 2. *Printed Material.*

AUTHENTIC LIFE OF LOUIS KOSSUTH . . . with a full report of his speeches delivered in England . . . to which is added His address to the people of the United States . . . London, 1851.

BACH, A. Rückblick auf die jüngste Entwicklungs-Periode Ungarns. Wien, 1857.

BECK, W. Memoiren einer Dame . . . London, 1851. 2 vol.

BECK, W. Personal adventures during the late war of independence. London, 1850. 2 vol.

BENSON, A.C. The letters of Queen Victoria. London, 1908. Vol. 2.

BENTLEY, R. The presecution and death of the Baroness von Beck. London, 1852.

CLARK, T.G. Hungary and the Hungarian struggle: three lectures. Edinburgh, 1850.

CORRESPONDENCE RESPECTING THE ASSAULT COMMITTED UPON MARSHALL HAYNAU. London, 1851.

CORRESPONDENCE RELATIVE TO THE AFFAIRS OF HUNGARY 1847-49; presented to both Houses of Parliament by command of Her Majesty, 15 August 1850. London, 1851.

CORRESPONDENCE RESPECTING REFUGEES FROM HUNGARY WITHIN THE TURKISH DOMINIONS. London, 1851. Accounts and Reports, Vol. 53.

Further CORRESPONDENCE RESPECTING THE REFUGEES FROM HUNGARY WITHIN THE TURKISH DOMINIONS . . . London, 1852.

DE GERANDO, A. De l'Esprit public en Hongrie depuis la révolution francaise. Paris, 1848.

DESPREZ, H. La révolution dans l'Europe Orientale. Paris, 1848.

DERFEL, R.J. Rhosyn Meirion; sef Pruddest wobrwyedig ar "Kossuth" . . . Rhuthym, 1853.

DERRA DE MORODA, C. A refutation... London, 1851.

EGRESSY, G. Törőkországi naplója, 1849-1850. Pest, 1851.

EŐTVŐS, J. Die Gleichberichtigung der Nationalitäten. Pest, 1850.

EŐTVŐS, J. The village notary; translated by Otto Wenckstern, with introductory remarks by F. Pulszky. London, 1850. 3 vol.

ESQUISE DE LA GUERRE EN HONGRIE. London, 1849.

GÁL, I. Kossuth's Danubian Confederation. Bp., 1944. (Source publication.)

GERANDO See: DE GERANDO.

GŐRGEI, A. Gazdátlan levelek. Pest, 1867.

HAJNAL, I. A Kossuth-emigráció Törőkországban. Bp., 1927. Fontes Historiae Hungaricae Aevi Recentioris.

HEADLEY, P.C. The life of Louis Kossuth, Governor of Hungary... with an introduction by Horace Greeley. Auburn, 1852.

HENNINGSEN, C.F. Kossuth and "The Times"... London, 1851.

HORVÁTH, Z. Teleki László, 1810-1861. Bp., 1964. 2 vol. (2nd vol. is source publication.)

HUNGARIAN ASSOCIATION, Highgate, near London, October 1849. B.P.L. Toulmin Smith Collection, 7215, Item 131. (See: Appendix 4).

IRÁNYI, D. - CHASSIN. Histoire de la révolution de Hongrie, 1847-49. II. tem. Paris, 1861.

JÁNOSSY, D. A Kossuth-emigráció Angliában és Amerikában, 1851-1852. Bp., 1940-48. 2 vol. Fontes Historiae Hungaricae Aevi Recentoris. (2nd vol. is source publication.)

JAY, W. The Kossuth excitement. New York, 1852.

KABDEBO, T. Kossuth Lajos azt üzente... IRODALMI UJSÁG, 1968. márc. 15. P. 6-7. (Exchange of letters between Kossuth, Cobden and Dudley Stuart.) (Source publication.)

KÁSZONYI, D. Ungarns fier Zeitalter... (N.p.), 1868. 4 vol.

KEMÉNY, Zs. Még egy szó a forradalom után. Bp., 1851.

KOLTAY-KASTNER, J. Mazzini e Kossuth: lettere e documenti inediti. Firenze, 1929.

KLAPKA, G. Memoirs of the war of independence in Hungary; translated by Otto Wenckstern. London, 1850.

KLAPKA, Gy. Emlékeimből; fűggelékül gr. Teleki László levelei. Bp., 1886.

KNIGHT, C. The English Encyclopaedia. London, 1854-1860. Vol. I-IV. Synoptical index, 1862./Esp. Vol. IV. articles on Hungarians contributed by Thomas Watts./

KOSSUTH e URQUHART, estrato di un corrispondenza. Londra, 1859.

KOSSUTH, L. Irataim az emigrációból; /ed. by I. Helfy and F. Kossuth/. Bp., 1891-1914. 14 vol. (Esp. Vol. 1-3, 9 and 13.)

KOSSUTH, L. Kossuth demokráciája . . . Közreadja Ács Tivadar. Bp., 1958.

KOSSUTH, L. Memories of my exile. London, 1880.

LEWITSCHNIGG. Silhuetten aus dem Nachmärz in Ungarn. Bp., 1850.

LUKÁCSY, S. Rabszolga Kossuth sirjánál: Kossuth emigránstársainak irásai Amerikából. Bp., 1953. (Source publication.)

The MANIFESTO OF THE REPUBLICAN PARTY . . . by Kossuth . . . London, 1855.

MAZZINI, G. Dei doveri dell'uomo. Milan, 1949. /1st ed. 1841-42./

MAURY, A., PULSZKY, F. and others. Indigenous races of the earth . . . Philadelphia, 1857.

NEWMAN, F.W. An appeal to the middle classes on the urgent necessity of radical reforms. London, 1848.

NEWMAN, F.W. The crimes of the House of Habsburg against its own liege subjects. London, 1853.

NEWMAN, F.W. Miscellanies. London, 1890. Vol. III.

NEWMAN, F.W. Reminiscences of two exiles /Kossuth and Pulszky/ and two wars /Crimean and Franco-Austrian./ London, 1888.

NEWMAN, F.W. Select speeches of Kossuth. London, 1853.

PAGET, J. Hungary and Transylvania. London, 1839. 2 vol.

PÁSZTOR, L. Lajos Kossuth nel suo carteggio con Adrianno Lemmi, 1851-1852. Roma, 1947. Bibliotheca Italo-Ungherese del Risorgimento, serie II.

PRIDHAM, C. Kossuth and the magyar land. London, 1851.

PULSZKY, F. Ábránd és valóság. 2nd e. Bp., 1886. Nemzeti Kvt., 40.

PULSZKY, F. A falu jegyzöje. MAGYAR SZÉPIRODALMI SZEMLE, 1847.

PULSZKY, F. Aus dem Tagebuch eines in Grossbritannien reisenden Ungarn. Pesth, 1837.

PULSZKY, F. Catalogue of the Fejérváry ivories in the Museum of Joseph Mayer, Esq. . . . preceded by an essay on antique ivories. Liverpool, 1856.

PULSZKY, F. Életem és Korom. Bp., 1880-1882. 4 vol.; 2nd ed.: Bp., 1884. 2 vol.; 3rd ed.: Bp., 1958. /Sajtó alá rendezte s a jegyzeteket irta Oltványi Ambrus./ 2 vol.

PULSZKY, F. Eszmék Magyarország története philosophiájához. Bp., 1880. /1st ed.: Bp., 1838./

PULSZKY, F. Jellemrajzok: Eötvös, Széchenyi, Deák, Dessewffy Aurél. Bp., 1888.

PULSZKY, F. Kisebb dolgozatai; sajtó alé rendezte Lábán Antal, bevezetéssel ellátta Merczali Henrik. Bp., 1914.

PULSZKY, F. On the verbal and nominal affixes in the Hungarian language. TRANSACTIONS OF THE PHILOLOGICAL SOCIETY, 1859. P. 92-124.

PULSZKY, F. Petöfi Sándor összes költeményei. MAGYAR SZÉPIRODALMI SZEMLE, 1847. P. 277-97.

PULSZKY, F. Uti vázlatok 1836-ból. In: EÖTVÖS, J. Budapesti Árvizkönyv. Köt.1. Bp., 1839. P. 70-122.

PULSZKY, F. Visszaemlékezések. BUDAPEST SZEMLE, 1884. 34 köt. P. 70-78.

Személyes leirása PULSZKY FERENCZNEK; Schlick fötábornok hirdetése. ABAUJ-KASSAI KÖZLÖNY, 1878. 46 sz. P. 2-3.

PULSZKY to COBDEN, London, 1851. SOUTH EASTERN AFFAIRS, Vol. VIII. p. 239-254. /Typescript supplied by Dr. I. Gál./

PULSZKY to KOSSUTH, 26 February 1849. NEMZET, 1884. 40 sz.

PULSZKY, F. and PULSZKY, T. White, Red and Black; sketches of society in the United States, during the visit of their guest. /L. Kossuth/ London, 1853, 3 vol.

PULSZKY, T. Three Christmas plays for children...London, 1858.

PULSZKY, T. and PULSZKY, F. Memoirs of a Hungarian lady; with a historical introduction by Francis Pulszky. London, 1850.

PULSZKY, T. and PULSZKY, F. Tales and traditions of Hungary. London, 1851. 3 vol.;/ vol.1. Popular tales and traditions of Hungary by T. Pulszky, vol. 2-3. The Jacobins in Hungary by F. Pulszky./; Separately: PULSZKY, F. The Jacobins in Hungary. Leipzig, 1851. 2 vol. In Hungarian: translated by Emil Beniczky, Pest, 1861-2; 2nd ed.: Pest, 1862. In German: Leipzig, 1851. 3 pts. Europaische Bibliothek, 507-509; 2nd ed.: Berlin, 1851. 2 vol.; 3rd ed.: Berlin, 1868. 2 vol. Shortened Hungarian version: Martinovits és társai. Pest, 1881. Olcsó Kvt. Reviewed in: FÖVÁROSI LAPOK, 1881. P. 277-89.

SCHLESINGER, M. The war in Hungary, 1848-49; translated by John Edward Taylor, edited with notes and an introduction by Francis Pulszky. London, 1850. 2 vol.

STILES, W.H. Austria in 1848-1849. New York, 1852. 2 vol.

SZÉCHENYI, I. Ein Blick auf den Anonymen Rückblick. London, 1859.

162 BIBLIOGRAPHY

SZEMERE, B. Graf Ludwig Batthyány, Arthur Görgei, Ludwig Kossuth
. . . Hamburg, 1853. 2 Vol.

TANÁRKY, Gy. Tanárky Gyula naplója, 1849-1866: a Kossuth-emigráció
szolgálatában. Bp., 1961. Magyar Századok.

TELEKI, L. The case of Hungary. London, 1849.

TELEKI, L. Question Austro-Hongroise et l'intervention Russe. Paris, 1849.

TELEKI. L. Válogatott munkái; szerkesztette Kemény G. Gábor. Bp.,
1961. 2 vol.

TESLAR, J.A. Unpublished letters of Adam Czartoryski and W. Janoski
. . . SLAVONIC AND EAST EUROPEAN REVIEW, Vo. 29. December
1958. P. 153-76.

THUN, L. Briefwechzel zwischen Leo Grafen von Thun und Franz von
Pulszky. VIERTELJAHRSCHRIFT AUS UND FÜR UNGARN, 1843.
Vol. I, 2., II, 1.

TOULMIN SMITH, J. The facts of the case of the pretended "Baroness
von Beck". . . London, 1852.

TÓTH, L. La Societé Hongroise de Presov. REVUE D'HISTOIRE COM-
PARÉE, XXV, Tom. V. No. 3. P. 50-59.

VERESS, S. A magyar emigratió a Keleten. Bp., 1878. 2 vol.

VÉRTESSI, J. Teleki László levelei Pulszky Ferenchez, 1849-51. IROD-
ALOMTÖRTÉNETI KÖZLEMÉNYEK, 1917. 2 füzet P. 217. - 3
füzet P. 313.

WAGNER, M. The tricolor on the Atlas, or Algeria and the French conquest;
from the German of Dr. Wagner and other sources by F. Pulszky.
London, 1854.

WALDAPFEL, E. A forradelom és szabadságharc levelestára, 1848-49.
Bp., 1950-65. 4 vol.

WENCKSTERN, O. History of the war in Hungary in 1848 and in 1849.
London, 1859.

III. SECONDARY SOURCES.

ÁCS, T. A genovai lázadás. Bp., 1968.

ÁCS, T. Magyarok az északamerikai polgárháboruban. Bp., 1964.

ANKERL, G. Képrombolás. . . IRODALMI UJSÁG, 1965. jun. 15.

ANDICS, E. Habsburgek és Romanovok szövetságe: az 1849 évi magyarországi cári intervenció elötörténete. Bp., 1961. (Reviewed by L. Péter

in: SLAVONIC AND EAST EUROPEAN REVIEW, December 1964.
P. 216-220.)

BAILEY, T. A diplomatic history of the American people. New York, 195o.

BELLOT, H. Hale. University College London, 1826-1926. London, 1929.

CONCHA, Gy. Emlékbeszéd Pulszky Ferenc fölött. Bp., 1903.

CONCHA, Gy. Pulszky Ferenc: élet és jellemrajz. Bp., /1903/.

DASENT, A.I. John Thaddeus Delane, Editor of the Times. . . London, 1908. Vol. 1.

DICTIONARY OF AMERICAN BIOGRAPHY. New York, 1928-36. 20 vol.

DICTIONARY OF NATIONAL BIOGRAPHY. London, 1885-1900. 63 vol. + suppt. vol. 1-3. /1901./

ENTREVES, A.P. d' The notion of the state. Oxford, 1967.

1848-1948 centenáris kiállitás. Bp., 1948.

FERENCZY, J. Pulszky Ferencz életrajza. Pozsony, /1897./ (With some primary material: letters of PULSZKY to KOSSUTH.)

FEST, S. Links between England and Hungary. HUNGARIAN QUARTERLY, vol. 2. 1936. P. 106-114.

FEST, S. Political and spiritual ties between England and Hungary. HUNGARIAN QUARTERLY, Vol. 1. 1936. P. 72-78.

GÁL, I. Arnold and Swinburne magyar tárgyú szonettjei. FILOLOGIAI KÖZLÖNY, 1967. 1-2. P. 84-101.

GÁL, I. Kossuth, America and the Danubian Confederation. HUNGARIAN QUARTERLY, Vol. 6. 1940. P. 417-433.

GRACZA, Gy. Kossuth Lajos élete és müködése. Bp., 1893.

HAJNAL, I. A Batthyány-Kormány külpolitikája. Bp., 1957. Értekezések a történettudományok köréböl. Uj. sorozat, 1.

HARASZTI, É. Az angol külpolitika a magyar szabadságharc ellen. Bp., 1951. (With source publications.)

HOBSON, J.A. Richard Cobden:the international man; 2nd ed. introduced by Neville Masterman. London, 1968. (With some primary material; letters of COBDEN to DUDLEY STUART.)

HOL LAKOTT LONDONBAN KOSSUTH? NEMZETI UJSÁG, 1935. Ápr. 6. XVII evf. 79 sz. P. 9.

HORVÁTH, J. A londoni magyar propaganda bizottság 1849-ban. BUDAPESTI SZEMLE, 1936. Vol. 242, P. 129-153.

HORVÁTH, J. Gróf Széchen Antal londoni küldetése 1849-ban. BUDAPESTI SZEMLE, 1937. Vol. 244, P. 364-7.

HORVÁTH, J. Kossuth and Palmerston, 1848-1849. SLAVONIC AND EAST EUROPEAN REVIEW, 1930-1. Vol. IX. P. 612-27.

HORVÁTH, J. Magyar diplomácia, 1815-1818. Bp., 1928.

HORVÁTH, M. Magyarország függetlenségi harcának története. Genf, 1865. 3 vol.

IVÁNYI, B.G. The working classes of Britain and the Eastern European Revolutions. SLAVONIC AND EASTERN EUROPEAN REVIEW, Vol. 26. P. 107-24.

JÁNOSSY, D. Die ungarische Emigration und der Krieg im Orient. Bp., 1935. Archivum Europae Centro-Orientalis, tom. V.

JÁNOSSY, D. Great Britain and Kossuth. /With Appendix./ Bp., 1937. Archivum Europae Centro-Orientalis, tom. III. fasc. 1-4. P. 53-190. (With Primary material in the Appendix.)

JÁSZAY, M. L'Italia e la rivoluzione ungherese, 1848-49. Bp., 1948. Biblioteca della Revue d'Histoire Comparée, VII.

JÁSZI, O. Magyarország jövöje és a Dunai Egyesült Államok. Bp., 1918.

JONES, Mrs. M. Wales and Hungary: a lecture given to the Cymmrodorion Society on 23 April 1968.

JONES, Mrs. M. Wales and Hungary: a talk. /Unpublished typescript of BBC transmission, 24 February 1957. 3.45-4.00 p.m./

KABDEBO, T. A legkozmopolitább nacionalista. /Pulszky Ferenc/ IROD-ALMI UJSÁG, 1964. szept. 15. P. 10-11.

KABDEBO, T. Igazság a legföbb illedelem. (Review of "László Teleki" by Z. Horváth.) IRODALMI UJSÁG, 1965. márc. 15. P. 6-7.

KOLTAY-KASTNER, J. A Kossuth-emigráció Olaszországban. Bp., 1960.

KOSÁRY, D. Kossuth Lajos a reformkorban, Bp., 1946.

KOSÁRY, D. Nationalisme et internacionalisme dans l'histoire des peuples danubiens. REVUE D'HISTOIRE COMPARÉE, tom. V. No. 3. P. 3-21.

KROPF, L. Memoir and letters of Francis W. Newman. By I. Giberne Sieveking. (Review) ERDÉLYI MUZEUM, 1912. VII évf. XXIX köt. P. 100-101.

KURAT, Y.T. The European Powers and the question of the Hungarian refugees. London, 1958. Ph. D. Thesis. (Typescript.)

LAUTERPACHT, H. Oppenheimers International Law; 6th ed. London, 1947. Vol. 1.

LENGYEL, T. The first Hungarian minister in London. HUNGARIAN QUARTERLY, Vol. 6. 1940. P. 82-94.

LENGYEL, T. The Hungarian exiles and the Danubian Confederation. HUNGARIAN QUARTERLY, Vol. 5. 1939. P. 450-461.

LENGYEL, T. Hungarians and the Crimean War. HUNGARIAN QUARTERLY, Vol. 5. 1939. P. 99-107.

LENGYEL, T. Teleki László. Bp., /n.d./

LUKÁCS, L., (and others). Kossuth Lajos. Bp., 1952.

MAGYAR IRODALMI LEXIKON; föszerkesztö Benedek Marcell. Bp., 1963-65. 3 vol.

MAGYAR NEMZETISÉGI ZSEBKÖNYV. Pest, 1861.

MAGYAR TÖRTÉNETI BIBLIOGRÁFIA; szerkesztette Tóth Zoltán. Bp., 1953. 3 vol.

MARCZALI, H. Pulszky a tudományban és a közéletben. Bp., 1914.

MOMIGLIANO, A. Da G.G. Zerffi a Sau-Ma Chien. RIVISTA STORICA ITALIANA, anno LXXVI, fasc. IV. P. 1058-1069.

MORLEY, J. The life of William Ewart Gladstone. London, 1903. 3 vol.

PEÉRY, R. Carl Schurz, londoni fogadáson Kossuth Lajosnál. IRODALMI UJSÁG, 1964 november 15. P. 4.

PÉTER, L. A magyar nacionalizmus. In: ESZMÉK NYOMÁBAN. München, 1965. P. 188-224.

PÉTER, L. The antecedents of the 19th c. Hungarian state concept. D.Phil. Thesis. Oxford, 1965. (Typescript.)

PETRIE, Sir Charles. The historical relations of England and Hungary. HUNGARIAN QUARTERLY, Vol. 3. 1937.

PULSZKY FERENC KÉZIRATAI. Article in : MAGYAR KÖNYV-SZEMLE, 1889-1890.

QUINTAVALLE, F. Storia dell'Unitá Italiana. Milano, 1926.

RANK AND TALENT OF THE TIMES. London, 1861.

ROBBINS, W. The Newman brothers: an essay in comparative intellectual biography. London, 1966.

SPROXTON, C. Palmerston and the Hungarian revolution: a dissertation. Cambridge, 1919.

SZABAD, Gy. A forradalom és a kiegyezés utján 1860-1861. Bp., 1967. (Reviewed in Times Literary Supplement, 14 November 1968, by Neville Masterman.)

SZABAD, Gy. Kossuth and the British "Balance of power" policy 1859-1861. Bp., 1960. Studia Historica Academiae Scientiarum Hungaricae 34.

SZENTKIRÁLYI, J. Magyar költemények angol forditásban. Bp., 1943. (Kölönlenyomat az "Angol filológiai tanulmányok" IV. kötetböl.)

SZILASSY, S. America and the Hungarian Revolution of 1848-1849.

SLAVONIC AND EAST EUROPEAN REVIEW, Vol. 44. January 1966. P. 180-196.

SZINNYEI, J. Magyar irók élete és munkái. Bp., 1891-1914. 14 vol. (Esp. Vol. 9.)

TESLAR, J.A. Biographical notes. Harrowby MSS. Vol. 451. Section 5. (Typescript.)

I. TÓTH, Z. Balcescu Miklós élete. Bp., 1958.

VAS, Z. Kossuth in England. NEW HUNGARIAN QUARTERLY, Vol. IX. 1968. P. 132-141.

WALDAPFEL, E. A független magyar külpolitika 1848-1849. Bp., 1962.

WALPOLE, S. The life of Lord John Russell. London, 1891. Vol. II.

NOTES

Notes to Introduction.

1. SZÉCHENYI papers, relative to his English voyages, O.L.

2. FEST, S. Links between England and Hungary. Hungarian Quarterly, Vol. 2, 1936. P. 106.; according to Dániel Székely of the Academy, Jeremy Bentham had not become a member of this learned body. (Communicated on 29 October 1968 from Budapest.)

3. The Correspondence of J. Bentham, Vol. 2: 1778-80. London, 1968. P. 333, 385, 389, 394, 421, 479.

4. Letter from Count I. Széchenyi to Lord Brougham, 11 June 1836. U.C.L. Brougham Collection, 39.964.

5. HORVÁTH, J. Magyar diplomácia, 1815-1918. Bp., 1928. P. 1.

6. "Kimüvelt emberfök sokaságát" akarta Magyarországon - untranslatable; paraphrasable as: *he wanted many people with a cultivated and open mind in Hungary.* For recent publications on Széchenyi consult: BARANY, A. Stephen Széchenyi and the awakening of Hungarian nationalism 1791-1841. Princeton, 1968; "Széchenyi, István." A Magyar Tudomágyar Akadémia Történeti Föbizottsága... tézisei...[szeakesztő Barta István]. Társadalmi Szemle XV, 30-55. (1960) *and* SPIRA, Gy. A Hungarian Count in the Revolution of 1848. Budapest, 1972.

7. PAGET, J. Hungary and Transylvania. London, 1839. Vol. II. P. 469-470.

8. BLACKWELL, A.J. Missions I-VI. Unpublished MSS. in the archives of M.T.A.

9. Correspondence, 1847-49. P. 64.

10. IRÁNYI, D.-CHASSIN. Histoire de la revolution de Hongrie, 1847-49. II. tom. Paris, 1860. Tom. I. P. 471. Count Latour addressing Pulszky on 2 August 1848 referred to "das königlish ungarische Ministerium des Aussern". HAJNAL, I. A Batthyány kormány külpolitikája. Bp., 1957. p.20.

11. HÁBORÚS FELELÖSSÉG. 1929 január. A Szabadságharc magyar diplomáciai levelei, 1848-49. Szemere pótutasitásai Szalayhoz...P. 267-8.

12. HORVÁTH, Z. Teleki László. Bp., 1964. Vol. 1. P. 206-7.

13. HORVÁTH, J. Kossuth and Palmerston. Slavonic Review, 1930-1. P. 616.

14. Correspondence, 1847-49. Item No. 78.

15. Ibid. No. 79.

16. Ibid. No. 80.

17. Lord Eddisbury: Stanley, Edward John, second baron Stanley of Alderley (1802-1869) was Under-Secretary for Foreign Affairs from 1846-52. (B.N.B.) cf. SPROXTON, C. Palmerston and the Hungarian revolution. Cambridge, 1919. P. 45.

18. Correspondence, 1847-49. Item. No. 82.

Notes to Chapter One.

1. HARASZTI, E. Az angol külpolitika a magyar szabadságharc ellen. Bp., 1951. P. 88.

2. HORVÁTH, J. Magyar diplomácia, 1815-1918. Bp., 1928. P. 39; HAJNAL, I.A. Batthyány kormány külpolitikája. Bp., 1957. P. 41.

3. WALDAPFEL, E. A független magyar külpolitika. Bp., 1962. P. 239.

4. PULSZKY, F. Életem és korom. Bp., 1880-2. 4 vols.; the present writer used the 3rd ed.: Életem és korom; sajtó alá rendszte... Oltványi Ambrus. Bp., 1958. 2 vol. (Abbreviated as É-K.). (Henceforth referred to as Memoirs).

5. Rand and talent of the times, published by Griffin and Co., London, 1861.

6. B.M. Add. MSS. 28,511. ff. 317-18.

7. Pulszky's family belonged to the Upper range of the Hungarian middle-nobility: *Lubócz* and *Cselfalva* being the family estates. Ferencz Pulszky was the son of Károly Pulszky - whose great grandfather Samuel Pulszky obtained Hungarian nobility on 13 September 1741 - and of Apollónia Fejérváry. SZINNYEI, Vol. IX, P. 221.; MAGYAR NEMZET-ISEGI ZSEBKÖNYV Nemes családok. Bp., 1905. P. 524.

8. PULSZKY, F. Aus dem tagebuche eines in Grossbritannien raisenden Ungarn. Pesth, 1837.

9. PULSZKY, F. Úti vázlatok 1836-ból. In: EÖTVÖS, J. Budapesti Árvizkönyv. köt. I. 1939. P. 70-122.

10. In É-K. Vol. I. P. 150. Pulszky relates that his election was due to a successful bet between his uncle, G. Féjerváry and the mayor of Sáros. The county of Sáros was somewhat like an English pocket-borough before the reform - still, Vipan, and English archaeologist, who visited the Pulszky estates in 1839 found that the Hungarian elections were more civilised than those in Ireland. (E-K. Vol. I. P. 142.).

11. Reform politician. (1809-1882).

12. "As secretary of the Committee he consulted Mittelmayer on a visit to Heidelberg, and the excellent scholar of criminal law approved of his contribution . . ." SZINNYEI, Vol. IX. P. 224; CONCHA, Gy. Emlékbeszéd Pulszky fölött. Bp., 1903. P. 26.

13. Palatine Archduke Stephen=István Főherceg, Palatine of Hungary in 1847-48.

14. Count L. Batthyány (1806-1849) was the leader of opposition then the first Prime Minister of Independent Hungary. He was executed by the Austrians on 6 October 1849. cf. PULSZKY, T. and F. Memoirs of a Hungarian lady . . . London, 1850. Vol. 2. P. 358-9.

15. Prince Paul Eszterházy (1805-1877) was Hungarian Minister to the King's person, thus virtually Hungary's Foreign Minister in 1848. HAJNAL, I. A Batthyány kormány külpolitikája. Bp., 1957. P. 28.

16. Hajnal refers to Pulszky's manifold diplomatic activities in Vienna. His tasks were: a) to help normalise contacts with other nationalities, b) endeavours to gain England's friendship, c) manouvres to get all Hungarian soldiers back from Austria's Italian campaign, d) to find out whether the Czar was behind the Serb's revolt, e) to investigate the possibility of a German alliance, f) to investigate the possibilities of sending an ambassador to Paris. (HAJNAL, I. A Batthyány kormány külpolitikája. Bp., 1957. P. 20, 34, 45, 67, 82, 116.)

17. Jellashich, Joseph. (1801-1859). Imperial general of Croatian origin and Ban of Croatia. He led an expeditionary force against Hungary, at the instigation of Count Latour, the Austrian Minister of War. Pulszky intercepted the despatches of Latour, sent an alarm to the Hungarian Parliament, whereupon a Hungarian force met and defeated Jellashich's army on 29 September 1848 near Sukoro. HEADLEY, P.C. The Life of Louis Kossuth . . . Auburn, 1852. P. 121. DIARY, Vol. 2. P. 399.

18. BEM. Joseph. (1795-1850). Took part in the Polish revolution of 1830, the defence of Vienna in 1848, the Hungarian war of independence in 1849, and finally emigrated to Turkey. He became a Hungarian general on Pulszky's recommendations. DIARY. Vol. I. P. 201.

19. Orders for Pulszky's arrest: a) Schlick fötábornok hirdetése. Kossuth Lajosnak, Pulszky Ferencznek, Petőfi Sándornak személyes leirása. In: Abaúj Kassai Közlöny, 1878, 46sz.; b) Imperial Court Martial, Pest, május 6. 1852. (E-K. Vol. II. P. 113-115).

20. BEZERÉDY, István. (1795-1865).

21. BEÖTHY, Ödön. (1796-1864). Hungarian Consul to Bucarest.

22. É-K. Vol. I. P. 464.

23. Ibid. P. 566.

24. Ibid. P. 480.

25. FERENCZY, József. Pulszky Ferencz életrajza. Bp., Pozsony, 1897.

26. Op. cit. Vol. 9. P. 225.

27. O.SZ.K.E. MSS. Quarto 5. Escape of Mr. Pulszky taken from memory of his relation . . . by Miss Susan Horner.

28. KNIGHT, C. The English Cyclopaedia, London, 1854, Vol. IV. P. 1012.

29. 10 July 1858.

30. HORVÁTH, J. Magyar diplomácia. . . Bp., 1928. P. 44.; Kossuth and Palmerston. . . Slavonic Review, 1930-31. Vol. 9. P. 617.

31. The letters of Teleki to Browne, and of Kossuth to Pulszky on the appointment, are in the VÖRÖS Collection, in the Hungarian National Archives. No. 1351/a and b.

32. É-K. Vol. I. P. 487.

33. K-e T. = HAJNAL, I. A Kossuth—emigráció' Törökországban. Bp., 1927. Fontes Historiae Hungariacae Aevi Recentoris.

34. K-e A. = JÁNOSSY, D. A Kossuth—emigráció Angliában és Amerikában, 1851-52. Bp., 1940-48. 2 Vol. Fontes Historiae Hungaricae Aevi Recentoris.

35. HARASZTI, E. Az angol külpolitika a magyar szabadságharc ellen. Bp., 1951. P. 88-89.

36. É-K. Vol. I. P. 15. (Introduction).

37. HORVÁTH, Z. Teleki László,1810-1861. Bp., 1964. Vol. I. P. 244-5.

38. WALDAPFEL, E. A független magyar külpolitika, 1848-49. Bp., 1962. P. 122-7.

39. The two versions: i) "1848 deczemberre nem emlékeztettelek Soha. Erre, jöhet idö, midön emlékeztetni foglak." KOSSUTH, L. Itataim az emigrációból. Bp., 1882. Vol. III. P. 543-4. ii) "1848 végén nehéz körülmények közt elhagytál - soha nem emlékeztettelek rá. Erre, jöhet idö, hogy emlékeztetni foglak." TANÁRKY, Gy. A Kossuth - emigráció szolgálatában: Tanárky Gyula naplója, 1849-1866. Bp., 1961. P. 226.

40. A HON. Esti kiadás. 1868 dec. 29, 30.

41. SZEMERE, B. Graf Ludwig Batthyány, Arthur Görgei, Ludwig Kossuth. . . Hamburg, 1853. Vol. II. P. 146-152.

42. 1848-1948 Centenáris Kiállítás. Bp., 1948. P. 64. Copies of both the 'official' authorisation dated 18 May 1849 and the Hungarian Foreign Minister's private letter to Pulszky dated 14 May 1849 were on public view in case 16 of this exhibition. For the *originals* of.: P.R.O. F.O. Turkey, Vol. 375. and JÁNOSSY, D. Great Britain and Kossuth. Bp., 1937. Appendix I.

43. Ibid. P. 65.

44. É-K. Vol. I. P. 488-9.

45. It was probably Sandford who recommended Pulszky to Forster. Undated letter of John Forster to William Sandford. MYERS CATALOGUE, No. 6. Spring, 1967.

46. Pulszky's wife, Theresa Walter, was a childhood friend of Lady Louise Howard, Lord Lansdowne's daughter. Pulszky's mother-in-law, Mrs. Walter, sent a letter of recommendation to the Lansdowne family, and later she herself visited them on several occasions. É-K. Vol. I. P. 489.

47. É-K. Vol. I. P. 490.

48. T.C. BANFIELD was a London lawyer and journalist; both letters are in the O.SZ.K. Pulszky Coll. and were referred to by Hajnal. K-e. T. P. 83.

49. Correspondence, 1847-49. No. 132. Zoltán Horváth (Teleki László, Bp., 1964. Vol. I. P. 244) was mistaken in believing that this letter was sent by Kossuth to Pulszky, and that it was a letter of authorisation.

50. DAILY NEWS, 3 March 1849.

51. Dudley Stuart sent word to Pulszky on 30 April that Palmerston was expecting him on the next day. K-e. T. P. 85.

52. Correspondence, 1847-49. P. 197.

53. É-K. Vol. I. P. 580.

54. Correspondence relative, 1847-49. P. 255-6. The date given here, as the date of issue, is - curiously enough - 14 April 1849.

55. Waldapfel (op. cit.) P. 208-210, gives the Hungarian text and its English and French translations.

56. ANDICS, E. Habsburgok és Romanovok szövetsége: az 1849 évi Magyarországi cári intervenció elötörténete. Bp., 1961. Reviewed by L. Péter: Slavonic and East European Review, December, 1964. P. 216-220.

57. In the second half of March Teleki handed in a memorandum to Broyn de l'Huys about the dangers of the Russian intervention; on 1 May he had an interview with the French Foreign Minister; on 12 and on 25 May he questioned Tocqueville on the Russian intervention, who gave evasive answers. HARASZTI op. cit.; TELEKI, L. The case of Hungary. London, 1849.

58. HÁBORÚS FELELÖSSÉG. Vol. I. P. 518-9.

59. Ibid. P. 520.

60. P.R.O. F.O.7. Vol. 363. Draft No. 59.

61. N.R.A.P.P. GC/PO/825/. Palmerston to Ponsonby, 21 January 1849. Copy.

62. N.R.A.P.P. GC/PO/830. Palmerston to Ponsonby, 4 April 1849. Copy.

63. N.R.A.P.P. GC/PO/574/4. Ponsonby to Palmerston, 16 June 1848.

64. N.R.A.P.P. GC/PO/588/1.

65. P.R.O. F.O.7. Vol. 364. Palmerston to Magenis, 2 July 1849. Draft 29.

66. 11 May 1849. K-e.T. P. 85.

67. O.SZ.K. Pulszky Coll. Vipan to Pulszky, 6 May 1849. According to Vipan: "Lord P. is very well disposed to act against Russia, but he does not, from want of English support *etc.*"

68. HANSARD, Vol. 105. P. 326.

69. Ibid. Vol. 107. P. 785-6.

70. Daily News, No. 986. 24 July 1849.

71. Ibid. No. 988. 26 July 1849.

72. P.R.O. F.O.7. Vol. 364. Palmerston to Ponsonby, 1 August 1849. Draft, 102. cf. N.R.A. P.P. GC/PO/831/1-3.

73. P.R.O. F.O.7. Vol. 364. Palmerston to Ponsonby. Draft 103. cf. N.R.A. P.P. GC/PO/432.

74. *See:* Appendix I.

75. 10 July 1849. (É-K. Vol. I. P. 545-7).

76. K-e. A. Vol. I. P. 52.

77. Daily News, 26 February 1849; e.g. 21 February news under the general headings: Germany and Austria. From June onwards, the paper had a correspondent in Hungary.

78. Ibid. 12 February 1849.

79. Ibid. 3 March 1849.

80. Ibid. 8 March 1849.

81. Vipan to Pulszky, 3 May 1849. O.SZ.K. Pulszky Coll.

82. Ibid. Vipan to Pulszky, 6 May 1849.

83. HORVÁTH, J. A londoni magyar propaganda-bizottság 1849-ben. Budapesti Szemle. 1936. Vol. 242, P. 129-153.

84. Daily News, 9 May 1849.

85. Pulszky's style could be detected in the following unsigned article in the Daily News: "A letter from Vienna" (7 May); "the Hungarian Declaration of Independence" (9 May); "Austria. . . .-from the Wiener Zeitung, Lloyd" (23 May); "Private letters" (30 May).

86. Vipan to Pulszky, 14 May 1849. O.SZ.K. Pulszky Coll.

87. Boldényi, J. *pseud.* (i.e. Pál SZABÓ). La Hongrie en 1848. Paris, 1848.

88. GÉRANDO, August de. De l'esprit public en Hongrie depuis la révolution francaise. Paris, 1848.

89. TELEKI, L. Question Austro-Hongroise et l'intervention Russe. Paris, 1849.

90. MINUTES OF the Hungarian Propaganda Committee, 1849. O.SZ.K. Pulszky Coll. Published in extracted form by J. Horváth. Budapesti Szemle. 1936. Vol. 242, P. 129-153.

91. Birkbeck had tackled Pulszky on this question and Pulszky replied on 22 May 1849. "From Travellers Club." "My dear Birkbeck, Vipan wrote me you want to know if the Hungarian notes have any value in London, what discount? The hungarian notes are not in circulation out of Hungary except Vienna where they are at present taken at 98% against *American paper*, the silver is at present, so as the foreign devisa's 27%. In Hungary, the Hungarian notes are in fact worth (al pari), the Austrian notes at 98." HARROWBY, MSS. Cracow Xerox Volume. Copy. (N.B. Pulszky's orthographical and stylistic faults are retained here as well as elsewhere in the quotations).

92. DAILY NEWS, 11 June 1849.

93. Ibid. 26 July 1849.

94. Vipan to Pulszky, 8 June 1849. O.SZ.K. Pulszky Coll.

95. Ibid. Pulszky to Vipan, 10 June 1849.

96. i.c. Csernátony.

97. cf. p. 59.

98. John Edward Taylor, proprietor of a private press, was a liberal and a friend of the Hungarians.

99. This was Pulszky's second trip to Paris since the end of February. He failed to meet Tocqueville and returned immediately.

100. *Examiner* 7, 14, 21, 25 July 1849. In the last number (p. 451) Vipan wrote: "if through Russian aid Austria be victorious, the last barrier is swept away from the road to Constantinople"- thus forcing the Crimean War.

101. On the same day, an article by Pulszky on the Russian intervention appeared in the *Globe*. The next day Colloredo complained to Schwarzenberg that Austria was attacked even in Palmerston's own paper. (HORVÁTH, J. Kossuth and Palmerston. Slavonic Review, 1930-1. P. 625).

102. LENGYEL, T. Teleki László. Bp., (n.d.) P. 98.

103. Vipan to Pulszky, 11 July 1849. O.SZ.K. Pulszky Coll.

104. Birkbeck expressed his satisfaction, that the Times' "Hungarian" had not replied to Pulszky's challenge to produce evidence against Kossuth's private life, nor did he publish a list of Hungarian officers serving in the Austrian army to which he alluded in his article of 10 July. (Birkbeck to Pulszky, 20 July. O.SZ.K. Pulszky Coll.).

105. Ibid. Vipan to Pulszky, 16 July 1849.

106. Pulszky fought against the further accusations of the anonymous writer in 21 August issue of the Daily News.

107. 30 September, 1, 8, 17, 20 October, 2, 21 November, 6, 10, 15, 22 & 25 December 1849. (HORVÁTH, J. Gróf Széchen Antal londoni küldetése 1849-ban. Budapesti Szemle, 1937. Vol. 244. P. 364-7).

108. Article 10/1790 under Leopold II. sanctioned upon oath by the King, that Hungary was a free and independent country with regards to its government, and not subordinate to any other state or people whatever, consequently that it was to be governed by its own customs and laws. cf. Declaration relative to the separation of Hungary from Austria. DIARY, Vol. II. P. 307-8.

109. August Gottlieb Wimmer (1793-1863), protestant theologian was Kossuth's first agent to visit England in the summer of 1848; he returned to London in July 1849.

Notes to Chapter Two.

1. K-e.A. Vol. I. P. 52.

2. É-K Vol. I. P. 550-553; HARASZTI, op. cit. P. 93. Sproxton, op. cit. P. 74-75.

3. HORVÁTH, M. Magyarország függetlenségi harcának története. Genf, 1865. Vol. III. P. 517-8.

4. Correspondence, 1847-49. No. 298 and Enclosures.

5. Daily News, No. 1003.

6. Ibid. No. 1004.

7. Report from the Manchester Examiner in Daily News, No. 1006. P. 2.

8. Ibid. No. 1007. 17 August 1849.

9. Sympathy-meetings are reported by the Daily News: 31 August - Hammersmith; 12 September - Norwich; 9 October - London Tavern; 11 October - Bristol.

10. Kiss, Aulich, Damjanich, Nagy S., Török, Lahner, Vécsey, Pöltenberg, Count Leiningen, Schweidel, Dessewffy, Knezich, Lázár.

11. HORVÁTH, Z. Teleki László. Bp., 1964. Vol. I. P. 300.

12. É-K. Vol. I. P. 510.

13. Teleki to Pulszky. Paris, 2 May 1849. É-K. Vol. I. P. 516.

14. Illustrated London News, 21 July 1849.

15. KLAPKA, Gy. Emlékeimböl. Bp., 1886. P. 293.

16. Pulszky refers to the same address as "Saint-Petersburgh place". É-K. Vol. II. P. 11; KLAPKA, Gy. op. cit. P. 294.

17. Daily News. No. 984. "HUNGARIAN REFUGEES AT FOLKSTONE."

18. É-K. Vol. II. P. 13.

19. TANÁRKY, P. 26.

20. Assoc. of the Hung. Political Exiles. Minutes. 2506. Quart. Hung., 102.

21. From the autumn of 1849 to June 1850, Teleki was chairman in Paris.

22. Klapka, (op. cit. P. 298), compares the Hungarian exiles to the English emigrants in Holland, as they were portrayed in Macaulay's History of England, hoping, planning, intriguing against James II.

23. É-K. Vol. II. P. 18-19; K-e.A. Vol. I. P. 80.

24. É-K. Vol. II. P. 14.

25. The connection between the German emigrant paper and the Hungarian was pointed out to me by Dr. T. Dénes of Geneva, in a private letter dated 28 March 1968.

26. For notes on Szulczewski: HARROWBY MSS. Vol. 451. Section V. Biographical notes by J.A. Teslar.

27. Április 8/9.

28. P.R.O. H.O. 45/2991. 1 November 1849; T. Dénes. Arménia hercege. Irodalmi Újság. 1967. dec. 15. P. 10.

29. Pulszky to Prince Charles II of Braunschweig. London, November 1850. Bibliothéque publique et Universitaire Genéva, MS. Bruns. 35.

30. Willich had a factory in London where some of the refugee soldiers found employment. K-e.A. Vol. I. P. 79.

31. Március 25/3., and Ch. II/3.

32. cf. JONES, Mrs. M. Wales and Hungary. (A talk transmitted on the BBC third programme, 24 February 1957); and JONES, Mrs. M. Wales and Hungary: a lecture given to the Cymmrodorion Society on 23 April 1968.

33. Professor Newman writes to Pulszky in this connection: "Do you see that the Welsh are beginning to sound the praises of Magyars in their own tongue? We are powerless, but God & justice are mighty." Newman to Pulszky (1850). O.SZ.K. -U.C.L.

34. É-K. Vol. II. P.16.

35. Ferenczy (op. cit. P.52), writes that apart from the requests for financial reliefs, Pulszky was overwhelmed by other petitions. L. Diószeghy, a Hungarian taylor asked P. to order his suits from him. Another emigrant who wrote on slavery, asked P. to place his article in an English journal. A sailor wanted recommendations to get into a shipping company. A man from Arad asked him to convey his best wishes to Kossuth. Another man, from Pest, asked him to present his work in the forthcoming great Exhibition at Crystal Palace.

36. From 'Appeal' (1836). Tr. by T. & F. Pulszky. DIARY, Vol. 2. P. 223.

37. KLAPKA, Gy. op. cit. P. 295-7.

38. WENCKSTERN himself came to write a dispassionate account of the Hungarian struggle. WENCKSTERN, Otto. History of the war in Hungary in 1848 and 1849. London, 1859.

39. KLAPKA, Gy. Memoirs of the War of Independence in Hungary; transl. by Otto Wenckstern. London, Chapman & Hall, 1850.

40. É-K. Vol. I. P. 511.

41. cf. MARCZALI, H. Pulszky Ferencz a tudományban és a közéletben. In: Pulszky Ferenc kisebb dolgozatai. Bp., M.T.A. 1914. P. xxvii.

42. K-e.A. Vol. I. P. 69-70.

43. Silhuetten aus dem Nachmärz in Ungarn. Budapest, 1850.

44. TOWNSON, R. Travels on Hungary with a short account of Vienna, London, 1797.; BRIGHT, R. Travels from Vienna through Lower Hungary, Edinburgh, 1813.

45. BEATTIE, William. The Danube, its history, scenery and topography, London 1842; Miss PARDOE. City of the Magyar or Hungary and her institutions in 1839-40. London, 1840. 3 Vol.; PAGET, John. Hungary and Transylvania, London, 1839. 2 Vol.

46. BOWRING, Sir John. The poetry of the Magyars, 1830. Used German rough translations; VARANNAI, Aurél. John Bowring and Hungarian Literature. Acta Littereria Ac. Sci. Hung., Tom 6, fasc. 1-4. P. 105-148, 288-319; CZIGÁNY, Lóránt. The reception of Hungarian literature . . . London, 1965. Typescript, Ph.D. thesis.

47. CLARK, Thomas Grieve. Hungary and the Hungarian struggle . . . Edinburgh, Hogg, London, Groombridge, 1850.

48. PULSZKY, Theresa and Francis. Memoirs of a Hungarian Lady, with a historical introduction by Ferenc Pulszky. London, Colburn, 1850. 2 vol. In German: Aus dem Tagebuche einer ungerischen Dame . . . Leipzig, 1850; 2nd ed. Altenburg, 1880. 2 vol.

49. Theresa Pulszky published other - though less successful literary works as well. Pulszky, T. Three Christman plays for children: the sleeper awakened, the wonderful bird, Crinoline . . . London, Griffiths, 1858; PULSZKY, T. and F. and PULSZKY, A. Regék olasz földröl. Bp., 1866.

50. É-K. Vol. I. P. 241.

51. PULSZKY, Theresa. Diary. 28 October. O.SZ.K. MSS. Germ. Vol. 19. N.B. This diary, full of interesting detail, is still unpublished in 1977-only snippets and quotes have appeared in print so far. Naturally, its relevant pages formed the basis of the Memoirs of a Hungarian Lady.

52. PULSZKY, F. to Toulmin Smith. London, 19 October 1849. Appendix 2.

53. "The hero of our days" by M. Lermontoff; translated from the Russian by T. Pulszky. London, 1847. The Parlour Library, Vol. 12; most probably Mrs. Pulszky worked from a German translation.

54. 21 November. TANÁRKY, P. 25.

55. DIARY, Vol. I. P.IV.

56. Published in five instalments in ATHENAEUM, 1838. II-ik. félév. Most probably it used Péczeli's work, a magyarok történetei, Debrecen, 1837, 2 Vol. as its chief source.

57. In his foreward to the second completed edition of the work. PULSZKY, F. Eszmék Magyarország története philosophiájához. Bp., Franklin-Társulat, 1880. P. 3.; The first complete edition: Bp., 1875. Olcsó Könyvtár. The theme is brought up again by Pulszky in his lecture to the Historical Society on 22 August 1881 in Eperjes - Századok, 1881. This was re-published as: A magyar történelem korszakai in Pulszky, F. Kisebb dolgozatai . . . Bp., 1914. P. 254-265.

58. DIARY, Vol. I. P. ci.

59. The Palatine is elected by the Diet for life. He is the President of the House of Peers, Captain-General of the country, etc... If a difference arose between the king and the realm, the Palatine was, according to the law, the mediator... If the King failed to convoke the Diet, it was the Palatine's duty to do it... As often as the Viennese Government attacked the Constitution, it always began by leaving the dignity of Palatine unfilled. Thus it was under Rudolf and Leopold I, thus under Maria-Theresa, under Emperor Joseph, and behold! in 1848 again. Ibid. Vol. I. P. 113.

60. DIARY, Vol. II. P. 1-22.

61. WENCKSTERN, O. History of the war in Hungary in 1848 and 1849. London, Packer, 1859. P. 319.

62. Whereas these charges have remained unsubstantiated Pulszky's part played in the Vienna revolution is undeniable. Furthermore, the Latour-Jellashich correspondence, which revealed the double-dealing of the Austrian Minister, was published by Pulszky on 6 October 1848, the day of Latour's murder by the populace.

63. É-K. Vol. II. P. 29.

64. N.R.A. P.P. GC/PO/839/3.

65. Ibid. Palmerston to Ponsonby, 19 October 1849.

66. PULSZKY, F. & T. Tales and traditions of Hungary. London, Colburn, 1851. 3 Vol. Vol. I.: Popular tales and traditions of Hungary (by Theresa Pulszky). Vol. 2-3: The Jacobins in Hungary (by Francis Pulszky). In German: Berlin, 1852. 2 Vol. Separately: PULSZKY, F. The Jacobins in Hungary. Leipzig, 1851. 2 Vol. In Hungarian: (translated by Emil Beniczky), Pest, 1861-62. 2nd ed.: Pest, 1862. In German: Leipzig, 1851. 3 pts. Europaische Bibliothek, P. 507-509. 2nd ed.: Berlin, 1851. 2 Vol. 3rd ed.: Berlin, 1868. 2 Vol. Shortened Hungarian version: Martinovits és társai. Pest, 1881. Olcsó könyvtár, 136. Ismertetve: Fövárosi Lapok, 1881. P. 277; Copies for an American edition were burnt in a fire in 1851.

67. Ibid. Vol. I. P. 1.

68. Ibid. Vol. I. P. 221-230. Népmondák. Emlény. Bp., 1840.

69. É-K. Vol. II. P. 17.

70. Vol. 2. P. 221-3. A misprint on P. 221 states that the poem was written 'seventy years earlier', in fact it was published in 1836.

71. The original was published in 1844.

72. PULSZKY, F.: Petöfi Sándor összes költeményei. Magyar szépirodalmi Szemle, 1847, P. 277-297.; Later, Pulszky returned to Petöfi again: PULSZKY, F.: Petöfi és a kritika a negyvenes években. A Petöfi-Társaság Lapja, 1877.

73. "Halálom", the original was published in 1843; this translation is by Pulszky. SZENTKIRÁLYI, J. Magyar költemények angol forditásban. Bp., 1943. P. 57. (Különlenyomat az 'Angol Filológiai Tanulmányok' IV. kötetéböl.)

74. Lóránt Czigány is right in assuming that this translation was produced by Mrs. Pulszky, although it was not a prose-translation as first stated by him. (London, Ph.D. thesis, 1965. P. 167.) Later, he corrected himself on this score (CZIGÁNY, L. Magyar irók portréi, Új Látóhatár, X, P. 263.).

75. Of the critical acclaim, the best reception was given by the Edinburgh Review, Vol. 94, 1851, P. 127-139.

76. Hardy, Horne-Tooke and other members of a corresponding society in England had been acquitted by the Jury. Tales and traditions, Vol. III. P. 140.

77. Cathéchisme du citoyen. . . (by J. Saige). En France, 1788.

78. FRAKNÓI, V. Martinovics és társainak összeesküvése. Bp., (18?).

79. DE GERANDO, A. De l'Esprit public en Hongrie depuis la révolution francaise. Paris, 1848.

80. FESSLER, Ignaz A. Die Geschichte der Ungarn und ihrer Landsassen. Leipzig, 1815-25.

81. Pulszky was a member of the parliamentary sub-committee On Guilt and Punishment which dealt with the revision of the Criminal Law.(cf. E-K. Vol. I. P. 184.) Stavi, one of the members of the secret society lived to see the modifications in the law of high treason in 1843.

82. "Despotism makes no lawsuits but sacks victims". Tales and traditions Vol. III. P. 294.

83. Reviewed in The Spectator 5 April 1851. Suppt. P. 3-4. Thomas Watts dismisses it as a "long and somewhat tedious story". KNIGHT, C. the English Cyclopaedia. Vol. IV. P. 1012.

84. A list of the Austrian and Hungarian ministers in the course of the years 1848 and 1849 are included in the Diary, Vol. I. P. 141-44.

85. EÖTVÖS, J. The village notary; tr. by Otto Wenckstern, with introductory remarks by Francis Pulszky. London, Longman, Brown, Green, 1850. 3 Vol.

86. EÖTVÖS, J. A falu jegyzöje. Bp., 1845.

87. PULSZKY, F. A falu jegyzöje. Magyar Szépirodalmi Szemle, 1847.

88. EÖTVÖS, J. Der Dorfnotair. . . übersetzt von Grafen J. Mailath. Leipzig, 1846. 3 Vol.

89. The critics received the book well in England. cf. *The Spectator* 16 February 1850. P. 161; *The Sun* 28 February 1850; *Frasers Magazine*, April 1850.

90. The best modern monograph on Eötvös is: Sötér, István. Eötvös József. második atdolgozott kiadás. Bp., 1967.

91. SCHLESINGER, Max. The war in Hungary, 1848-49; tr. by J.E. Taylor, ed. by F. Pulszky. London, Bentley, 1850. 2 Vol. (Reviewed in Blackwood Magazine, January 1851. P. 89-106.).

92. Op. cit. Vol. I. P. lxviii.

93. Ibid. Vol. I. P. lxii.

94. MAURY, A., PULSZKY, F. and others. Indigenous races of the earth. . . Philadelphia, 1857.

95. Maury, A. op. cit. P. 87.

96. Ibid. P. 192.

97. In 1854 Pulszky translated and abridged a work by the Bavarian naturalist Moritz Wagner on Algeria, bringing the work up to date, by making use of the official Blue Book: *Tableau de la situation des Etablissements francais dans l'Algéria, 1850-52.* WAGNER, M. The tricolor on the Atlas. . . from the German of Dr. Wagner and other sources by F. Pulszky. London, 1854.

98. In 1859 Pulszky was elected Member of the Philological Society and published an essay: On the verbal and nominal affixes in the Hungarian language. Transactions of the Philological Society, 1859. P. 97-124; augmented ed. in Hungarian: A magyar kópzök és ragok. . .*In: Életem és korom*; 2-ik kiadás. Bp., 1884. Vol. 2. P. 231-285. P. took private lessons in Sanscrit from Dr. Goldstücker, prof. of Comp. Phil. in University College.

99. Catalogue of the Fejérváry ivories in the Museum of Joseph Meyer, Esq., preceded by an essay on antique ivories by F. Pulszky. Liverpool, 1856. Pulszky's uncle, the archaeologist Gábor Fejérváry, left his collection of ivories to him. An English friend nominally bought the collection in Budapest and then arranged for it to be delivered to Pulszky in London. Pulszky first offered the collection to the B.M. but eventually

sold it to Joseph Meyer of Liverpool for 18,000 forints. (Communicated by Mr. Bentley-Bridgewater of the B.M.; É-K. Vol. II. P. 134-6.) The collection is at Liverpool City Museum now. The catalogue was partly the work of Imre Henszlmann, who joined the Pulszkys in London.

100. Arnold was the secretary of Lord Lansdowne, when P. first came to London. (cf. GÁL, I. Arnold és Swinburne magyar tárgyú szonettjei. Filológiai Közlöny. 1967, No. 1-2. P. 68-89.) His sonnet, "To the Hungarian nation" was first published in the Examiner, 21 July 1849.

101. See: Ch. V/2.

102. American biographer of Lafayette and Josephine, wife of Napoleon, dedicated his life of Kossuth: "to Count Francis Pulszky, the Hungarian hero and statesman". HEADLEY, P.C. The life of Louis Kossuth . . . with an introduction by Horace Greeley. Auburn, 1852.

103. Watts was Pulszky's close friend, a Keeper in the B.M. who learned Hungarian. From his contributions to KNIGHT'S English encyclopaedia (London, 1854-62), 4 vol. + Suppt., the following were consulted for this thesis: Vol. I. Batthyány, Count C. P. 547; Batthyány, Count L. Ibid.; Bem, J. P. 638; Vol. 2. Eötvös, J. P. 782, Vol. 3. Klapka, G. P. 772; Kmety, G. P. 733; KOSSUTH, L. P. 746; Vol. 4. Petöfi, S. P. 767; Pulszky, F. P. 1012; PULSZKY, T. P. 1013; Suppt. Széchenyi, I. P. 877; Vörösmarty, M. P. 450.

104. March 25/3. April 24/3.

105. BECK, W. Personal adventures during the late war of independence. London, 1850. 2 Vol.

106. BECK, W. Memoiren einer Dame . . . London, 1851. 2 Bd.

107. Ibid. Vol. II. P. 360.

108. SMITH, Toulmin. The facts of the case of the pretended "Baroness von Beck". . . London, 1852. P. 12.

109. Ibid. P. 13.

110. The Household Narrative, September 1851. P. 197.

111. Dickens mis-spelt some of the names: Derra as Darra, Hajnik as Hajvik.

112. DERRA DE MORODA, Constantine. A refutation . . . London, 1851.

113. Ibid. P. 14.

114. Ibid. P. 16.

115. Ibid. P. 18.

116. Thade Idzikowski and Xavier Gorsky.

117. Derra, op. cit. P. 23.

118. 6 September 1850 and 19 September 1850. cf. Derra, op. cit. P. 26.

119. Derra, op. cit. P. 39.

120. K-e.A. Vol. I. P. 80-83.

121. JOURNAL OF THE HOUSE OF LORDS, Vol. 84. P. 200, 285, 378, 492.

122. HANSARD, 3rd. S. Vol. 121. P. 1275-1288.

123. D.N.B. Vol. 53. P. 94-95.

124. The Birmingham correspondence shows that the two families were on friendly terms too, invited one another, etc.. See: Appendix 2; and PULSZKY to Toulmin Smith. London, 9, 10 1849. Birmingham Public Library. 7215 item 133/1. This friendship between Pulszky and T. Smith lasted well into the sixties, when Pulszky was in Italy and exchanged letters with T. Smith until he returned to Hungary. 11 Pulszky letters to T. Smith written between 1861-63, were sold at Sotheby's on 20 February 1967 to the highest bidder: O.SZ.K. (cf. SZÁSZ, B. Kossuth levelei a kalapács alatt. IRODALMI, UJSÁG, 1967. Márc. 15-ápr. 1.p.6; RÓNAY MIHÁLY, András. A Pulszky iratok hazatérnek. Magyar Hirek - 1967. apr. 15). U.C.L. took part in the bidding and lost the letters at £300.

125. SMITH, Toulmin. op. cit. P. 16.

126. Interrogatories to be administered to Louis Kossuth. K-e.A. Vol. II. Document 528. P. 1025-1030.

127. K-e.A. Vol. II. P. 993-4.

128. Memoiren einer Dame, London, 1851. Vol. I. P. 227.

129. STILES, W.H. Austria in 1848-9. New York, 1852. Vol. 2. P. 156.

130. BENTLEY, R. The persecution and death of the Baroness von Beck . . . London, 1852.

131. Ibid. P. 12 and 18.

132. K-e.A. Vol. II. P. 962.

133. Bentley, op. cit. P. 12.

134. Karl Marx referred to her as "Kossuth's spy". cf. ANDERL, G. Képrombolás avagy Kossuth-Kép a marxista Klasszikusok leveleiben. IRODALMI ÚJSÁG. 1965. jún.15. p.9.

135. Pulszky to Kossuth. Southampton, 6 October 1851. K-e.A. Vol. I. P. 664.

136. 24 St. Peterburgh Place, Bayswater. O.SZ.K. -U.C.L.

137. N.R.A. P.P. GC/BL/5.

138. SMITH, Toulmin. op. cit. P. 23.

139. KÁSZONYI, D. Ungarns fier Zeitalter. . .4 Bd. 1868. Reference to the Beck affair in Vol. 3. P. 72-88.

140. The case damaged Kossuth's in London, cf. Times, 1 June 1852.

Notes to Chapter Three.

1. K-e.T. P. 182.

2. *See*: The stipulations of their treaties in the Introduction.

3. cf. Oppenheimer's International Law; 6th ed. by H. Lauterpacht, London, 1947. Vol. I. P. 645.

4. F.SZ. Vol. IV. P. 348-9.

5. N.R.A. P.P. GC/PO/834. Palmerston to Ponsonby. F.O. 22 August 1849.

6. N.R.A. P.P. GC/PO/835. Palmerston to Ponsonby. F.O. 25 August 1849.

7. N.R.A. P.P. GC/NE/2. 1849. (September).

8. Canning to Sir W. Parker, 17 September 1849. cf. Sproxton, op. cit. P. 120.

9. N.R.A. P.P. MM/TU/39-40. Brouillons of despatches from Lord Palmerston to the Lords of the Admiralty, etc. and ibid. MM/TU/41. 6 October 1849. Draft letter from Lord Palmerston to the Lords of the Admiralty.

10. Ibid. GC/PO/837. F.O. 6 October 1849. Palmerston writes to Ponsonby "in my verbal communications with Brunnow and Colloredo I have said nothing about our Squadron being ordered up to the Dardanelles. But it is right that you should know and understand that the Government is resolved to support Turkey."

11. cf. K-e.T. P. 302.

12. cf. Ibid. P. 204-5.

13. Veress, S. A magyar emigráció Keleten. Bp., 1878. Vol. I. P. 34.

14. Kossuth wrote to Palmerston via Pulszky, on 28 September 1849; "Mr. Francis Pulszky, our diplomatic agent at London, has received full informations upon the causes of this sudden and unlooked for changes in the Hungarian war and is ordered to make communication of them to Your Excellency. . . I put ourselves under the protection of England and for it in the name of humanity." O.SZ.K. KOSSUTH Collection. cf. K-e.T. P. 482-6.

15. EGRESSY, G. Törökországi naplója. Pest, 1851. P. 70-72.

16. K-e.T. (P. 679-683), refers to 492 persons, counting women and children, when the emigrants were transferred from Widdin to Sumla.

17. S. Veress estimated that about 300 soldiers had died of that illness. op. cit. Vol. I. P. 300.

18. KOSSUTH, L. Irataim. Vol. II. P. 271 and Vol. IX. P. 268 and 358.

19. Leipzig, 1849. Verlag Von Otto Wigand; Its full Hungarian test was first published in 1915 by Gy. KACZIÁNY in MAGYARORSZÁG. 233-254 sz. cf. K-e.T. P. 472-4.

20. The present writer had no chance to examine the correspondence between Wigand and Pulszky, which is preserved in the Pulszky Collection of the O.SZ.K.

21. See: Ch. IV/1. for more detailed discussion of Stuart's role.

22. HENNINGSEN, C.F. Eastern Europe and the Emperor Nicholas. London, 1846; and the more famous: Revelations of Russia. London, 1844.

23. It cannot be ascertained exactly when Henningsen arrived at Widdin; Hajnal thinks it was the middle of September, we would rather think it was in the first days of October, as an eye-witness, Gábor Egressy, writes in his diary on 7 October 1849: "In the last few days . . . a tall thin man arrived here on horse-back . . . His name: Thomson." (Egressy, op. cit. P. 58).

24. K-e.T. P. 54; we could not consult these letters which, like most others, are in the Pulszky Coll. of O.SZ.K.

25. Roger Casement, the Indian traveller was to deliver this letter in October to Palmerston, and the others to Pulszky and Teleki.

26. Vol. II. App. 7.

27. HEADLEY, P.C. The life of Kossuth. Auburn, 1852; Authentic life of Louis Kossuth. London, 1851. Kossuth nach der Capitulation von Vilagos . . . Weiner, 1852; DERFEL, R.J. Rhosyn Meirion; sef Pryddest wobrwyedig ar "Kossuth" . . . Rhuthyn, 1853.

28. K-e.T. P. 379.

29. Egressy, op. cit. P. 63.

30. Alternative spellings: Kiutahia=Kutaya=Kutayya.

31. N.R.A. P.P. GC/PO/838.

32. Ibid. GC/PO/843. 30 November 1849.

33. Veress (op. cit. Vol. I. P. 117), supplies the full list of names.

34. EGRESSY, G. op. cit. P. 237.

35. From Sumla he still preferred to write in German, to those Englishmen who spoke the language; e.g. to Guyon on 7 December 1849 (K-e.T. P. 555), and to Henningsen, on the same date (Ibid. P. 559-562).

36. MASSINGBERD, A. Letter on Kossuth and the Hungarian question. London, 1851.

37. Kossuth to Pulszky. Kiutahia, 18 April 1850; (to Teleki with ref. to Pulszky); 8 November 1850; 21 December 1850; É-K. Vol. II. P. 35-51; 7 February 1851; 13 March 1851; 31 May 1851; 20 June 1851; Ferenczy, op. cit. P. 51-62.

38. Jánossy, D. Great Britain and Kossuth. Bp., 1937. P. 99.

39. Pulszky to Kossuth, London, 30 July 1850. K.H. O.L. Bp., cf. K-e.I. P. 78.

40. Ibid. London, 30 January 1851.

41. HARROWBY MSS. Vol. 453. Section 13. cf. Memorials . . . 1851 (664) XXXI. P. 327. (cf. General Index to the Accounts and Papers, Reports of Commissioners, Estimates . . . printed by order of the House of Commons . . . 1801-52. London, 1938.).

42. Correspondence respecting Refugees.

43. March, May and June. Hansard, Vol. 114, P. 1317-8; Vol. 116, P. 769-70; Vol. 117, P. 782-3.

44. P.R.O. Draft No. 130, F.O. 1849. Turkey.

45. F.SZ. Vol. IV, P. 409; É-K. Vol. II. P. 15, 58.

46. K-e.A. Vol. I. P. 88.

47. É-K. Vol. II. P. 62.

48. Hansard, 3rd series. Vol. 118. P. 1888-89.

49. K-e.A. Vol. I. P. 90-1. Jánossy's evidence is based on the Ambassadorial reports of these conversations.

50. P.R.O. F.O. Austria. No. 182. 30 September 1851.

51. Pulszky to Kossuth. 6 October 1851. KH.OL. Bp. Published as: Document 66, by Jánossy, K-e.I. P. 663-5.

52. First Deák, later Kossuth then Garibaldi and finally Deák again.

53. 1841, 71 sz. Szabad föld; 1842, 116-119 sz. Centralisatio; 157-159 sz. Központositás és középités; 1843, 123 sz. Vámszövetséghezi csatlakozás; 272-275 sz. Adalákok a városi kérdéshez.

54. No. 72. Wien, 19 February 1847. Ludwig Kossuth . . . .

55. Veress, op. cit. Vol. I. P. 217-22.

56. 29 October. The Times, 7 October 1851. Re-printed in K-e.A. Vol. I. P. 623-5. Pulszky (É-K. Vol. II. P. 63) noted the origin of the motto, which Kossuth was to repeat many times and in various forms and contexts during his tour of England and America.

57. Karády, Török, his personal secretary, Col. Ihász, 4 Poles, and Lemmi with his family.

58. É-K. Vol. II. P. 64.

59. For three weeks from 1 November to 22 November 1851, the *Illustrated London News* described Kossuth's every move, reported all his speeches and drew nearly two dozen pictures of his journey in England. 1 Nov. 1851, P. 537-8, 544-6. Supplement, P. 558-9; 8 Nov. P. 565, 567-8; 570, 582-3; 22 Nov. P. 609-11. In the Supplement to 15 Nov. issue, there appeared an *Authentic Life of L. Kossuth* (p. 587-91) which was soon reprinted and issued in book form by Bradbury & Evans. Practically the same material was used by P.C. Headley. *The life of Louis Kossuth*, Auburn, Derby & Miller, 1852. When, adding the description of Kossuth's tour in America, he brought out the most detailed biography of Kossuth in English.

60. Cobden to Pulszky, Midhurst, 4 October. Letter VIII. of Cobden in *South Eastern Affairs*, materials relative to the history of Central Europe and the Balkan Peninsula. Ed. by J. Horvath. Vol. VIII-IX. 1938-40. (Typescript copies kindly communicated by Dr. I. Gál.) In his letters, Cobden was of the opinion that Kossuth should have gone to America first, then come to Britain. He also offered to take Kossuth around the Great Exhibition, before it closed. - Ibid. Letter VII. 22 September, and Letter X. (undated).

61. É-K. Vol. II. P. 65.

62. *Appendix 3*. Exchange of letters between Lord Dudley Stuart and Lord Palmerston. Harrowby MSS. Vol. 453. Unpublished sources, Section 13. 3 Xerox copies. cf. N.R.A. P.P. GC/ST/144-145.

63. BENSON, A.C. The letters of Queen Victoria, London, 1908. Vol. II. P. 324; WALPOLE, S. The life of Lord John Russel. London, 1891. Vol. II. P. 132-3.

64. JÁNOSSY, D. Great Britain and Kossuth. Bp., 1937. P. 134-8.

65. Kossuth e Urquhart, estratto di una corrispondenza. Londra, 1859.

66. K-e.A. Vol. I. P. 403-4.

67. On 27 October 1851 Marx wrote to Engels: "Mr. Kossuth is, like the Apostle Paul, all things to all men. In Marseilles he shouts: 'Vive la

republique', and in Southampton 'God save the Queen!' VAS, Z. Kossuth in England. New Hungarian Quarterly, Vol. IX. P. 140. In fact the letter was written by Engels to Marx. Marx-Engels Werke, Berlin, 1962. Vol. 28. P. 368.

68. Peéry, R. Carl Schurz, Londoni fogadáson Kossuth Lajosnál. IRODALMI ÚJSÁG. 1964. 15 November. P. 4.

69. HORVÁTH, Z. Teleki László. Bp., 1964. Vol. II. P. 52-7, 78-9, 81.

70. Pulszky, for instance, wrote in the *Eclectic Review* (January 1850, P. 59): "Centralisation is the political bane of our age. Its . . . results have long been visible in paternal systems and despotisms of Europe." This was the very clue to many of Kossuth's speeches in England.

In the unexplored parts of the vast Pulszky MSS Collection in the Széchényi Library there is a folder of sketches of articles and drafts of speeches. A comparative analysis of this material and Kossuth's speeches might have revealed interesting clues to the origin of Kossuth's 'cribs' but the present writer had no access, at the time of writing, to this material. Although the summer vacation in 1964 was spent in research in the Széchényi Library, subsequent visa applications were denied, until 1975.

71. Authentic life . . . P. 51.

72. The Birmingham speech referred to the city's beginnings from the time of Julius Caesar. Headley, op. cit. P. 379.

73. The Constitutional parallels between Engalnd and Hungary were enhanced by historic parallels, such as: "As the Czar has brought back the Hapsburgs to us, Monk once brought the Stuarts back to you . . . we are now, where you were after 1665." Ibid. P. 387; Prof. Newman wrote: "at Southampton, Toulmin Smith boarded his ship . . . handed to him a precise manuscript that gave details concerning the local history and affairs of Southampton. Not many hours later, the great Hungarian . . . seemed to have a truly marvellous acquaintance with our English municipalities." (Reminiscences of two exiles. London, 1888. P. 5).

74. According to contemporary reporting there were 200,000 people at Copenhagen Fields.

75. Morley, J. The life of William Ewart Gladstone. London, 1903. Vol. I. P. 402.

76. DASENT, A.I. John Thaddeus Delane, Editor of the Times . . . London, 1908. Vol. I. P. 144.

77. 9 October, 16 October, 17 October 1851.

78. HENNINGSEN, C.F. Kossuth and the Times. London, 1851. The author did not print his name.

79. Kossuth's letter to Nicholas Kiss. Cincinnati, 15 February 1852. K-e.A. Vol. II. P. 554.

80. First stanza of a poem by Frigyes Kerényi, which remained in fragment. (LUKÁCSY, S. Rabszolga Washington sirjánál. Bp., 1953. P. 10.).

81. This number is an approximation, based on Pulszky's estimate in his Memoirs. Jenő Piványi, the historian, mentions the same number but refers it to the period of the American Civil War. Tivadar Ács, on the other hand, estimates that by the 1860's a total of 3,000 Hungarians were living in the States.

82. É-K. Vol. II. P. 69-70.

83. As on 4 July, on board ship, on the way back to England. cf. É-K. Vol. II. P. 115.

84. PULSZKY, F. & T. White, red, black; sketches of society in the United States. London, Trubner, 1853. 3 Vol. Henceforth referred to as: White, red, black.

85. SZILASSY, S. America and the Hungarian revolution of 1848-49. Slavonic and East European Review, Vol. 44. January 1966. P. 180-96.

86. F.SZ. Vol. IV. P. 305.

87. He was a brother of Senator Charles Sumner. (1811-1874; D.A.B.)

88. Published in: New York Daily Times, 20 October 1851; Union (Washington), 21 October; New York Herald, 20 October 1851.

89. BAILEY, T. A diplomatic history of the American people. New York, 1950. P. 287.

90. LUKÁCS, L. & others. Kossuth Lajos. Bp., 1952. P. 162. At one instance he went even further: "But I may be answered,'Well, if we (the United States) make such a declaration. . . and Russia will not respect our declaration, then we might have to go to war.' . . . Well I am not the man to decline the consequences of my principles." Headley, op. cit. P. 293.

91. JAY, W. of New York. The Kossuth excitement. New York, 1852.

92. GÁL, I. Kossuth, America and the Danubian Confederation. HUNGARIAN QUARTERLY, Vol. 6. 1940. P. 430.

93. Kossuth to Nicholas Kiss. Cincinnati, 15 February 1852. "Mun-

kásságom célja: hazánk függetlenségi nyilatkozatának valósitása. A Habsburg-házzal semmi transaetio, sem ezen territoriumoknak akár nemsetiségi akár más tekintetbőli földarabolása. Népsuverenitás . . . etc." (Kossuth-Hagyaték, O.L. Közli: Jánossy, K-e. A. vol. II. p. 551.

94. December, 1851.

95. 30 December 1851.

96. TELEKI, L. Válogatott munkái. Bp., 1961. Vol. 2. P. 84. HORVÁTH, Z. Teleki . . . Bp., 1964. Vol. 2. P. 297; S. Vukovics too joined the polemics defending Kossuth. Daily News, 17 January 1852. cf. NEWMAN, F.W. Select speeches of Kossuth. London, 1853. P. 365-69.

97. 9 December 1851, a letter by Szemere and 10 December 1851 by Batthyány.

98. 7 January 1852 and 16 March 1852. Both articles were reproduced in K-e.A. Vol. II. P. 420-6 and ibid. P. 606-13 respectively.

99. ÁCS, T. Magyarok oz északamerikai polgárháborúban. Bp., 1964. P. 18.

100. KOLTAY-KASTNER, J. A Kossuth - emigráció Olaszországban.Bp., 1960. P. 36-41.

101. Pulszky and Mrs. Pulszky to Newman. Niagara Falls, 25 May 1852, and New York, 18 June 1852. O.SZ.K. - U.C.L. cf. K-e.A. Vol. II. P. 847-49, 883-88.

102. É-K. Vol. II. P. 106.

103. Ibid.

104. The Eclectic Review, May 1853. P. 530-48; Fraser's Magazine, April 1853. P. 477-85.

105. Op. cit.

106. BANCROFT, G. History of the United States . . . Edinburgh, 1848.

107. White, red, black. Vol. II. P. 212.

108. GRACZA, Gy. Kossuth Lajos élete és müködése. Bp., 1893.

Notes to Chapter Four.

1. HARROWBY MSS. 4th Series. Vol. 1062. P. 305-6. The present writer published the letter with commentary and Hungarian translation in: IRODALMI ÚJSÁG, 1968. március 15. P. 6-7.

2. Kossuth's orthography is preserved.

3. HARROWBY MSS. 4th Series, Vol. 1062. P. 313-4.

4. É-K. Vol. II. P. 154.

5. K-e.A. Vol. I. P. 408.

6. Letter of Maine Reid in the Morning Post, 17 February 1853. What in fact did happen was that Kossuth sent a proclamation to the Hungarian soldiers in Italy to Mazzini in 1851 from Kiutahia. They agreed that Mazzini could only use it when the time was ripe for it in Kossuth's judgement. In 1853 Mazzini up-dated the document, changed its text and faced Kossuth with a fait accompli.

7. The Eclectic Review, April 1853. P. 487.

8. Ibid. P. 493, 496.

9. Tanárky, P. 31.

10. É-K. Vol. II. P. 118-20.

11. Jánossy, D. Die Ungarische Emigration und der Krieg im Orient. Bp., 1939. P. 155-6.

12. New York Daily Tribune, No. 3756. 30 April 1853. P. 5.

13. cf. HANSARD, Third series, Vol. 125. P. 1208-15.

14. New York Daily Tribune, No. 3757. 2 May 1853. P. 5.

15. Ibid. No. 3768. P. 5.

16. In 1851 Prussia raised repeated objections to the activities of exiles in London. Palmerston, as Foreign Secretary, instructed his Ambassador to reply: . . . "we had no power of expelling from the country any persons foreign or otherwise who did not render themselves subject to legal proceedings for the infringements of the laws of the Country". P.R.O. H.O. 45.O.S.3514. 5 April 1851.

17. K-e.A. Vol. I. P. 438.

18. K-e.A. Vol. I. P. 445.

19. April 8/9.

20. PULSZKY-NEWMAN. June 1853. O.SZ.K. -U.C.L.

21. Appearing in No. 3789. 1 June 1853.

22. Ibid. No. 3790. 9 June 1853.

23. Ibid. No. 3815. 9 July 1853 and No. 3819. 14 July 1853.

24. Ibid. No. 3824. 20 July 1853 and No. 3828. 25 July 1853.

25. Ibid. No. 3850. 18 August 1853.

26. Ibid. No. 3862. 2 September 1853.

27. Ibid. No. 3869. 10 September 1853.

28. Ibid. No. 3880. 23 September 1853 and No. 3886. 30 September 1853.

29. Pulszky-Newman, 20 July 1853. O.SZ.K. -U.C.L.

30. Progress of Russia in the West, North and South, by opening the

sources of opinion and appropriating the channels of wealth and power. By David Urquhart. London, Trübner, 1853. The Eclectic Review, August 1853. P. 225-39.

31. Pulszky quotes pages from the proofs of the third printing in the New York Daily Tribune. No. 3875. 17 September 1853.

32. Ibid. P. 233.

33. HARROWBY MSS. 4th Series, Vol. 1062. P. 408-9. The present writer had communicated this letter to Mr. Neville Masterman, who published it in August 1968. cf. HOBSON, J.A. Richard Cobden: the international man; new ed. with introd. by Neville Masterman. London, 1968. P. 411-2.

34. Jánossy, D. Die Ungarische Emigration und der Krieg im Orient. Bp., 1935. P. 119-35. The facts relating to Kossuth's plans in the Crimean War are based on Jánossy's work, who was, however, less critical of Kossuth than the present writer.

35. NEWMAN, F.W. Reminiscences of two exiles... and two wars... London, 1888. P. 85-6.

36. National Library of Scotland. Adam Black MSS. 3713. (Unpublished letter of Kossuth, communicated by Mrs. Marion Jones.).

37. Pulszky-Newman, 1 September 1853. O.SZ.K. -U.C.L.

38. Draft (in Lord Palmerston's handwriting) from the final three paragraphs of the Declaration of War against Russia. N.R.A. P.P. MM/RV/20. 28 March 1854.

39. Pulszky-Newman, Ventnor, Isle of Wight. 9 October 1854. O.SZ.K. -U.C.L.

40. The basic tenets of Mazzini's creed were best expressed in his "Dei doveri dell'uomo" first published in the *Apostolo Popolare* from 1841 to 1842, then in *Pensiero ed Azione* from 1858-9; for our summary we used the Rizzoli edition, Milan, 1949, especially P. 67, 73.

41. The *Manifesto* was published by Holyoake, London 1855.

42. N.R.A. P.P. MM/AU/2. 5 June 1854. Although the late Zoltán Horváth, author of Teleki's monograph, knew about the Count's intention to send this memorandum (op. cit. Vol. I. P. 376), he did not trace the document itself with Palmerston's comments. His death has frustrated the present writer's intention to send a photocopy of this document to him.

43. Edinburgh Review, Vol. 90, 1849. P. 238.

44. cf. Pulszky-Newman. ('Spring' 1854). O.SZ.K. -U.C.L.
45. É-K. Vol. II. P. 133.
46. For this information I am grateful to Professor László Országh.
47. É-K. Vol. II. P. 151.

Notes to Chapter Five.

1. D.N.B. Vol. 55. P. 76-7; for family connections: WHO'S WHO, 1967. P. 1334, Burke's Peerage, 1967. P. 1192; D.N.B. Vol. 50. P. 44-5; for general appraisal: Examiner, 25 November 1854. P. 747, Gentlemen's Magazine, 1855, i. P. 79-81, the Times, 21 November 1854, Illustrated London News, 1843. iii, P. 325 and xiv, P. 124.

2. HARROWBY MSS. Vol. 451. Section V. Biogr. notes by J.A. Teslar.

3. cf. J.A. Teslar, Unpublished letters of Adam Czartoryski and W. Janoski to Lord Dudley Coutts Stuart and the Earl of Harrowby, 1832-61. The Slavonic and East European Review, Vol. 29. No. 72. December 1950. P. 153-76.

4. In 1836 he published a "speech on the policy of Russia, delivered in the House of Commons".

5. *See:* I/2.

6. Ibid. Vol. 108. P. 481; the full debate: P. 480-501.

7. *See:* II/2.

8. Ibid. P. 496.

9. HARROWBY MSS. Vol. 28. P. 338-9.

10. cf. "Noble people of Hungary": Address of the public meeting held . . . at Regent's Park, 30 July 1849. HARROWBY MSS. Vol. 28. P. 337.

11. HARROWBY MSS. Vol. 28. P. 282-3.

12. Ibid. P. 221-2.

13. Ibid. Vol. 25. P. 231-2.

14. Ibid. Vol. 25. P. 120-22. London, 23 October 1849.

15. Ibid. Vol. 27. P. 312. 20 September 1849.

16. Ibid. Vol. 25. P. 217-8. Brighton, 3 September 1849.

17. Ibid. Vol. 27. P. 65-6. Duke Street, St. James's. 4 January 1850.

18. Ibid. Vol. 114. P. 885-6.

19. Accounts & Reports, 1851. Vol. 53.

20. HARROWBY MSS. Vol. 453. Unpublished sources, section 13. P. 224-7. (Xerox copy).

21. Ibid.

22. HANSARD, 3rd Series. Vol. 120. P. 943-50.

23. Its full title contains two errors: . . ."in continuation of papers presented to Parliament on *August 15, 1850* . . . Presented in pursuance of their Address of *April 20, 1852*". In fact it was the continuation of papers presented on *28 February 1851*, while the date of the Address was *21 April 1852.*

24. K-e.A. Vol. I. P. 353.

25. HANSARD, 3rd Series. Vol. 120. P. 477-96.

26. K-e.T. P. 114.

27. K-e.A. Vol. II. P. 328-31, 413, 616.

28. With the exception of the letters quoted or referred to in this, or in previous chapters, Dudley Stuart's letters in the O.SZ.K. were reported missing.

29. *See*: Appendix 4.

30. HARROWBY MSS. Vol. 28. P. 1.

31. Dudley Stuart to Count Paul Eszterházy. 15 February 1852. O.SZ.K. Pulszky Coll. A copy of this document was found in O.L. undated by Jánossy. cf. K-e.A. Vol. III. P. 582-5.

32. Horváth, J. Magyar diplomácia . . . Bp., 1928. P. 66 and Kossuth & Palmerston. Slavonic Review, 1930-1. P. 621. One of Lord Dudley's letters, written on 24 May was transmitted to Bem through Pulszky, via Bucarest.

33. K-e.A. Vol. I. P. 670.

34. M.P. for Westminster.

35. K-e.A. Vol. I. P. 693.

36. Ibid. P. 825.

37. Several historians (lately Mrs. M. Jones) tried & failed to trace the Minutes.

38. The O.SZ.K. acquired Pulszky's letters to Newman a year after his death in 1898. "Newman, Francis William. Précieuse correspondence avec le célébre homme d'Etat et homme politique grand savant, archéologue et grand patriote hongrois, M. Francios de Pulszky." Only a small portion of these letters has been reproduced in print by Jánossy in K-e.A. as indicated in the references. Many of Pulszky's letters to Newman & his to Pulszky lack precise dating: in such cases we give the catalogue dates in crossed brackets: ⟨ ⟩.

39. cf. D.N.B. 1st Suppt. Vol. 3. P. 221-3. Further biographical accounts: Times, 6 October 1897; Inquirer, 9 October and 27 October 1897; Christian Reformer, 1853. P. 386.

40. cf. É-K. Vol. II. P. 164-5.

41. cf. BELLOT, H. Hale. University College, London, 1826-1926. London, 1929.

42. Reminiscences of two exiles, Kossuth and Pulszky . . . London, 1886. P. 6-24.

43. The committee included: Lord Dudley Stuart, Joshua Toulmin Smith, Francis W. Newman, John Edward Taylor, Charles Gilpin, M.P., Richard Cobden, Lord Nugent (chairman), William Lloyd Birkbeck, Rev. W. Nicolay, Professor at King's College, and a certain Mr. Prout and Mr. Witton referred to by Lord Dudley Stuart but otherwise not identified.

44. Newman in 1888 cut down on the original text omitting point eleven, presumably because after the *reconciliation* of 1867 the House of Habsburg was accepted again by the Diet.

45. cf. SIEVEKING, O.I. Memoir and letters of Francis W. Newman. London, 1909. P. 364-73; reviewed by L. Kropf, Erdélyi Muzeum, 1912. VII. évf. XXIX. köt. P. 100-101.

46. Carlyle was hostile to Kossuth and Dickens could hardly conceal his animosity for the ex-Governor. So Newman chafed both of them in a letter dated 19 December 1851 to Dr. Nicholson: "Dickens is in my judgement a foolish man, he writes on centralisation and despotism like an Austrian: however so does Carlyle often . . . " Sieveking, op. cit. P. 146.

47. Newman-Pulszky, 18 October 1851. O.SZ.K. -U.C.L.

48. K-e.A. Vol. I. P. 820-22.

49. Newman-Pulszky, August 1853. O.SZ.K. -U.C.L. Pulszky advised Newman to use the translation from Stiles's book instead of the version from the *Diary*, which was done by Banfield.

50. Select speeches of Kossuth . . . London, Trubner, 1853.

51. cf. Pulszky-Newman (1853). O.SZ.K. -U.C.L.

52. Hungary in principle was bound by the Pragmatic Sanction to help out the Monarchy with troops against foreign attack. Kossuth's speech in the Parliament swayed the votes in favour of sending Hungarian troops helping Austria in Italy.

53. The crimes of the House of Hapsburg against its own liege subjects. London, 1853.

54. The Eclectic Review, April 1853. P. 478-98.

55. Coxe, W. History of the House of Austria. . . London, 1807. 2 vol.

56. Grattan, T. The History of the Netherlands. (London), 1830.

57. Robertson, W. The History of the reign of the Emperor Charles V. London, 1769. 3 Vol.

58. It is interesting to contrast that Newman believed that by 1867 the Austrians exculpated their sins as regards to Hungary. Re-reading the *Crimes* he wrote in 1868 to Pulszky that he felt as "though reproaching a penitent criminal". Newman-Pulszky, 22 December 1868. O.SZ.K.- U.C.L.

59. Pulszky-Newman. (1853). O.SZ.K.-U.C.L.

60. P. 637-8.

61. August 1853. P. 244.

62. K-e.A. Vol. II. P. 644.

63. O.SZ.K. -U.C.L.

64. K-e.A. Vol. II. P. 760.

65. Ibid. P. 851-2. The agent was Adolf Magyoródy, a lieutenant, sent with special instructions to the Croatians.

66. Ibid. P. 995.

67. O.SZ.K. Pulszky Coll.

68. Pulszky-Newman, 26 July 1852. O.SZ.K. -U.C.L.

69. Ibid. Pulszky-Newman (1853). This house has been demolished since.

70. Ibid. Newman-Pulszky, 1 January 1854, (1854) and 31 August 1854 respectively.

71. Ibid. Newman-Pulszky (1859).

72. Ibid. Pulszky-Newman, 23 September 1854 and 20 September 1855.

73. Ibid. Newman-Pulszky, 20 August 1875.

74. Ibid. Newman-Pulszky (1850).

75. Ibid. Newman-Mrs. Pulszky, 9 January 1850. He helped it by an excellent review in Fraser's Magazine, April 1850. P. 477-85. Newman so much got into the habit of correcting Pulszky's style that he even corrected the personal letters written to him by Pulszky.

76. Ibid. Pulszky-Newman, 1 September 1855, (1859), 15 November 1864.

77. Phases of faith; or passages from the history of my creed. London, 1850.

78. The soul, her sorrows and her aspirations: an essay towards the natural history of the soul... London, 1849.

79. Knight, C. The English Cyclopaedia. Vol. IV. P. 465-6.

80. Robbins, W. The Newman Brothers: an essay in comparative intellectual biography. London, 1966. P. 141.

81. An appeal to the middle classes on the urgent necessity of numerous radical reforms...London, 1848.

82. London University Magazine, June 1859 repr. in F.W. Newman, Miscellanies. London, 1890. Vol. III. P. 45-53.

83. Ibid. P. 54-86.

84. He wrote to Pulszky in 1887: "Under the pressure of my friend Anna Swanwick (a lady whom I fancy you once knew), I wrote *Reminiscences* which included you and Kossuth and the whole time from 1848 to 1860 with an *Outline* of Hungary under the Hapsburgs sufficient to make your war of 1848-49 intelligible." Newman-Pulszky (1887). O. SZ.K. -U.C.L.

85. Robbins, op. cit. P. 30.

Notes to Chapter Six.

1. É-K. Vol. II. P. 186.

2. Newman, F.W. Reminiscences... London, 1888. P. 110.

3. 19 March 1859. TELEKI, L. Válogatott munkái. Bp., 1961. Vol. II. P. 142.

4. 15 January 1859. TANÁRKY, P. 44.

5. O.SZ.K.2501. Quart Hung. (Pulszky's MSS. *Notebook*, 24 April 1859 - 29 July 1859, henceforth referred to as *Notebook* was set up in diary fashion. The writing is difficult to read, words and phrases are crossed out, and the Hungarian text is interspersed with passages in French, German and occasionally English. The Notebook contains letters and press-cuttings).

6. Ibid. 27 April 1859.

7. Ibid. 28 April 1859.

8. Ibid. Letter attached to f.4 of *Notebook*.

9. Ibid. 3 May 1859.

10. Ibid. f.5-6 and on 2 separate sheets loose in the *Notebook*. cf.

Kossuth's own account of this interview: Kossuth, L. Memoirs of my exile. London, 1880. P. 155-181.

11. P.R.O. F.O.7. Vols. 568, 569 esp. despatches of Loftus to the Earl of Malmesbury, 28, 29 March 1859.

12. Report in the Daily Mail, 21 May 1859. The Daily News gave a full coverage to the meeting on the same date. Pulszky's cuttings are inserted in the Notebook.

13. Times, 25, 26, 27 May 1859.

14. cf. Ács, T. A genovai lázadás. Bp., P. 98-101.

15. Kossuth, L. Memoirs of my exile. London, 1880. P. 265-76.

16. Ibid. Gilpin to Kossuth, 11 June 1859. P. 271.

17. Henceforth referred to as the Directory.

18. É-K. Vol. II. P. 194.

19. Ibid. P. 192.

20. Daily News, No. 4098. P. 5.

21. Daily News, No. 4099. cf. TANÁRKY. P. 74-7.

22. Ács, T. A genovai lázadás. Bp., 1958. P. 102, 108-9, 151-2; Veress, op. cit. Vol. II. P. 350-77.

23. Kossuth, L. Memories. . . P. 381-6.

24. SZABAD, Gy. Kossuth and the British balance of power policy, 1859-61. Bp., 1960. Studia Historica Academiae Scientiarum Hungaricae, 34. P. 19; cf. Kossuth, L. Memories . . . P. 361.

25. Ibid. P. 20-1.

26. Newman-Pulszky, 28 June 1859. O.SZ.K. -U.C.L.

27. Notebook, 30 June 1859.

28. É-K. Vol. II. P. 201-2.

29. Ibid. P. 202-7. On the same day Pulszky wrote to Newman: "I have still no other news from Kossuth but a telegraphic message dated Turin, July 15th when he was in despair about the extent of treachery which he could not at once believe." Pulszky-Newman, 18 July 1859. O.SZ.K. -U.C.L.

30. É-K. Vol. II. P. 203. Kossuth in his letter to Pulszky quoted Cavour in Hungarian, later in French.

31. cf. Quintavalle, F. Storia dell'Unità Italiana. Milano, 1926. P. 132.

32. K-e.O. P. 183.

33. Kossuth to Pulszky, 31 August 1859. ÁCS, T. A Genovai lázadás. Bp., 1958. P. 274-6.

34. cf. Ács, T. A genovai lázadás. Bp., 1958. P. 314; M.I.L. Vol. 2. P. 542-5; Szinnyei, Vol. 5. P. 656-71.

35. TANÁRKY, P. 118-9; K-e.O. P. 181; for Kossuth's own account in a letter to Teleki: Ács, T. A genovai lázadás. Bp., 1958. P. 315.

36. Printed in London, 1859 as a reply to Alexander Bach's anonymous: Rückblick auf die jëngste Entwicklungs-Periode Ungarns. Wien, 1857.

37. Quintavalle, F. op. cit. P. 138.

38. TANÁRKY, P. 140.

39. Kossuth, L. Irataim. Bp., 1880. Vol. 2. P. 513.

40. É-K. Vol. II. P. 217-8.

41. Pulszky to Newman, 27 October 1860. O.SZ.K. -U.C.L.

42. cf. HORVÁTH, Z. Teleki. . . Bp., 1964. Vol. I. P. 444-64.

43. É-K. Vol. II. P. 263.

44. Kossuth, L. Irataim. Bp., 1880. Vol. 3. P. 543-4; É-K. Vol. II. P. 259-62, 277-85.

45. SZABAD, Gy. A forradalom és a kiegyezés útján. Bp., 1967. P. 414.

46. Magyarország, 8 March 1861.

47. This is convincingly argued in great detail by L. Péter. The antecedents of the nineteenth century Hungarian state concept. D.Phil. thesis. Oxford, 1965. P. 41-58.

Notes to Epilogue.

1. From: 'Appeal' by Mihály Vörösmarty (1836); prose translation by D.Mervyn Jones. Five Hungarian writers. London, 1966. P. 143.

2. Péter, L. A magyar nacionalizmus. In: Eszmék nyomában. München, 1965. P. 188-244. cf. Kedourie, C. Nationalism. London, 1961.

3. cf. KOSÁRY, D. Nationalisme et internationalisme dans l'histoire des peuples danubiens. Revue d'Histoire Comparée, Tom. V. No. 3. P. 3-21.

4. GÁL, I. Kossuth, America and the Danubian confederation. Hungarian Quarterly, Vol. 6. P. 425.

5. Blackwell to Ponsonby. 13 April 1848. Correspondence, 1847-49. Inclosure 3-16.

6. e.g. Zoltán Horváth and Jenő Horváth.

7. The term itself is not used by Hungarian historians, but was given by the present writer, to differentiate them from orthodox nationalists,

from whom the idea of federalism in whatever shape or form remained alien.

8. *Diary*, Vol. I. P. cix.

9. The present writer's italics; this recurrent statement was perhaps best argued in *Dei deveri dell'uomo*.

10. PÉTER, L. The antecedents of the nineteenth century Hungarian State concept. D.Phil. Thesis. Oxford, 1965. P. 41.

11. Dr. I. Gál has called the present writer's attention to Anglo-Hungarian treaties of the seventeen forties, which mention Hungary as an independent state. Chronologically, these should certainly precede Croatian equivalents.

12. Vierteljahrschrift aus und für Ungarn, 1843. Briefwechzel zwischen Leo Grafen von Thun und Franz von Pulszky, I.2., II.2.

13. Marczali, H. Pulszky Ferencz a tudományban és a köséletben. In: PULSZKY, F. Kisebb dolgozatai . . . Budapest, 1914. P. xv-xvi.

14. Desprez, H. La Révolution dans l'Europe Orientale. Paris, 1848.

15. É-K. Vol. I. P. 434.

16. K. Batthyány to Pulszky. 14 July 1849. É-K. Vol. I. P. 550.

17. EÖTVÖS, J. Die Gleichberichtigung der Nationalitäten. Pest, 1850.

18. K-e.T. P. 171-4.

19. Ibid. Hajnal's description is based on Balcesco's Memoirs; cf. I. TÓTH, Z. Balcescu Miklós élete. Bp., 1958. P. 153.

20. KOSSUTH, L. Kossuth demokráciaja . . . közreadja Ács Tivadar. Bp., 1943. P. 35-50.

21. In greater detail, cf. his speech on 15 December 1851 in America. Newman, F.W. Select speeches of Kossuth. London, 1853. P. 57-74.

22. K-e.A. Vol. I. P. 434.

23. The whole question has a voluminous literature on the Hungarian side alone- here, the present writer must restrict himself to call attention to those research workers who have fairly recently contributed to the field: István Hajnal, Imre Deák, Gábor Kemény, Endre Kovács, Tamás Lengyel, Imre Milo and Gyula Merei.

24. JÁSZI, O. Magyarország jövöje és a Dunai Egyesült Államok. Budapest, 1918.

25. In the 1 May 1862 issue of the Milan weekly *Alleanza*.

26. JÁSZI, O. op. cit. p. 48.

27. GÁL, I. Kossuth's Danubian Confederation. Budapest, 1944.

28. ENTRÉVES, A.P. d' The notion of the state. Oxford, 1967. P. 179-80.

Notes to Appendix One.

    1. N.R.A. P.P. GC/PO/833/1-3.

Notes to Appendix Two.

    1. B.P.L. Toulmin Smith Collection, 7215, item 133/2.

Notes to Appendix Three.

    1. HARROWBY MSS. Vol. 453. Unpublished sources, section 13, P. 219-21.

Notes to Appendix Four.

    1. B.P.L. Toulmin Smith Collection, 7215, item 131.

NAME INDEX

PULSZKY, Francis (Ferenc), being the subject of this book *was not given a separate entry*, either under his real name, or his assumed name of *Lipót Kánitz* or *Joseph Andrews*.

EAST EUROPEAN MONOGRAPHS

The *East European Monographs* comprise scholarly books on the history and civilization of Eastern Europe. They are published by the *East European Quarterly* in the belief that these studies contribute substantially to the knowledge of the area and serve to stimulate scholarship and research.

1. *Political Ideas and the Enlightenment in the Romanian Principalities, 1750-1831.* By Vlad Georgescu. 1971.
2. *America, Italy and the Birth of Yugoslavia, 1917-1919.* By Dragan R. Zivojinovic. 1972.
3. *Jewish Nobles and Geniuses in Modern Hungary.* By William O. McCagg, Jr. 1972.
4. *Mixail Soloxov in Yugoslavia: Reception and Literary Impact.* By Robert F. Price. 1973.
5. *The Historical and National Thought of Nicolae Iorga.* By William O. Oldson. 1973.
6. *Guide to Polish Libraries and Archives.* By Richard C. Lewanski. 1974.
7. *Vienna Broadcasts to Slovakia, 1938-1939: A Case Study in Subversion.* By Henry Delfiner. 1974.
8. *The 1917 Revolution in Latvia.* By Andrew Ezergailis. 1974.
9. *The Ukraine in the United Nations Organization: A Study in Soviet Foreign Policy. 1944-1950.* By Konstantin Sawczuk. 1975.
10. *The Bosnian Church: A New Interpretation.* By John V. A. Fine, Jr., 1975.
11. *Intellectual and Social Developments in the Habsburg Empire from Maria Theresa to World War I.* Edited by Stanley B. Winters and Joseph Held. 1975.
12. *Ljudevit Gaj and the Illyrian Movement.* By Elinor Murray Despalatovic. 1975.
13. *Tolerance and Movements of Religious Dissent in Eastern Europe.* Edited by Bela K. Kiraly. 1975.
14. *The Parish Republic: Hlinka's Slovak People's Party, 1939-1945.* By Yeshayahu Jelinek. 1976.
15. *The Russian Annexation of Bessarabia, 1774-1828.* By George F. Jewsbury. 1976.
16. *Modern Hungarian Historiography.* By Steven Bela Vardy. 1976.
17. *Values and Community in Multi-National Yugoslavia.* By Gary K. Bertsch. 1976.
18. *The Greek Socialist Movement and the First World War: the Road to Unity.* By George B. Leon. 1976.
19. *The Radical Left in the Hungarian Revolution of 1848.* By Laszlo Deme. 1976.

20. *Hungary between Wilson and Lenin: The Hungarian Revolution of 1918–1919 and the Big Three.* By Peter Pastor. 1976.
21. *The Crises of France's East-Central European Diplomacy, 1933–1938.* By Anthony J. Komjathy. 1976.
22. *Polish Politics and National Reform, 1775–1788.* By Daniel Stone. 1976.
23. *The Habsburg Empire in World War I.* Robert A. Kann, Bela K. Kiraly, and Paula S. Fichtner, eds. 1977.
24. *The Slovenes and Yugoslavism, 1890–1914.* By Carole Rogel. 1977.
25. *German-Hungarian Relations and the Swabian Problem.* By Thomas Spira. 1977.
26. *The Metamorphosis of a Social Class in Hungary During the Reign of Young Franz Joseph.* By Peter I. Hidas. 1977.
27. *Tax Reform in Eighteenth Century Lombardy.* By Daniel M. Klang. 1977.
28. *Tradition versus Revolution: Russia and the Balkans in 1917.* By Robert H. Johnston. 1977.
29. *Winter into Spring: The Czechoslovak Press and the Reform Movement 1963–1968.* By Frank L. Kaplan. 1977.
30. *The Catholic Church and the Soviet Government, 1939–1949.* By Dennis J. Dunn. 1977.
31. *The Hungarian Labor Service System, 1939–1945.* By Randolph L. Braham. 1977.
32. *Consciousness and History: Nationalist Critics of Greek Society 1897–1914.* By Gerasimos Augustinos. 1977.
33. *Emigration in Polish Social and Political Thought, 1870–1914.* By Benjamin P. Murdzek. 1977.
34. *Serbian Poetry and Milutin Bojic.* By Mihailo Dordevic. 1977.
35. *The Baranya Dispute: Diplomacy in the Vortex of Ideologies, 1918–1921.* By Leslie C. Tihany. 1978.
36. *The United States in Prague, 1945–1948.* By Walter Ullmann. 1978.
37. *Rush to the Alps: The Evolution of Vacationing in Switzerland.* By Paul P. Bernard. 1978.
38. *Transportation in Eastern Europe: Empirical Findings.* By Bogdan Mieczkowski. 1978.
39. *The Polish Underground State: A Guide to the Underground, 1939–1945.* By Stefan Korbonski. 1978.
40. *The Hungarian Revolution of 1956 in Retrospect.* Edited by Bela K. Kiraly and Paul Jonas. 1978.
41. *Boleslaw Limanowski (1835–1935): A Study in Socialism and Nationalism.* By Kazimiera Janina Cottam. 1978.
42. *The Lingering Shadow of Nazism: The Austrian Independent Party Movement Since 1945.* By Max E. Riedlsperger. 1978.
43. *The Catholic Church, Dissent and Nationality in Soviet Lithuania.* By V. Stanley Vardys. 1978.

44. *The Development of Parliamentary Government in Serbia.* By Alex N. Dragnich. 1978.

45. *Divide and Conquer: German Efforts to Conclude a Separate Peace. 1914-1918.* By L. L. Farrar, Jr. 1978.

46. *The Prague Slav Congress of 1848.* By Lawrence D. Orton. 1978.

47. *The Nobility and the Making of the Hussite Revolution.* By John M. Klassen. 1978.

48. *The Cultural Limits of Revolutionary Politics: Change and Continuity in Socialist Czechoslovakia.* By David W. Paul. 1979.

49. *On the Border of War and Peace: Polish Intelligence and Diplomacy in 1937-1939 and the Origins of the Ultra Secret.* By Richard A.

50. *Bear and Foxes: The International Relations of the East European States.* By Ronald Haly Linden. 1979.

51. *Czechoslovakia: The Heritage of Ages Past.* Edited by Ivan Volgye and Hans Brisch. 1979.

52. *Prime Minister Gyula Andrassy's Influence on Habsburg Foreign Policy.* By Janos Decsy. 1979.

53. *Citizens for the Fatherland: Education, Educators, and Pedagogical Ideals in Eighteenth Century Russia.* By J. L. Black. 1979.

54. *A History of the "Proletariat": The Emergence of Marxism in the Kingdom of Poland, 1870-1887.* By Norman M. Naimark. 1979.

55. *The Slovak Autonomy Movement, 1935-1939: A Study in Unrelenting Nationalism.* By Dorothea H. El Mallakh. 1979.

56. *Diplomat in Exile: Francis Pulszky's Political Activities in England, 1849-1860.* By Thomas Kabdebo. 1979.

57. *The German Struggle Against the Yugoslav Guerrillas in World War II: German Counter-Insurgency in Yugoslavia, 1941-1943.* By Paul N. Hehn. 1979.

58. *The Emergence of the Romanian National State.* By Gerald J. Bobango. 1979.

59. *Stewards of the Land: The American Farm School and Modern Greece.*

58. *The Emergence of the Romanian National State.* By Gerald J. Bobango. 1979.

59. *Stewards of the Land: The American Farm School and Modern Greece.* By Brenda L. Marder. 1979.